Picturing South Asian Culture in English:
Textual and Visual Representations

Edited by Tasleem Shakur and Karen D'Souza

Open House Press
Liverpool

First published in Great Britain by Open House Press in 2003
153 Green Lane
Liverpool
UK L31 8BD

www.openhousepress.co.uk

ISBN 0-9544463-0-5

Designed and produced by Open House Press

Cover design: Ruth Owen

Cover photographs ©Clive Grey Front cover: Taj Mahal in wartime, spring 1943: British servicemen pose in front of the landmark. Back cover: Rural Indian woman in 1943

Printed by: Riverside Press, 443 Mill Street, Liverpool, L8 4RD

Contents

Part 3: Communicating Identity: Language and the Popular Cultures

Part 4: Negotiating Postmodernity: Culture, Hybridity and Critique

Preface

This project has its beginnings in a starry-eyed idea to introduce a module on 'Popular Culture of South Asia' to our third year undergraduate students at Edge Hill, an option which was initially taken up by a small but intrepid group of interested, or merely curious students, but whose positive response to the course encouraged us to venture further in promoting this rich field of study.

With the participation of mainly College staff, a workshop was subsequently organised by EMRAU (Ethnic Municity Research Action Unit) an offshoot of ICDES (International Centre for Development and Environmental Studies) and held on 21 March 2002 at Edge Hill College of Higher Education based at Ormskirk, Lancashire, UK. A further impulse behind the workshop was the desire to continue the interests and explorations initiated at a previous interdisciplinary gathering under the banner *Hangovers, Hybridity and Heritage: Nationhood, Identity and New South Asian Englishes* which was held to commemorate fifty years of Indian and Pakistani independence and twenty five years of Bangladeshi independence. The workshops brought together a group of individuals from various disciplines and professions (including contributions from an Indologist from Paris, a dramatist from Birmingham and an architect from Liverpool) with an interest in textual and visual images of South Asian culture produced through the medium of English. A diverse array of interests were reflected in the last workshop, yet recurring themes and concerns were echoed and amplified throughout the sessions. Significantly, as a consequence of cross-discipline debate, a questioning of the relationship and interaction between South Asian cultures and those of the west emerged which needed to be addressed.

Initially there were obvious practical reasons for examining South Asian culture through the medium of English, and likewise a practical reason for the broad nature of the theme; namely the acquisition of a group of enthusiastic contributors without specific professional academic interests in the cultures and languages of south Asia. But in the genesis of this volume, this pragmatic approach developed in substance. We suppose the unavoidable implication of any picturing of South Asian culture in English assumes some degree of interaction between south Asia and Britain (or the West). It is this notion which lies at the heart of this volume – that by examining the representations of South Asian culture in English we cannot escape the fact we are holding up a mirror to two cultures simultaneously, and are therefore attempting some sort of assessment as to the impact these have made on each other and continue to do so.

Therefore in addition to our students, we are indebted to our contributors for sustaining their initial inspiration and bearing with our various requests for revisions and changes. We are grateful to Open House Press, for publishing this volume. However, in reaching the stage at where we actually produce a completed volume, our sincere thanks must go to the tireless work and patience of Ann Chapman during the whole publication process. Special thanks goes to Dr Clive Grey for proofreading the final manuscript and providing linguistic improvement as necessary. Without Siraz Natha's management expertise the appearance of the volume would have been significantly delayed.

We also acknowledge our gratitude to Edge Hill College (Equal Opportunities Unit, and the Departments of English and Natural, Geographical and Applied Sciences) for their funding and support in the production of the volume. Thanks also to Dr A K Shakoor MBE and Imtiaz Patel of Rais Academy for their enthusiastic support. Finally, a deep appreciation to our families for their constant encouragement and indulgence.

Tasleem Shakur and Karen D'Souza

Lancashire, England, January 2003

Introduction

Exploring South Asian Culture through English

Representations

Tasleem Shakur and Karen D'Souza

The investigation of textual and visual production as a means of understanding cultural representation offers a rich field of opportunity for research. The location of a South Asian cultural space however, produced through the medium of English, is perhaps an area of study which is particularly diverse, complex and challenging. With the maturing of postcolonial south Asia and the ever growing diaspora communities situated in the West, it follows that such issues as continuity and transformation of tradition; the impact of imperialism; the 'Indianization' of English; are increasingly seen as areas of debate. While South Asian literature in English continues to receive a degree of recognition, film and television texts along with other forms of visual representation (including sculpture and video games) are yet to receive serious attention. A new breed of South Asian film (mainly in English or with English subtitles) Radio and TV programmes (such as Goodness Gracious Me! BBC,1999-2000) and cartoons (for example The Simpsons which includes the strong presence of South Asian character Apu) made in Britain and America are attracting increasing international critical acclaim as well as commercial success. Accordingly, this volume seeks to address notions of hybridity, and diversity, but also to acknowledge the resistance of unique traditional cultural forms to the tensions created by transformative social conditions.

Originally the focus of the volume was to be on popular culture. However, the contributions and discussions during a workshop on the theme of *Picturing Popular South Asian Culture in English* (ICDES, 2002) and the subsequent submission of papers suggested a wider representation of culture. The generic development of four thematic parts grew organically from the submitted contributions and efforts were made in ordering the parts into a somewhat chronological historical time frame. Such categorisation is probably more obvious in sequencing the first two parts which refer specifically to the colonial and post-colonial periods while the latter two parts attempt to address contemporary cultural texts and visual representations.

With regard to actual geographical location under review in this volume, there will be discrepancies between the articles featured here dependent upon the actual time and place of representation being considered. The inclusive term 'south Asia' is being used here as an umbrella term for the region which includes Bangladesh, India, Nepal, Pakistan, Sri Lanka – that is the modern nation states of the area. However, for historical reasons and as a result of the representations examined here, 'India' is often used generically rather than simply as a representation of modern geographical and political circumstances and is therefore frequently used as an inclusive term. What binds this volume together is not its being situated in any specific and accurate geography, nor as stated is it bound by an attempt to form a comprehensive analysis of South Asian culture, but rather by its focus on how this region is represented in western produced or largely western targeted forms of communication.

Deconstructing History: Canonising Critical Constructions

'Tale of hunting would be different if lions had historians'
(African proverb)

Part one of the volume brings together two papers which deal with writers who are representative of particular literary traditions of their time and place, and whose work is indicative of a range of critical responses to, and examinations of, British colonisation of south Asia and its implications during the post-colonial period.

As a systematic study of popular South Asian culture in English our investigation begins with the early colonial period of the East India Company in Bengal. Baron charts the development of colonial Calcutta within a few generations from three nondescript fishing villages to a city of 250,000 people, including perhaps 2,500 Europeans by 1775 (Baron, A. 2001, p.60). He summarises the speedy development of European culture in India and the rise of a bourgeois class:

> Calcutta boasted two French hairdressers, several theatres and newspapers, a celebrated performance of Handel's Messiah and a Masonic temple. But though all this aped London society, the British inhabitants were much of fast-set, too macho, raucous, even vulgar, for this to set the real tone in Calcutta. (ibid. p.61)

With the advent of South Asian imports into Britain as early as the end of the seventeenth century, and the East India Company merchants of the eighteenth century, opportunism was exacerbated.

The "new 'nabobs' of the Company's service were returning with fortunes equalling those of the landed aristocracy, and without either too much effort or ability it would appear. A corrupt political system at Westminster combined jealousy with morality to curb the corruption of Company rule in India". (Farrrington, A. 2002, pp.114-115)

Stephen Gregg's essay offers a significant reading of 18th century popular English literature outlining concepts of Orientalism, as Foote's satirical depiction of the English merchant classes calls upon the device of stereotypical constructions of the East in order to deride the merchants and make his point. Gregg demonstrates that it is the pragmatic concerns of the dramatist which encourage Foote to draw on these stereotypes. Whatever the motive or intent, this strategy as revealed by Gregg is indicative of an oft-repeated trend in English literature, and consequently an examination of Foote's work is an appropriate place to begin this volume of articles.

Moving on a hundred and forty years or so, in a reiteration of the parallels claimed between Ireland and India under British rule, Claire Spencer-Jones assesses Joyce's references to the Indian mutiny in his novel *Ulysses*. The 'Citizen' chapter in Joyce's novel simmers with the oppositional undertones previously absent from English writings of the period, and therefore a counterbalance to the literature of which Foote is an example. Joyce mobilises the oft made comparison between the plight of Ireland under British rule with that of India, hence India is invoked as a political symbol, a device in order to progress the debate regarding the complexities of Irish nationalism and British imperialism. Joyce himself is complex in his stance towards Irish politics and nationalism, but that aside, the question arises as to how far Joyce is ultimately similar to writers such as Foote, as the Indian mutiny is invoked to comment on the domestic situation rather than for any specific concern or interest regarding India itself.

The extent to which the Indian mutiny continues to be exploited by western writers is further illuminated by Spencer-Jones' investigation of J.G. Farrell's *The Siege of Krishnapur* as a complementary text. Spencer-Jones takes a particular reading with regard to Farrell's novel; where some critics read the Anglo-Irish writer's account of the mutiny as a parody of the genre of Anglo-Indian fiction, Spencer-Jones situates Farrell's limited representation of the Indian perspective within a specific tradition of the colonial novel, and identifies it as further evidence of British imperiousness, displaying the conventional hallmarks of indifference towards Indian culture and customs.

This article is also an attempt to provide readers with parallel colonialism and its variable impact on other cultures. Although a significant proportion of the sensitive documents relating to rebellion by colonial Indian forces remain out of the public domain, modern historians have indicated Irish sympathy with Indian mutinies. Not surprisingly then, the conflict in Northern Ireland of 1972, ('Bloody Sunday') was instantly evoked as the 'Massacre of Amritsar' by Irish nationalists. In this context, this article could form an alternative subaltern study of British Imperialism written by Irish writers. Claire Spencer-Jones recalls some of the chilling accounts of public executions of the Indian Sepoys; the voice of the anti-imperialist who disapproved the barbarity; and acknowledges the homage paid to the manner in which the mutineers met their death some hundred and fifty years ago. Yet even before the 'Sepoy Mutinee' of 1857, as Spencer-Jones emphasises, the first edition of the Irish nationalist daily newspaper The Nation (15 October 1842) gave a disturbing account of the burning of Hindu widows, demonstrating that the 'Irish were fascinated with death and more particularly with the funeral customs of India' (*See Spencer-Jones's article*).

It is interesting to note that what Joyce captures is in fact not only the morbid interest of the Irish, but more significantly in his recording of social phenomena emerges a regional individuality rather than a standardised western response or outlook with regard towards south Asia.

Revisiting Colonialism: The Persistence of the Raj

As an attempt to assess the role and impact of popular culture, part two of this volume explores more specifically the cultural interaction and changing relationships between south Asia and the West in the latter half of the twentieth century, but with a backward glance to the imperial situation of the earlier half. Reading this section one is reminded of the huge changes which have taken place during the twentieth century in terms of socio-economic and geo-political relationships between Britain and India, and within south Asia itself. In fictional terms this section picks up chronologically at the time of Joyce's bar-room debates with their allusions to the cultural practices and political concerns of India in support of the nationalist aspirations of the Irish. Yet in Britain the inevitable death-knell for British India had already been sounded, intellectually and economically. However it is the cultural complexities pertaining to the decline of empire and the birth of nation states which are perhaps more wide reaching and pervasive, long after conquering armies have sailed home!

John Simons and Sylivia Woodhead introduce a personal and individual quality to their papers as they consider the significance of place and literature in colonial and postcolonial contexts. Simons writes an engaging account of Gamini Salgado, an immigrant Sri Lankan professor of English at Exeter University, in which he identifies continuities between Salgado's native Sinhalese culture and his scholarship on English Renaissance literature. Among other things, this article demonstrates the possible consequences of a colonial education; the absorption of the imaginative spheres of English literature and the real, lived experiences of Ceylon. Here is an incisive insight which contrasts with the negative portrayals of such colonial collision often found in postcolonial literature and theory. Simons' thoughtful, and compassionate celebration of Gamini Salgado's life identifies a less abrasive indoctrination of British values through the digestion of its literature. For Salgado there seems to be a happy marriage between the rhythms of his local language and culture and British literary classics through which he was educated, and he stands as an example of the integration and assimilation of South Asian culture with English. The inside cover jacket of Salgado's posthumous publication *(The True Paradise)* introduces the author as an 'exceptional person growing up in one culture and gradually being possessed by European attitudes' (Salgado, 1993). An expression of such experience is aptly formed by the Indian poet A.K. Ramanujan, whose voice seems to connect with Salgado as a fellow writer vaguely searching for an identity in middle age, which is neither entirely South Asian, nor entirely English.

> English and my disciplines (linguistics, anthropology) give me my 'outer' forms – linguistic, metrical, logical and other such ways of shaping experience; and my first thirty years in India, my frequent visits and fieldtrips, my personal and professional preoccupations with Kannada, Tamil, the classics and folklore give me my substance, my 'inner' forms, images and symbols. They are continuous with each other, and I no longer can tell what comes from where. (quoted in Mehrotra, 1998, p.3)

However the leap of imagination required to achieve this state seems to be firmly on the part of the colonised rather than the coloniser. Simons' article makes complementary reading alongside Sylvia Woodhead's account of suburban Britain and its collective perception of south Asia in the mid-twentieth century. This article illustrates a contrasting lack of cultural diversity. Woodhead recounts the institutional representation of south Asia through a consideration of contemporary geography text books, contrasted with an appraisal of how personal knowledge may be gained through the representation of place and culture in the popular romantic novel. Such an account offers illumination with regard to understanding South Asian culture through popular novels in English, as Woodhead's article reminds us of the seductiveness of fictional representation, and the potential power of such images.

The paucity of educational interest in a region which had only recently relinquished strong connections is perhaps indicative of the legacy of imperialist ideology. It is within such a context Woodhead examines the scope of the popular romantic novel to enhance cultural knowledge of place, and to penetrate such bold statements found in the texts books that described India simplistically as a chaotic mixture of religious, linguistic and cultural groups. Woodheads' confessions of being introduced to South Asian culture through *The Far Pavilions* (1978) raises similar moral and ethical questions concerning the reception and impact of other similar fiction or films. In the film *Bhowani Junction* (Dir. George Cukor, 1956) Ava Gardner plays a Eurasian girl torn between a British Army Officer and her Anglo-Indian fiance. The themes of Anglo-Indian fictions (e.g. *Passage to India, The Far Pavilions, Jewel in the Crown)* tend to emphasise the problematic circumstances of divided loyalties in both pre and post colonial India. One thing becomes clear that in almost all cases, the film or the television adaptations of these novels are invariably manipulated to match the socio-cultural aspirations and desires of western audiences at the time of production. Philip French, a respected film critic acknowledges this phenomenon in the film *Bhowani Junction*. In a review for *The Observer* he notes that the 'producers changed the ending of John Masters' novel after the American preview audiences objected to Gardner marrying an Indian' (The Observer, 2002).

The third article in this section, *From Heat and Dust to East is East,* by D'Souza and Shakur draws together many of the issues which arise in the previous two, as it explores three literary texts and their film versions, which when read together, map out in a literary context responses to 20th century experiences of colonialism, and its consequential impact on the cultural identity of both South Asian and British communities. Comparison of these texts and films identifies schematic and thematic links but also examines differences in representation of South Asian culture arising from the cultural positioning of the author/director, and the assumed reader and audience. The authors of the texts under review offer the voice of the insider, but owing to their hybridity or multicultural positioning are also situated to some extent outside the culture with which they engage. *Heat and Dust* offers an image of imperialism viewed through the lens of the post-colonial age. Through the novel's juxtapositioning of the two periods, Jhabvala is able to examine the continuity between colonial and post-colonial time and space, and the relationship between East and West. Desai's novel *In Custody* presents a portrayal of a small town college lecturer in contemporary India. In terms of cultural perception the novel presents an important study of South Asian culture as it deals with the representation of a marginal sub-culture in a Hindu dominant society and charts the changing socio-economic landscape. Alternatively *East is East* explores the South Asian diaspora community and its relationship with the host English culture, evoking colonial collision of the past. The popular forms of Islam depicted here provide an engaging site in which to examine critical debate such as Bhabha's analyses of 'hybrid culture'.

Essentially this article demonstrates a concern with regard to the creation and reception of images of South Asian culture pictured in English and read in conjunction with John Simons' account of a colonial childhood, and Sylvia Woodhead's reflections on an education in the aftermath of empire, the powerful significance of fiction to construct and shape both individual and collective cultural perceptions is evident. The strategic positioning of this article at roughly the mid point of this volume may also be seen as an attempt to erect a metaphorical bridge between representations of the colonial past and the post-colonial present (which inevitably includes the cultures of post-independence south Asia and the diaspora communities living in the West).

Communicating Identity: Language and the Popular Cultures

While politics are never far away from any discussion of colonial and postcolonial issues, it is perhaps in this section of the volume where politics surface more obviously and assertively. The articles in this section tend to deal with issues which engage with an exploration of politics in independent, modern India: politics of language; politics of gender; and the politics of architecture.

Yet underlying the modern political positioning, is also the combined force of history in determining the responses of modern society and culture. Particularly in the first and third essays in this section the authors directly consider the positioning of modern India as a direct consequence of interaction between south Asia and the west. Considering the imperialism of language and taking a cue from the British Home Secretary, David Blunkett's controversial remarks of December 2001, Clive Grey considers the issue of language as an expression of identity in South Asian contexts. In his discussion of the contrasting attitudes towards the use of English in Britain and in south Asia, Grey places an emphasis on the issues of ownership of language, English in particular, in a political and cultural context. What emerges from Grey's discussion is that despite a common language, generally there is an on-going lack of mutual awareness and a continued circulation of stereotypical perceptions.

French Indologist, Annie Montaut's article discusses the relationship between history and myth in the shaping of modern Indian culture, and questions their relevance in constructing identity with particular attention to gender through an examination of social protest in the writing of Mrinal Pandey. Montaut remarks upon the general representation of Indian postcolonial culture in English, commencing her analysis with Naipaul's sociological observations and descriptions of India, and the implicit acknowledgement of the end of the Nehruvian vision, and contrasting this with Pandy's work, whose characters she identifies as subaltern voices which forge a link between legend and history in contradistinction to the general tenets of social historians.

Iain Jackson's contribution to this volume provides a stimulating approach to the consideration of constructions of south Asia through the lens of Europe in his discussion of architectural development of Chandigarh. During the 1950s, while commissioning the then renowned French architect Louis Corbusier for the design of post-independent Chandigarh (as the new capital of Punjab, India), the Indian Prime Minister Jawaharlal Nehru and many other Indians looked on Chandigarh as the promise of the future and accordingly the new town was placed a little way off the Grand Trunk Road on a site 'free from existing encumbrances of old towns and old traditions' (Nilsson, S. 1973, p.89). The environment that Le Corbusier planned bore a striking resemblance to the Viceroy's sheltered enclave in Delhi (designed by Liverpool-based British Raj architect Lutyens in the early twentieth century). In his critical review of the new capitals of south Asia, Sten Nilsson (an accomplished Swedish academic) commenting on the role of the European architects in India suggested that 'although Lutyens and Le Corbusier might seem to represent two different eras... their conception was similar, and they had great deal in common that originated in the European tradition' (op. cit. p.99).

Fifty years on Chandigarh has gained the reputation of having both the examples of one of the finest modernist designs and a typical dysfunctional, unequal city inappropriate to the overwhelming poor inhabitants.

Iain Jackson, a recent graduate of architecture from Liverpool, presents his view of a 'new identity' of the politicised space of Chandigarh (Punjab, India), as one of the better- known examples of modernist agendas promoted by Le Corbusier and his team of European architects. Documenting the work of the well-established anarchic sculptor Nek Chand, whose street sculpture developed from systematically collected and reassembled discarded household rubbish, Jackson provides readers with a passionate portrait of a post-independent art expression, arguing that such work is indicative of a change in the political and cultural mindset of contemporary India. The author charts the process of ruin in Corbusier's modernist city while observing the growth of Nek Chand's 'mini city' (Rock Garden) through the perspective of an emerging spatio-cultural, politicised, Indian identity.

Iain Jackson's article demonstrates the emergent tension between modernist and postmodernist aesthetics in the visual representation of Chandigargh, that makes a link with the next section of the volume, which explores more directly the relationship between south Asia and the postmodern situation.

Negotiating Postmodernity: Culture, Hybridity and Critique

The articles in this part of the volume demonstrate a concern with diaspora and postmodern forms of presentation, although interestingly there are parallels and similarities in the constructions of character and identity to be found in more traditional media. These three essays explore the critical spaces of post-colonial South Asian identities, imaginative, hyper-ironic, and anthropomorphic. These 'spaces' articulate hybrid and transformative constructions of South Asian culture, at once both a critique of Western mainstream cultures and contemporary South Asian identity. Each essay leaves us with not only questions about the future of South Asian Culture through English, but also tempts us to re-interpret the history, emergency and transformations of South Asian culture witnessed throughout the collection.

Anna Claydon's article on *Bhaji on the Beach* in fact identifies new forms of identities within British South Asian culture; in particular her analysis of post-colonial masculinities depicted in the film expands in some detail on observations made by D'Souza and Shakur with regard to the problematic male identity experienced within both the colonial and post-colonial society. Claydon's identification of the film as representative of the new British cinema is a refreshing commentary on the hybridity of South Asian cultural space within Britain. The film interweaves strands of social commentary along with fantasy sequences typical of Bollywood films, and in which Blackpool is configured as a creative materialisation of both the imperial and post-imperial within British culture. Claydon's article in fact identifies a significant trend in the British arts world as both film and fiction of this genre seem to be on the increase. Aspects of Anglo-Asian space, culture clash and the departure from homogeneity towards heterogeneity in British cinema is analysed through the film narrative while constantly seeking links with the theoretical discourses of 'Otherness', 'post-colonial masculinity' and 'contemporary hybrid Britishness'.

Through a critical reading of the character of Apu, the South Asian shopkeeper in the American cartoon *The Simpsons*, Paul Rodaway argues that characters, spaces and storylines of the cartoon open up a 'critical cultural space' which questions South Asian American immigrant identities. Moving on from Claydon's article on South Asian hybridity, Rodaway presents an equally hybrid identity of a character (fictionally born in Pakistan, educated in India, and possibly given a surreal Sri Lankan name), Apu, who proudly claims to be an 'American Indian' (not to be confused with 'Native American'!). Adopting Tingleff's notion of cartoon characters as iconographic rather than representational (Tingleff, S. 1998), that is Apu as a 'conflict of ideas', Rodaway argues that through hyper-irony the *South Asian in Springfield* has a performativity of radical openness, critiquing South Asian immigrant culture (represented by Apu, his shop, his family and storylines) and mainstream American culture (represented by Homer and the community of Springfield). Furthermore, like Claydon, Rodaway adopts the notion of 'Critical Othering' to explicate the reversal of the relationship of oppressed (immigrant) and the oppressor (citizen), demonstrated through the mutual friendship of Apu and Homer, and argues that 'critical cultural spaces' of the cartoon, and the hyper-irony that articulates them, produces a critical potential for cultural transformation and counter-hegemonic practice. All through the colonial and post-colonial novels (from *Passage to India* to *White Teeth*) we find heartening friendships at the juxtaposition (and conflict) of cultures, but it is through recognising these - to borrow bell hooks' concept of 'spaces of radical openness' (hooks, b. 1991) - that the political and critical potential of such spaces as sites of resistance and transformation become realised. Reflecting on Apu in *The Simpsons*, Rodaway raises the big question: 'whether humour, satire, parody, and irony can genuinely progress social critique or does it dilute, diffuse and ridicule it and therefore, ultimately dis-empower, de-motivate and neutralise the counter-hegemonic? A question which is present in various guises in this volume and is addressed, sometimes implicitly, by several authors.

As we move in a generally chronological fashion through these articles it is perhaps apposite to end the volume with a critical textual reading of the anthropomorphism in a contemporary popular videogame, written jointly by James Newman and Claire Molloy 'How the elephant forgot its politics. Cultural identity and difference in the videogame: Taj the elephant genie in Rare's *Diddy Kong Racing*.' Inspired by Homi Bhabha's 'Colonial Stereotypes' (Bhabha, H. 1997) the authors (similar to that of Paul Rodaway's previous article) find discursive currency in the hegemonic relationship between the South Asian subservient non-playable elephant character and the player.

Newman and Molloy attempt to explain the complex relationship between Hindu mythology, colonial identity and national identity that are presumably inscribed upon the videogame. In its discussion of 'cultural identity' through representation of Taj's (the elephant genie) 'Indian-ness' and 'Indianicity', this article establishes links with the other two authors in this part. Indeed it is thought provoking to find references to hunting by the Mughals, an activity which was later commandeered by the British elite classes (e.g. nabobs, See Stephen Gregg's article in this volume). It may be noted that picturing animals in Mughal miniatures and painting was one of the essential features of pre-colonial south Asia. During the colonial period, as remarked in the Newman and Molloy essay the 'Indian elephant is routinely pictured carrying English ladies'. Anglo-Indian fiction and film has frequently included scenes of hunting or leisure activities with the use of elephants. Works of fiction such as Jim Corbett's *Man-eaters of Kumaon* appearing in 1944 (Hawkins, R.E. 1978, p6) describes the tracking and shooting of tigers which roamed the jungles and foothills of the Himalayas (with the hunter safely on the elephant's back). Such adventure stories were included in many of the secondary schools of south Asia, up to the 1970s, and in some instances remain yet on the school curriculum. A comparable account of the domestication and commodification of the Indian elephant can be found in Amitav Ghosh's novel *The Glass Palace* (2001). Ghosh narrates how the British recognised and exploited the strength and character of the Indian elephant, and taught the Indians and Burmese how to use them in the logging and rubber trades which made up a significant part of the imperial commercial enterprise.

Collectively the articles in this volume underline the prevailing power of fictional and stereotypical representations of South Asian culture but they also raise questions with regard to how they are digested and understood. A lasting impression is of how images in English have created a social construct of south Asia and the extent to which these are perpetuated. It is also evident from Foote, through to Joyce, Forster and beyond (and perhaps including British Asian writers such as Khan-Din and Kureishi) the construction of South Asian culture in fiction can be identified as a means to underpin and explore British or Western identities. Ironically, modern historical research, such as that found in William Dalrymple's (2002) *White Mughals* charts a time of integration in India before the Victorianism of the Raj, engendered by prejudice and fear, took hold, effectively segregating the races. Such accounts only serve to emphasise the need to engage with cultural differences. This presents us with the question of whether fictions such as *The Far Pavilions*, *Heat and Dust* or *Passage to India*, *Bhaji on the Beach, East is East*, and so on, whether produced as romanticised, comic or hard-hitting film versions, can offer ways of understanding, or whether despite the inherent orientalism, such images can be productive.

Holistically, the representations of South Asian culture interrogated in this volume throw up two further points. Firstly it is evident that the potent idea of an homogenised identity of south Asia still prevails very much in the west, despite the phenomenal growth of regional art and cultural development in post-colonial nation states. However some of the more recent images of South Asian culture do reveal emerging diverse identities among the diaspora communities to be found in Britain, America and possibly in the continent of Africa, some of which has been touched on here, but is worthy of further exploration. In light of these conclusions an interesting point of speculation would be whether non-English texts picturing South Asian culture would disclose similar findings.

Bibliography

Baron, A. (2001) *An Indian Affair,* Channel 4 Books, London.

Bhabha, H. (1997) *The location of Culture,* Routledge, London.

Dalrymple, W. (2002) *White Mughals,* Harper Collins, London.

Farrington, A. (2002) Trading Places: The East India Company and Asia 1600-1834, The British Library, London.

Forster, E.M. (1989) *A Passage to India*, Penguin, London (first published 1924).

Ghosh, A. (2001) *The Glass Palace,* Harper Collins, London.

Hawkins, R.E. (ed) (1978*) Jim Corbett's India*, Oxford University Press.

Hooks, bell (1991) Yearning: Race, Gender and Cultural Politics, Turnaround, London.

ICDES (2002) *Picturing Popular South Asian Culture in English: Textual and Visual Reprsentations*, an unpublished book of abstracts of the one day workshop held at Edge Hill College Ormskirk, Lancashire UK on 21 March 2002.

Kaye, M.M. (1978) *The Far Pavilions*, Penguin, London.

Mehrotra, A.K. (1998) *Twelve Modern Indian Poets*, Oxford University Press, Delhi.

Nilsson, S. (1973, reprinted 1975, 1978) *The New Capitals of India, Pakistan and Bangladesh,* Scandinavian Institute of Asian Studies, Monograph Series No 12, Curzon Press, London.

Salgado, G. (1993) *The True Paradise*, Carcanet Press Ltd.

Scott, P. (1966) The Jewel in the Crown, Penguin, London.

Smith, Z. (2000) *White Teeth*, Hamish Hamilton, London.

The Observer 2002, OTVFILMS:9

Tingleff, Sam (1998), *The Simpsons* as a Critique of Consumer Culture
http://www.snpp.com/other/papers/st.paper.html

Filmography

Bhowani Junction (1956). Director: George Cukor.

Goodness Gracious Me! BBC TV 1998-2000.

A Passage to India (1984) Director: David Lean.

The Simpsons TV Cartoon Series 1989-present (original concept 1987), Fox TV. (Creator & Executive Producer: Mat Groening).

The Far Pavilion (1984) Director: Peter Duffell.

The Jewel in the Crown (1984) Directors. Jim O'Brien, Christopher Morahan.

Part 1: Deconstructing History: Canonising Critical Constructions

Representing the Nabob: India, Stereotypes and Eighteenth-century Theatre

Stephen Gregg

By the 1770s there were a variety of satires on the men who worked in India for the East India Company in the eighteenth century. These agents were the 'nabobs', Englishmen who aspired to be Oriental princes by mimicking the manners and advantages of the nawabs of Indian states (Spear, 1963, p.37). The returning nabob had become a popularly recognisable figure by 1772 and was portrayed in contemporary writings as an avaricious and fabulously wealthy parvenu, corrupted by unfettered access to power, riches and vice in India.[1] These figures were the targets of satirical squibs such as the anonymous 'The Nabob or the Asiatic Plunderer' (1776), or Timothy Touchstone's 'Tea and Sugar: or the Nabob and the Creole' (1772) in which the nabobs are described as 'assassins, pampered high, by luxury's treats' (Touchstone, in Juneja, 1992, p.185). Sentimental moral outrage had its say in Henry Mackenzie's The Man of Feeling, when the novel's hero asks of his companion:

> When shall I see a commander return from India in the pride of honourable poverty? – You describe the victories they have gained; they are sullied by the cause in which they fought: you enumerate the spoils of those victories; they are covered with the blood of the vanquished! (Mackenzie, 1967, p.103)

Harley here displays his finer humanity typical of the sentimental fiction of this period of the eighteenth century.

Samuel Foote's *The Nabob* - first performed in 1772 - is one of the most famous of the satires against the nabobs and will be the critical lever to analyse the relations between satire, popular theatre, and the perceptions of India. The nabob of Foote's play is Sir Matthew Mite, who has been variously thought to refer to Robert Clive, Nabob Gray, General Richard Smith, or Sir Matthew White, all of whom worked for the East

---

[1] For an account of the distaste felt towards the nabob in the eighteenth century see Holzman's (1926) still excellent study. For an account of the politics of the East-India Company, see Bowen (1998)

India Company (Trefman, 1971, p.204; Taylor, 1984, p.13). Clive, in particular, was the *bête noire* of the times – an archetypal nabob who, while substantially consolidating British influence in India, netted himself fabulous riches. Foote's play is topical: the year before its performance, and for the next two years, the East India company and Clive in particular were under investigation by the Government for corrupt commercial practices.

The representation of the nabob in literature has received recent attention, with critics noting the way in which the occasion of nabobery is a symptom of anxieties over virtuous commerce and consumption, and that Indian culture itself is the implied background to concerns over English gentility. Further, such concerns become the occasion for a more pervasive management of the Indian provinces by the British government.[2] As Said has famously set out, 'Orientalism... has less to do with the Orient then it has to do with "our" World' (Said, 1995, p.12).

However, previous discussions of Foote's *The Nabob* have ignored its context within popular Georgian culture. As Stallybrass and White have noted, 'an utterance is legitimated or disregarded according to its place of production' (Stallybrass and White, 1986, p.80). Georgian theatre was a site of popular discourse, one in which satire, morality, the political sphere, and the economic sphere forged alliances. Yet it was also a site in which these discourses fought for dominance. Foote's play, interceding in these debates over morality and imperial economics, deserves close attention to the way in which it negotiates between these discourses within the context of popular culture. The problem is that *The Nabob* is in a long tradition of satires against mercantilism and, unfortunately, it is these very merchants who were the popular theatre's patrons, so that Foote's satire indicted the very audience which ensured its popularity. The problem for Foote to solve is how to reconcile these conflicting demands with moral satire. I will argue that while Foote's comic satires sought to rectify the audience's morals, the play maintained its popularity by ideological sleight-of-hand. Its satirical thrust is tempered by the effects of the formal idiosyncrasies of the 'afterpiece'; namely, the virtuous pronouncements by the merchant Thomas Oldham and his part in the sentimental closure of the play, and the farcical horseplay of Sir Matthew Mite's servants. However, the play's satire is also underpinned by stereotypes of the Orient, which provide the play's most subtle ideological safety-valve, neutralizing the potential for damaging satire on the practices of its professional and merchant audience.

---

[2] See Juneja (1992) pp.183-98, Singh (1996) and Bhattacharya (1998)

Foote and his audience: popular theatre and satires on merchants

The Nabob is an example of the most popular form of Georgian theatre: the short, three-act 'afterpiece' designed to accompany the main five-act play as part of the evening's bill of fare. Between 1737 and 1777 around two thirds of the plays sent to the Licenser were of this form, and by the later eighteenth century the afterpiece was reportedly the most popularly-attended form over the main attraction (Bevis, 1980, p.99). Bevis ties this form's popularity with the rise of a patron class of 'bourgeois merchants and businessmen' who were open to less traditional and more frivolous forms (Bevis, 1970, pp.vii-viii). Most of the afterpieces of the Georgian period were comic and had a 'penchant for social satire' (Bevis, 1980, p.121), so that clearly a comedy on one of the leading commercial interests of the day - the East India Company - would speak to this section of the urban classes. Foote's own characterisation of his comedy, in a 1760 letter to a critic, is that it is to be the moral mirror of his times; it is 'for the correction of individuals... as an example to the whole community' (Foote, in Bevis, 1980, p.151). Yet the relationship between a satire on the abuses of imperial profit and the status of the implied audience is a potentially tricky one for Foote to negotiate. In other words, the very merchant classes who saw satiric theatre as their own form, might well be faced with unpalatable truths.

Foote's prologue to *The Nabob* - added in 1773 - grants the author a degree of hubristic awareness as to the dangers of his satire. After warning the audience of his 'Humour with arched brow and leering eye' (Foote, 1778, p.v), Foote bemoans the possibility that his satiric wit may fail him:

> But should infirmities with time conspire,
> My force to weaken or abate my fire,
> Less entertainment may arise to you,
> But to myself less danger will ensue. (Foote, 1778, p.vi)

Here he clearly equates the force of comedy and the success of the play with danger to himself: the more pointed his satire, the more popular, but the more liable he is. His comment that 'No foe I fear more than a legal fury, | Unless I gain this circle for my jury' (Foote, 1778, p.vi) suggests that a satire against a specific person - resulting in a charge of libel - may be justified by a general and popular acclaim. It also suggests the need to smooth the consciences of his audience and yet for them to exercise a judgment upon the moral thrust of the play.

Indeed, such danger was not misplaced. An idea of the problems faced by Foote by baiting his audience of merchants is clear in the following story. Subsequent to a performance of *The Nabob*, an unverified report has it that Foote was accosted in the street by two nabobs who were out for revenge. Notably, Foote apparently appealed to the dictates of popular culture by claiming that he was nothing more than a 'wholesale popularmonger' and that his play was a not a satire on individual gentlemen such as they; reportedly, he then charmed them over dinner (Trefman, 1971, p.207). Another account has it that two nabobs, Sir Matthew White and General Richard Smith, thinking that they were the intended target of the play, invited Foote to dine with them - again Foote's wit and charm is said to have come to his rescue, assuring them that they were not the intended satirical targets, and that the virtuous character Thomas Oldham was meant to represent them (Taylor, 1984, p.13).

What might have been most problematic was that the play was steeped in a tradition of satires against the urban merchant classes: undoubtedly, *The Nabob* partakes of this wider satire on barbaric commercial practices and the ambivalence felt towards *parvenu* merchants. In fact conservative reactions were a commonplace in satirical comments against the trading and merchant classes and find their typical articulation in Tobias Smollett's novel of 1771, *Humphry Clinker*. The splenetic Matthew Bramble - the novel's dominant voice - delivers this broadside against 'every upstart of fortune' in fashionable Bath:

> Clerks and factors from the East Indies, loaded with the spoil of plundered provinces; planters, negro-drivers, and hucksters, from our American plantations, enriched they know not how; agents, commisaries, and contractors, who have fattened, in two successive wars, on the blood of the nation; usurers, brokers, and jobbers of every kind; men of low birth, and no breeding, have found themselves suddenly translated into a state of affluence, unknown to former ages; and no wonder that their brains should be intoxicated with pride, vanity, and presumption. Knowing no other criterion of greatness, but the ostentation of wealth, they discharge their affluence without taste or conduct, through every channel of the most absurd extravagance (Smollett, 1984, pp.36-37).

So the popular distaste for the East India factor is part of a larger critique on the 'presumption' of the merchant-classes - Bramble's litany of upstart men modulates from the nabob to men of 'low birth, and no breeding'. For him, clearly, moral attributes of propriety are anathema when espoused by the ranks of the urban commercial class. Further, the vainglorious display of wealth as a marker of status is another confirmation of a conservative ideology of class here; part of the wider concern over, what McKeon terms, a 'crisis of status inconsistency' (McKeon, 1987, p.171). Indeed, the origins of Foote's villain, Sir Matthew, are ignominiously revealed when, Putty, a glazier's apprentice, asks him about their boyhood friendship at 'Blue-Coat' school and whether he was the same 'Mat Mite, son of old John and Margery Mite, at the Sow and Sausage in St. Mary Axe' (Foote, 1778, p.59).

The Nabob holds some further uncomfortable truths on the commercial practices of the day - at home as well as abroad. In an aside to the audience at the end of act two, Sir Matthew voices a cynical appraisal of the use of riches:

> Riches to a man who knows how to employ them, are as useful in England as in any part of the East: There they gain us those ends in spite and defiance of law, which, with a proper agent, may here be obtained under the pretence and colour of law. (Foote, 1778, p.50)

Sir Matthew's claim that there is little difference between the commercial dealings in England and India, and that the law in England is merely the means to enable corruption and greed, would have been a bitter pill to swallow for the professional and urban classes sitting in the theatre. However, as we shall see, misdirection, stereotyping, buffoonery, moral sops, and flattery all temper the acerbic and dangerous sallies of Foote's satirical voice.

Parvenu servants and low farce

Foote himself sought to dignify his short plays as serious moral comedy, and objected to the label farce (Belden, 1969, p.173). However, contemporaries found it difficult to distinguish comedy from farce, and reaction to Foote's plays recognised farcical elements in his work (Belden, 1969, p.174; Bevis, 1970, p.xi). The Nabob is no exception: the clowning of Sir Matthew's servants is the play's farcical centrepiece.

Conserve, a porter, and Janus, who 'drudge[s] pretty much at the door' (Foote, 1778, p.19) exemplify the common comic trope of the 'upstart' servant: Conserve can barely 'own the place of a porter' (Foote, 1778, p.18). As the demigod of Sir Matthew's doors, Janus's lofty remarks on the visitors to Mite's residence show us comic disparities between his own sense of rank and the status of the tradesmen and minor aristocracy he keeps waiting on the doorstep. That Janus partakes of his master's own sense of status is clear: 'In my last place, indeed, I thought myself bound to be civil; for as all the poor devils could get was good words. It would have been hard to have been sparing of them' (Foote, 1778, p.18). He contrasts his last master's relative poverty with his present place: 'But here we are rich; and as the fellows don't wait for their money, it is but fair they should wait for admittance' (Foote, 1778, p.18). Conserve and Janus carry their equation of their master's wealth and their own status with them in their sociable hours, pilfering their evening victuals and aping their masters' own luxurious supper rituals: 'We all contribute, as usual: The substantials from Alderman Sirloin's; Lord Frippery's cook finds fricasees and ragouts: Sir Robert Bumper's butler is to send in the wine; and I shall supply the dessert' (Foote, 1778, p.22). The sheer delicacy and richness of their supper hints at the perceived corrupting effects of luxurious consumption and especially the importation of foreign foods and spices.[3]

Janus and Conserve, however, stand in for more than a satire on servants: the satire on improper status reversals reflects on reversals in a wider social order. Janus and Conserve are a microcosm of the reversal of the proper relations between imperial master (Britain) and commercial servant (the East India Company's factors in India). This context is made clear when Janus calms Conserve's anxiety at the vehement knocking at the door:

> *Janus*. No; sit still! That is some aukward body out of the city; one of our people from Leadenhall-Street; perhaps a director; I sha'n't stir for him.

> *Conserve*. Not for a director? I thought he was the commanding officer, the Great Captain's captain.

> *Janus*. No, no; quite the reverse; the tables are turned, Mr. Conserve: in acknowledgment for appointing us their servants abroad, we are so obliging as to make them directors at home. (Foote, 1778, p.20)

The plural pronoun again indicates the satirical and symbolic relationship between them and Sir Matthew. The link between the reversal of the social order at home and the reversal of the imperial centre and the periphery is symbolised by Janus's refusal to heed his master's 'captain'. Janus's explanation of how the East India company works similarly exploits this topos of reversal: the 'director' of the company is obliged to the 'servants' in India.

---

[3] See Brown (1757)

Such an anxiety was apparent when, eleven years later, the East India Company was again under investigation. Edmund Burke's speech to Fox's East India Bill incorporates virtually the same rhetoric:

> All the relations of the Company are not only changed, but inverted. The servants in India are not appointed by the Directors, but the Directors are chosen by them. ... The seat of the supreme power is in Calcutta. The house in Leadenhall Street is nothing more than a change for their agents, factors, and deputies to meet in, to take care of their affairs, and support their interests. (Burke, in Marshall, 1981, p.437)[4]

The fact that a topos of reversal is employed in two very different discourses, may suggest a serious satiric thrust. However, the scene between Janus and Conserve, coming at the end of the first act, is a self-contained piece of farce. It even includes a satire on a member of Parliament known for his tallness and long speeches in the person of Sir Timothy Tallboy.[5] Such an attack on a specific personage was deemed to be inappropriate to the seriousness of moral comedy that Foote claimed for his work. The drive for popularity forces Foote away from moral comedy, so that he is like the author 'who bounds his less-aspiring views | To Farce, the Combrush of the Comic Muse', as Joseph Reed (a contemporary farce-writer) puts it (Reed, in Bevis, 1970, p.xi). The merchant classes sitting in the audience would be content to 'laugh a thoughtful hour away' (Reed, in Bevis, 1970, p.xi). Further, they would be able to distance themselves ideologically from the buffoonery of such 'low' types: Janus is the comic butt of a 'conservative ideology' (McKeon, 1987) towards social mobility and status and part of a caricatured and stereotypical tradition of upstart servants.

Virtue wins the day

Mr. Thomas Oldham, like Sir Matthew, is a merchant himself, and like Sir Matthew is successful. Yet there the similarities end; Foote draws a distinction between the two, in that Thomas Oldham is virtuous. His comments to the anti-mercantile Lady Oldham (his sister-in-law), offer an ideal of the imperial commercial trader:

---

[4] Burke's cause for concern is the manipulation of the company's directors: the interest on the stock in the company that directors were required to hold was – so Burke argued – virtually worthless compared to the profits that were capable of being made from India. What they were worth, however, was the price of votes on the General Court, the meeting of stockholders.

[5] This would be Sir Thomas Robinson (Belden, 1969, p.149).

> There are men from the Indies, and many too, with whom I have
> the honour to live, who dispense nobly and with hospitality here
> what they have acquired with honour and credit elsewhere; and, at
> the same time that they have increased the dominions and wealth,
> have added virtues to their country. (Foote, 1778, p.13)

Thomas Oldham's comments would pour balm into the soul of
Mackenzie's Harley, displaying, as they do, an ideology of trade as an
empire of sociable and peaceful commerce. As a propagandist for
virtuous commerce, Sir Thomas's sentiments would go down well with
the mercantile patrons of Georgian theatre, as they reportedly did with
Foote's assailants.

Importantly, Thomas Oldham is the means by which his Matthew's
plans are thwarted and the Oldham's lineage kept free from pollution. Sir
Oldham is the moral victim of the play, a member of Parliament from an
ancient family who has spent a fortune on bringing charges of corruption
against Sir Matthew. Unfortunately, Sir Matthew has bought Sir
Oldham's debt, and now wants to marry his daughter, holding the threat
of foreclosure and bankruptcy over the family and estate. Thomas
Oldham's money - the profits of imperial trade - has saved Oldham's
estate and provided a suitable match for the daughter in the person of his
son. Thomas Oldham functions to align virtuous commerce with a stable
social order: he has thwarted Mite, and enabled the young lovers to marry.
The final words of the play ring with a resounding sound-bite that is a
paean to virtuous imperialism and civic duty:

> Then be happy, my children! And as to my young cousins within, I
> hope we shall settle them without Sir Matthew's assistance: For,
> however praiseworthy the spirit of adventure may be, whoever
> keeps his post, and does his duty at home, will be found to render
> his country best service at last! (Foote, 1778, p.71)

As Bhattacharya has noted, the emphasis on virtue in economic dealings
was ostensibly aimed at aligning public and private virtue (Bhattacharya,
1998, pp.80-84).[6] The equation of personal prosperity and civic virtue –
as idealised in the figure of Thomas Oldham - ensures no threat to the
social order, since the threat of individual economic desire would be
sublimated to the exigencies of the national good – unlike Sir Matthew's

---

[6] Interestingly, Robert Clive, in defence of his actions before the House of
Commons in 1773, would make exactly this claim; that after 'a life full of
employment for the public welfare' he could not suspect that he would lose 'my
honour and reputation' (Marshall, 1968, p.171).

damaging and unrestrained desires which threaten to wreck the social stability of the landed classes.

While Foote satirised the moral sententiousness of the fashion for sentimentalism in the drama of the period, his own plays are not free from this mode. The marriage of the 'true lovers' and the moral coda smacks of sentimental drama: Thomas Oldham is the family's saviour and the play's virtuous centre. Clearly, his character is a moral bribe to those of the commercial classes in the audience, insuring the play's popularity. Thomas Oldham, then, has a key function in the play's ideological manoeuvering between moral and economic discourses; between the demands of satire and popularity with the merchant classes.

Stereotypes of the Orient

Thomas Oldham's moralising on Sir Matthew's rise to excessive wealth and power echoes Smollett's concerns over parvenu merchants:

> These new gentlemen, who from the caprice of Fortune, and a strange chain of events, have acquired immoderate wealth, and rose to uncontroled [*sic*] power abroad, find it difficult to descend from their dignity, and admit of any equal at home. (Foote, 1778, pp.17-18)

This ironic stab at Sir Matthew's acquired 'dignity', however, also locates the source of this love of power 'abroad' - in other words, in India. Sir Matthew's characteristics are themselves stereotypes of the Orient and mobilise popular and hegemonic conceptions of Indian culture and civilisation. Stereotypes play an important role in the piece's popular appeal and its ideological conservatism. As Bevis notes, 'the art of the afterpiece is stereotypic' (Bevis, 1970, p.xiii; his emphasis) and Foote's reliance on this form ultimately provides the play's ideological safety valve, ensuring that unpalatable truths about its audience are neutralized by stereotypes of the Orient. Indeed, in an apposite comment, Edward Said notes the theatricality of Orientalism, as if a whole parade of ideas and myths of the East existed in a theatre of the Western imagination: 'the Orient is the stage on which the whole East is confined. On this stage will appear figures whose role it is to represent the larger whole from which they emanate' (Said, 1995, p.63).

Sir Matthew Mite's haughty manners and amoral attitudes to political and personal power - bribing local mayors to ensure his election to Parliament and his manipulation of Oldham's debt to gain their estate and their daughter - would be viewed as a typically Oriental despotism. As Lord Robert Clive noted in a speech to the Commons in 1772, 'Industan was always an absolute despotic government (Clive, in Horn and

Ransome, 1957, p.809). Similarly, in the satirical poem 'The Nabob or the Asiatic Plunderer' (1776), the anonymous poet declares 'in Asia's realms let slavery be bound' (anon., in Juneja, 1992, p.191). In Adam Ferguson's *An Essay on the History of Civil Society* (1767) Indian slothfulness coexists with tyranny, that demon of British nationalism: 'The sun, it seems, ... inspires a degree of mildness that can even assuage the rigours of despotical government' (Ferguson, 1966, p.111).

In a similar way, Sir Matthew's interest in gaming and an over-precious sense of dress ally him to the perceptions of Oriental luxury. In Ferguson's *Essay*, in a section detailing the characteristics of the 'torrid zone', Oriental luxury is hinted when he describes the 'love of ease and of pleasure' (Ferguson, 1966, p.111). Oriental passive resistance, tyranny and vice are yoked together:

> Transferred, without any great struggle, from one master to another, the natives of India are ready, upon every change, to pursue their industry, to acquiesce in the enjoyment of life, and the hopes of animal pleasure ... even the barbarous invader leaves untouched the commercial settlement which has not provoked his rage: though master of opulent cities, he only incamps in their neighbourhood, and leaves to his heirs the option of entering, by degrees, on the pleasures, the vices, and the pageantries his acquisitions afford: his successors, still more than himself, are disposed to foster the hive, in proportion as they taste more of its sweets; and they spare the inhabitant, together with his dwelling, as they spare the herd or stall, of which they are become the proprietors. (Ferguson, 1966, p.111)

As a justification for the ease with which Indian subjects are ruled it sounds suspiciously like imperial propaganda. However, there are also stereotypes of Indian culture: the passive ease of luxury, the addiction to 'animal pleasure'. It also confirms the dangers of an infectious love of tyranny and vice that Thomas Oldham sees in Mite: successive rulers seem to unavoidably 'taste more of its sweets'. Sir Matthew's sexual desires too - he uses a procuress, Match'em, to find suitable women who are in debt so he can buy their favours and he has had 'some thoughts of founding in this town a seraglio' (Foote, 1778, p.37) - all smack of the stereotypes of Indian love of sensual pleasure. Similarly, Ferguson assigns to the 'torrid zone' all the sexualised fantasies and desires of the European towards the Orient: it is a place of 'melting desires ... fiery passions ... the burning ardours, and the torturing jealousies, of the seraglio and the haram [sic]' (Ferguson, 1966, p.115).

The British nabobs' imported despotism was perceived to corrupt commercial trading practices at home, as Lady Oldham's stentorian indictment of Sir Matthew's effect on the country suggests: 'Preceded by all the pomp of Asia, Sir Matthew Mite, from the Indies, came thundering amongst us ... profusely scattering the spoils of ruined provinces' (Foote, 1778, p.4). Burke's speech to Fox's East India Bill in 1783 echoes very closely Foote's moral rhetoric when he imagines 'some man of power who has made an obnoxious fortune in India' returning 'that he may shower the spoils of the East, "barbaric pearl and gold," on them, their families, and dependents' (Burke, in Marshall, 1981, p.437). The Miltonic reference only serves to underline the anxieties surrounding the inversion of the proper relations between the centre and its peripheries, between Parliament and trade: the barbarism of the imported riches is synecdochic for the barbarism of the British company-men.

Intertwined with Burke's ostensibly humane indictment of the East India company's practices is a distinctly Orientalizing voice whereby Indian culture is deemed as an agent for corruption. His concern, then, is as much for the corruption of the British merchant while in India: 'English youth in India drink the intoxicating draught of authority and dominion before their heads are able to bear it' (Burke, in Marshall, 1981, p.402). The stereotype of Indian despotism is employed here as an emblem for the 'infection' of British youth. As Singh has noted, such images 'create a suggestive picture of a land *breeding* immorality in Englishmen' (Singh, 1996, p.57). Indeed, Sir Matthew's exasperated comment to a flower-seller, Crocus, reveals that he has been symbolically infected by the East: 'You know my complexion has been tinged by the East, and you bring me a blaze of yellow' (Foote, 1778, p.31). Lady Oldham's comment that 'with the wealth of the East, we have, too, imported the worst of its vices' (Foote, 1778, p.13) echoes exactly the metaphoric contagion of the British nation.

Sir Matthew's corruption is a product, then, not of mercantile practices endemic in Britain, but of vices native to India. Foote's satiric thrust at the nabobs is not a laughter at the expense of the morality of imperial commerce, but rather a comedy of stereotypes. As Sander Gilman says of stereotypes 'they buffer us against our most urgent fears by extending them, making it possible for us to act as though their source were beyond our control' (Gilman, 1985, p.16). The distancing effect of such a mode of representation locates the source of moral corruption beyond 'our' shores; beyond, even, the popular space of Georgian theatre. Ideologically, stereotypes let the English merchant off the hook of Foote's satire.

'This circle for my jury'

Attacks on the East India company grew throughout the 1770's: such a rich potential object for popular moral comedy was the quintessence of Foote's œuvre. His 'arched brow and leering eye' had singled out a most topical subject - one that was definitely close to home - and one that was guaranteed to pique the interest of the London theatre audience. But was it perhaps too near the bone?

His intercession on this topic was fraught with peril, since he was doubtless aware that the very merchants who would be closely aligned with the imperial commercial project were also the ones with an investment in the very theatrical space that Foote was claiming to reform. The 'circle' of this popular theatre had to have their consciences pricked, but he had to gain them for the play's 'jury'. His negotiations between the discourses of imperial economics, politics, satirical morality, and popular comedy indicate the competing tensions between these spheres.

Was, however, the appeal to popularity – at the expense of moral bite – an attempt to pre-empt the jury's decision? While Foote may well have constructed an 'ultimately ridiculous figure of the nabob' (Juneja, 1992, p.196) there is no sense in which this shows 'a developing conscience about the treatment of colonial subjects' or that it is 'free from any overt or implicit racism' (Juneja, 1992, p.195). By reproducing the ideological morality of imperial commerce, the merchant-audience's conscience was assuaged. Further, Foote's reliance on the form of the afterpiece, with its corresponding generic pressures to include farce, crude plot resolutions, and stereotypes enabled an audience to laugh away their fears, to dilute the moral outrage of his satire. To ensure his 'circle for my jury', Foote's satire has become as Swift has it, is 'a sort of glass, wherein beholders do generally discover everybody's face but their own' (Swift, 1986, p.104).

Bibliography

Belden, Mary Megie, (1929, 1969) *The Dramatic Work of Samuel Foote*, Archon Books.

Bevis, Richard, ed. (1970) *Eighteenth-century drama: afterpiece*. Oxford University Press, Oxford.

Bevis, Richard, (1980) *The Laughing Tradition: Stage Comedy in Garrick's Day*, University of Georgia Press, Athens.

Bhattacharya, Nandini, (1998) *Reading the Splendid Body: Gender and Consumerism in Eighteenth-Century British Writing on India*, University of Delaware Press, Newark; Associated University Presses, London.

Brown, John, (1757) An Estimate of the Manners and Principles of the Times, London.

Bowen, H.V. (1998) 'British India, 1765-1813: The Metropolitan Context', in P. J. Marshall (ed.) *The Oxford History of the British Empire, vol. 2: The Eighteenth Century*, Oxford University Press, Oxford, pp.530-51

Foote, Samuel, (1778) The Nabob; A Comedy in Three Acts, London.

Gilman, Sander, (1985) *Difference and Pathology: Stereotypes of Sexuality, Race, and Madness*, Cornell University Press, Ithaca and London.

Holzman, James M. (1926) The Nabobs in England: A Study of the Returned Anglo-Indian, 1760-1785, New York.

Horn, D. B. and Mary Ransome, eds. (1957) *English Historical Documents, 1714-1783*, Eyre and Spottiswoode, London.

Juneja, Renu, (1992) 'The Native and the Nabob: Representations of the Indian Experience in Eighteenth-Century Literature', *Journal of Commonwealth Literature*, 27:1, pp.183-98.

Mackenzie, Henry, (1771, 1967) *The Man of Feeling*, ed. by Brian Vickers, Oxford University Press, London.

Marshall, P.J. (1968) *Problems of Empire: Britain and India 1757-1813*, George Allen and Unwin, London.

Marshall, P.J. ed. (1981) The Writings and Speeches of Edmund Burke. Volume V. India: Madras and Bengal 1774-1785, Clarendon Press, Oxford.

Marshall, P.J. ed. (1998) The Oxford History of the British Empire, vol. 2: The Eighteenth Century, Oxford University Press, Oxford.

McKeon, Michael, (1987) *The Origins of the English Novel 1600-1740*, The Johns Hopkins University Press, Baltimore.

Said, Edward, (1978, 1995) *Orientalism: Western Conceptions of the Orient*, Penguin, London.

Singh, Jyotsna G. (1996) Colonial Narratives / Cultural Dialogues: 'Discoveries' of India in the Language of Colonialism, Routledge, London.

Smollett, Tobias (1771, 1984) *The Expedition of Humphry Clinker*, ed. by Lewis M. Knapp and Paul-Gabriel Boucé, Oxford University Press, Oxford.

Spear, Percival, (1963) The Nabobs: A Study of the Social Life of the English in 18th Century India, Oxford University Press, London.

Stallybrass, Peter and White, Allon, (1986) *The Politics and Poetics of Transgression*, Methuen, London.

Swift, Jonathan, (1702, 1986) *The Tale of the Tub and other works*, ed. by Angus Ross and David Woolley, Oxford University Press, Oxford.

Taylor, George, ed. (1984) *Plays by Samuel Foote and Arthur Murphy*, Cambridge University Press, Cambridge.

Trefman, Simon, (1971) *Sam Foote, Comedian, 1720-1777*, New York University Press, New York.

Making Sport of Violence: the Presence of The Sepoy Mutiny in James Joyce's *Ulysses* and J.G. Farrell's *The Siege of Krishnapur*

Claire Spencer-Jones

Despite the geographical distance of Ireland from India, the Sepoy Mutiny becomes part of the bar room conversation in Barney Kiernan's pub in the Dublin of 1904. This is the setting for the 'Citizen' chapter of James Joyce's Ulysses. Joyce juxtaposes history and parody in order to present an image of Dublin that is seething with discontent for the English occupation. Ulysses presents a picture of the disunity of Irish politics in the Dublin of 1904. This chapter will consider the presence of the Sepoy Mutiny in Joyce's work and the more recent J.G. Farrell text The Siege of Krishnapur. How does the Sepoy Mutiny, an Asian cultural moment, fit into the complex schema of the history of Ireland and Irish literature written in English? The first part of this discussion will consider the presence of the Sepoy Mutiny in James Joyce's novel Ulysses. After an opening review of the causes of the Sepoy Mutiny, the parodic relationship between the Mutiny, Irish nationalism and the sport of hurling will be examined. The intention here is to explore the connections between these apparently diverse issues and to consider why the Mutiny becomes part of the Irish political landscape of 1904 and how these seemingly disparate issues are linked in the 'Cyclops' episode of Ulysses. An overview of other publications in English, including J.G. Farrell's 1973 novel The Siege of Krishnapur, that have contributed to the continuing discourses surrounding the Sepoy Mutiny will form the latter part of this examination of representations of South Asian culture in English. Unless we are historians of Indian and British colonial history, the Sepoy Mutiny is an event that may not be at the forefront of our knowledge of history. Therefore, using eyewitness accounts of the uprising, written by British soldiers, the context of the Mutiny will now be considered. The Sepoy Mutiny occurred between January 1857 and April 1859. It consisted of a series of insurrections across the 'North-West Provinces' in India that included massacres, looting and warfare that culminated in executions. The suppression of the Sepoys became another infamous chapter in the history of British colonial oppression. There are many accounts of the Mutiny written by the victors but there are few written records produced by the losing side: 'fear, if not terror, inhibited Indians from putting on paper what they saw and heard during the Mutiny.' (Hewitt, 1972, p.v)

It can be gauged from contemporaneous written accounts that the origins of the Mutiny were unclear to the British, in fact, the overwhelming lack of preparation by the British suggests that they were unaware of the consequences of the provocative nature of their behaviour in India. George Bourchier in *Eight Months Campaign Against the Bengal Sepoy Army, During the Mutiny of 1857* remarked:

Many reasons have been assigned for the rising; but to use the words of the late lamented General Nicholson, than whom none more fully understood the native character, 'neither greased cartridges, the annexation of Oude, nor the paucity of European officers were the causes. For years,' he said, 'I have watched the army, and felt sure they only wanted their opportunity to try their strength with us.' (Bourchier, 1858, p.2)

Bourchier is suggesting here that the Sepoys were eager to engage in battle with the British because they relished a trial of their strength. There is an absolute lack of consideration of the cause and effect of the British disregard for religious customs. Although other accounts cite the growing missionary zeal to convert the Indians to Christianity as provocative, blaming the missionaries was regarded at the time as 'an idle absurdity' (Kay, 1880, p.523). There were undoubtedly a number of factors which conspired to produce the Mutiny including the destabilisation of the caste system through changes in transport, forcing different castes to travel together, the redundancies of large numbers of Indian soldiers and shifts in the balance of power through newly appointed administrative authorities (Hewitt, op. cit. pp.2-4). The cavalier attitudes that prevailed following the Mutiny can be heard clearly in the voice of Sir John William Kay. He accuses the natives of being 'obstinate' in their convictions regarding the British desire to 'pollute' the Sepoys. (Kay, op. cit. p.523)

Another account of the Mutiny, *Incidents in the Sepoy War 1857-8* edited by Henry Knollys, remarked that the accusation that the greased cartridges had provoked the Mutiny were 'so trumpery in its nature that a modern Swift, might have employed it to typify the origins of the wars of Lilliput or Laputa' (Knollys, 1873, p.15). Knollys' words represent the paternal authority of the colonial master in the act of rebuking the foolish native/child. He infers that the Indians' objections can be filed under imaginary fiction only suitable for the entertainment of children. In these circumstances Knollys' slender appreciation of the philosophical nature of Swift's work is ironic if not tragic. Despite this apparent lack of regard for the potential problems caused by the greased cartridges, Knollys does eventually explain why they did actually cause offence:

> For some years previous to the Mutiny, the old pattern rifle had been in use among Indian troops. The bullet was enveloped in a patch of cloth, which was smeared with a mixture of wax and oil, and the natives had used it without offering any objection. In 1856, however, the improved Enfield rifle was introduced, the projectile for which was lubricated with grease to facilitate its passage down the bore. Ere long it was rumoured that this grease was composed of the fat of pigs and cows- substances regarded with equal horror by Hindoos and Musselmans. (Ibid. p.17)

Knollys is clearly aware that by biting off the end of the cartridge, as was the common practice, the Indians would consider themselves 'defiled' (Ibid. p.17). Knollys attempts to deflect further blame by remarking that it was a low caste Lascar who provoked the higher caste Sepoy into mutinying by informing him that they would all share the same low caste because of the new cartridges. Knollys' account demonstrates that the colonial masters laid the blame for the commencement of the conflict firmly at the door of the native population.

The arrogant disregard for religious beliefs and customs from the colonial rulers was the major overarching influence that caused the Mutiny. The Mutiny that ensued was bloody and barbarous in many respects. However, it was the aftermath of the Mutiny that became infamous. Eric Hobsbawm, for example, comments in *The Age of Capital* that the 'Mutiny' was 'suppressed in a welter of blood' (Hobsbawm 1995, p.124). The *Encyclopaedia Britannica* (1998) supports this opinion: 'In the end the reprisals far outweighed the original excesses.' There were voices raised in protest against the executions carried out. But from the far-flung location of the British Parliament it was difficult to relay concern regarding the severity of the punishments meted out in India. Telegraphed messages were often corrupted in transit and took months to arrive at their destination.

The Earl of Ellenborough, speaking in the House of Lords on February 15th, 1858 raised some objections to the reprisals inflicted on the mutineers by Sir Hugh Rose:

> While this is the national character of the Natives of India - while the sufferers evince this heroism - instead of preventing the

commission of similar offences, you rather add grace and dignity to the cause in which they have so nefariously engaged. (Hansard, 1858, p.1362)

Ellenborough's objections, evinced above, voice the concerns of the British regarding the deterrent value of the executions rather than disapproval of their barbarity. His fears also express an admiration for the heroic manner in which the mutineers met their death.

There are a number of journals that recorded the executions and one of the eyewitnesses to these events was Lieutenant-Colonel F.C. Maude. Maude was also one of the soldiers in charge of the punishments. Part of Maude's first hand testimony relates the following conversation between himself and Brigadier-General Sir Henry Havelock:

Havelock asked me if 'I knew how to blow a man from a gun?' Naturally this had not formed part of our *curriculum* at Woolwich; but I had no hesitation in at once answering in the affirmative. For it will be obvious to anyone that three pounds of good powder (the service charge of a brass nine-pounder) would be pretty sure to effect the desired purpose. (Hewitt, op. cit. p.149)

Maude gives further explicit details concerning the events of the execution of a 'fine-looking young sepoy' witnessed by a crowd of onlookers. The whimsical tone of the recount jars with the grim reality of the execution. Following the recoil from the gun, the only remains of the 'brave man' left were his head and legs.

How are these events reflected in the work of James Joyce? The next part of this discussion of the presence of South Asian culture in English will consider the relationship between Irish nationalism, the Irish sport of hurling and the Sepoy Mutiny. Some research has already pinpointed the events of the Mutiny in Joyce's work. Vincent Cheng refers to the Sepoy Mutiny reference in *Ulysses* in his book, *Joyce, Race and Empire.*[1] Cheng concentrates his attentions on the reference to the Mutiny in *Finnegans Wake* in his chapter entitled 'The General and the Sepoy: imperialism and power in the Museyroom' (Ibid. pp.278-288). He demonstrates how, in *The Wake,* Joyce uses metonymy to connect the activities of the Duke of Wellington (the Iron Duke), King Billy and the Sepoy Mutiny. Cheng also highlights how the coloniser's religious 'intolerance', an issue revealed in the British accounts of the Mutiny, precipitates conflict (Ibid. p.284). Although Cheng briefly draws attention to the Mutiny reference in

---

[1] Cheng, 1995b, p.203

Ulysses, this exploration will consider Joyce's references to the Mutiny in *Ulysses* in more detail. (Ibid. p.203)

Ulysses by James Joyce follows a day in the life of Leopold Bloom in the Dublin of 1904. Although the text was published without chapter titles, Joyce provided a guide explaining the complexity of the individual sections of *Ulysses* to Carlo Linati in 1920 (Ellmann, 1983, p.519). The schema revealed that the travels of Odysseus in Homer's *The Odyssey* provided the structure for the text. In other words, each episode could be considered alongside Odysseus' adventures as the exiled king made his way home to Ithaca. It is to one of these chapters that we will now turn our attentions to because it contains a direct reference to the Sepoy Mutiny. The chapter in question is known as 'Cyclops' in the Linati schema, its alternative title has become 'the Citizen Chapter' for reasons that will now be explained.

The citizen, a character introduced in this chapter, is modelled on an individual who was called Michael Cusack. Cusack referred to himself as 'Citizen Cusack' (Ibid. p.61) and he was renowned for his short temper. There is evidence linking him to the IRB (Irish Republican Brotherhood), and S.J. Connolly argues in *The Oxford Companion to Irish History* that the GAA (Gaelic Athletic Association) may have been started as an IRB initiative designed to foster its own militant military agenda (Connolly, 1998, p.213). Cusack was founder of the Gaelic Athletic Association; an Association dedicated to the revival of Irish sports, including hurling (Gifford, 1988 p.316). Irish sports and nationalism were closely linked-the regular presence of prominent nationalists at hurling games is a testimony to the games' propaganda purposes. Hurling is an activity that Joyce, as we will see, links to the events of the Mutiny.

Although the 'unofficial' title of this episode is the 'Citizen' chapter the title given to Linati by Joyce was 'Cyclops'. Why was 'Cyclops' chosen for the title of this episode and how does the legend of Cyclops tie in with the events of the Sepoy Mutiny? The Cyclops we may remember was one of the race of Titans, a giant race that fathered the race of Mount Olympus gods led by Zeus and it is worth taking time to explore this Homeric allusion. Polyphemus was one of the race of one-eyed Cyclops who captured Odysseus and his crew as they journeyed home from the Trojan War. Odysseus blinded Polyphemus in order to make his escape from captivity and certain death (Homer, 1991, p.137). The giant one-eyed Titan is rather stupid but he was also violent and bloodthirsty and Joyce, as we have already observed, connects the Fenian 'citizen' to this one-eyed fiend. The citizen seated in Barney Kiernan's pub is easily provoked (Joyce, 1992, p.396). Bloom, a latter-day Odysseus, seems unaware of the effect he has on the Citizen and the Citizen's anger eventually turns to violence in a re-working of the friction-laden relationship between the coloniser and the colonised.[2]

On an intertextual level the citizen's temper also echoes the temperament of the voracious though rather stupid Polyphemus. Polyphemus killed his prisoners by various barbaric methods that included *hurling* stones at them; this is another Joycean pun that works in several ways. The issue of hurling will be discussed soon but it is interesting to note that Michael Cusack also put the shot; he really did have something in common with Polyphemus.[3] Shot is associated in military terms with cannons- the word is literally loaded. The executed Sepoys as we have seen are also associated with the violence of the cannon. These layers of language in *Ulysses* present the Citizen as an intimidating, stupid individual with nationalist pretensions who is easily goaded into violent action and Joyce links the Sepoy Mutiny and its aftermath with the intentions of nationalists in the 'Cyclops' episode of *Ulysses*. Moreover, this stratification of language: the historical, the biographical, the comic, and the mythic, combine to produce what Mikhail Bakhtin identifies in the novel form as 'several heterogeneous stylistic unities, often located on different linguistic levels and subject to different stylistic controls' (Bakhtin, 1994, p.262. Joyce employs several genres simultaneously: the comic ignorance of the Citizen is juxtaposed with the historical role of the Fenians in Irish history and the events of the Sepoy Mutiny. This clashing of literary dimensions creates a dissonance in the chapter as a whole that reflects a social disorder that is both comic and tragic. Joyce's complex form echoes the confusion and instability of the society of the period. In 'Cyclops' the subject of Irish games, the game of hurling, become magnified in importance because the sport was aligned with Irish nationalism. The suppression of games such as Hurling influenced the public sphere beyond the tittle-tattle of the public bar. In order to understand the political nature of Irish games it is necessary to consider why such sports were discouraged by the British in Ireland. Part of the Imperial project of subduing Irish nationalism consisted in the banning of Irish games and so the playing of Irish games in Dublin's Phoenix Park was a political act and provided an opportunity to publicly disrupt the hegemony of English domination. Anti-games legislation had been part of the English attempts to subdue the Irish for centuries as may

---

[2] One of the central discussions of 'Cyclops' concerns the right to be called a citizen. Bloom confounds the citizen when he states that his nation is Ireland. (Joyce, *Ulysses*, p.430)

[3] Bloom is of course the victim of Cusack's hurling abilities when a biscuit tin is aimed at him at the conclusion of the chapter. (Gifford, *Ulysses Annotated*, p.342)

be demonstrated in the 1366 *The Statute of Kilkenny* (Irish Archaeological Society, 1842, p.23).

If we consider the conversations in *Ulysses* it can be demonstrated that Irish games were considered to be an important aspect of an Irish identity. Sitting among the drinkers in Barney Kiernan's bar is the character of Joe Hynes. He is taking part in the general bar room banter and, at this point in the afternoon, he has raised the issue of cattle transportation. Hynes has actually gone to the bar to give 'the citizen' the 'hard word' about the cattle traders meeting that he had attended at the City Arms Hotel. Cattle transportation, however, becomes a side issue as the conversation develops into an exchange concerning the playing of Irish games. Hynes also tells the citizen that Irish issues are to be debated in the British House of Commons by Joseph Nannetti MP (1851-1915), referred to in *Ulysses* as 'Nannan'. The issue of the cattle and the playing of games are thus juxtaposed. However, in *Ulysses* these 'innocent' matters become manifestations of the violence that nationalism can engender. The conversation in Barney Kiernan's pub then swiftly changes location to the primary location of legislative activity - the British House of Commons (Joyce, *Ulysses, op. cit.* p.409).

Joyce parodies the decorum of the House by simulating the language and the decorum of the proceedings of this venerable institution. He playfully combines the issues of cattle slaughter with the problem of playing games in Phoenix Park. However, the records of the British House of Commons do in fact reveal that disparate issues, such as agriculture and recreation, were debated under the remit of 'Irish affairs'. This political system of grouping such a hotchpotch of Irish matters together because they were 'Irish' has an important political effect: it deflates the important issues because they are in the company of the trivial. The proceedings lose their gravity and become rather superficial. Joyce takes reality and reveals its inherent comic nature.[4] Joseph Nannetti MP did actually raise the question of playing games in Phoenix Park:

> I beg to ask the Chief Secretary to the Lord Lieutenant of Ireland whether he is aware that, while the game of polo is allowed to be played in that part of the Phoenix Park known as the Nine Acres, the members of Sluagh na h-Eireann are not allowed to play Gaelic games there; and, if so, will he state under what authority the Commissioners of Police are under an obligation not to increase

---

[4] Interestingly, it was the MP William Field (b.1848) who actually asked the question regarding the transportation of cattle on the 14th June 1904. (*Hansard's Parliamentary Debates*, 1914, p.20)

the enclosures or a number of allotments in the park; whether the Commissioners have authority to enforce prohibitive measures against the games played by most of the young men in Dublin, seeing that the history of the Phoenix Park clearly shows that the park belongs to the citizens of Dublin. (Ibid. p.286)

Mr. Wyndham, the Secretary of State for Ireland, replied that the games were not allowed owing to 'the damage to the turf' (Ibid. p.286). Wyndham elides the political nature of the request by commenting on the material damage done to the grass by the playing of such Gaelic games; it seems that English polo did little harm to the turf. The repartee in the British House of Commons is as comic as the dialogue in Barney Kiernan's. There is, however, a serious side to this apparently comic exchange because the dialogic provenance of the 'history of Phoenix Park' mentioned by Nannetti possessed a darker side. Orelli's reference to 'human animals' slaughtered in the park could be an oblique reference to the murders of the Chief Secretary for Ireland, Lord Frederick Cavendish and Thomas Henry Burke his Permanent Under-Secretary. Joyce is alluding to the assassinations that took place in May 1882 (Fairhall, 1995, p.11). There are several hints in 'Cyclops' that would support the argument that the murders in the park are on the minds of the drinkers, for example, there are a number of references to the Invincibles including one of their members, Joe Brady.

The Invincibles were the group of Irish activists held responsible for the murders in Phoenix Park in May 1882 (Welch, 2000, p.162). Here, another link between the murders in the Park, *Ulysses* and the Sepoy Mutiny exists. Although the Irish group calling themselves The Invincibles had formed in 1881 there was an earlier group of soldiers who were also known as 'The Invincibles', and they form part of history of the Sepoy Mutiny. These soldiers also went under the title of Carnegie's 'gallant Burkundauzes'[5]. According to James Lawrence's eyewitness account, these soldiers fought in the Sepoy Mutiny during the Battle of Chinhut on 30th of June 1858 (Ibid. p.131). On the day of the battle of Chinhut they deserted the British ranks and joined the Mutiny:

Our side was perfectly passive; Carnegie's *Invincibles* had deserted, and while I was looking about for them, a bustle in my rear attracted my attention. The rascally gunners were cutting their traces, and were galloping away... (Ibid. pp.132-3)

---

[5] A Burkundauze is defined in the *OED* as 'a matchlock man, but commonly applied to a native of Hindustan, armed with a sword and a shield, who acts as a doorkeeper, watchman, guard or escort.' (Hewitt, 1972, p.131

It is not beyond the bounds of possibility that Joyce was aware of the links between the Irish and the Indian Invincibles. Betrayal is a feature of Irish politics that Joyce reprised in his writings. The desertion and betrayal by the Indian Invincibles of their colonial masters finds an uncanny repetition in the actions of the Irish Invincible, James Carey, who turned Queens Evidence and betrayed his fellow conspirators (Welch, op.cit. p.262). The betrayal of the Irish by their own people is a recurrent theme in the history of Irish nationalism.[6] In Joyce's novel, *A Portrait of the Artist as a Young Man*, Stephen Dedalus openly refers to the presence of informers amongst Irish rebels thus illustrating that internecine betrayal featured in the discourse of college students (Ibid. p.231). The earlier text of *A Portrait of an Artist as a Young Man* also demonstrates the connections between hurling, nationalism and the theme of betrayal (Ibid. p.231).The innocuous subject of Gaelic sports becomes dialogically inseparable in Barney Kiernan's bar in *Ulysses* to the issue of gaining independence through violent means. Joyce's employment of parody illustrates that the futility of the proceedings in the British House of Commons provides a motive for nationalists taking the alternative path of violent extremism.

The violence of revolution is an underlying theme of 'Cyclops' in the Dublin of 1904. As already suggested, the citizen's ferocious nature is one of the more obvious manifestations of violence in the chapter. The references to the Invincibles and the execution of Robert Emmet are further allusions to the conflict and deaths that nationalist aspirations inevitably result in when they are faced with an intransigent ruling élite and a British House of Commons that is a laughing stock. Although the conversation takes place within the confines of Barney Kiernan's public house in Dublin, *Ulysses* also crosses international borders as other revolutionary events from far-flung places in the Empire find a dialogic echo in the text. There is, for example, a direct reference in 'Cyclops' to the 1857 Sepoy Mutiny (Joyce, *Ulysses*, pp.401-2.). The Sepoy Mutiny reference clearly demonstrates that cannons facilitate a sickening potential for violence and are not simply landmarks of a glorious Imperial past. The punishment that the Sepoys underwent was barbaric and the graphic language of *Ulysses* that describes the callous nature of their executions at the cannon mouth demonstrates that the events of the Mutiny remained fresh in the Irish mind. Furthermore, the inference is that the Imperial executioner, Tomkin-Maxwell, was the same individual responsible for

---

[6] The betrayal of Charles Stewart Parnell by Richard Piggott's fabricated letters that suggested that Parnell approved of the Phoenix Park assassinations is an infamous example of the Irish betraying their own people. (McCormack, 2001, p.464)

the Sepoys' punishment. (In 'Cyclops' Tomkin-Maxwell is also named as the executioner of Robert Emmet).[7] The 'mailed gauntlet' of Tomkin-Maxwell demonstrates that the personal risks that rebels run are high.

Joyce was not the first writer to employ references to the Sepoy Mutiny. The Sepoy Mutiny is, as we will now witness, at the forefront of another Irish writer's work. Padraic Pearse, the leader of the Easter 1916 Rising, was an author who was keen to keep the behaviour of the Imperial forces in the minds of his readership. In his 1912 pamphlet entitled *The Murder Machine* Pearse wrote:

A French writer has paid the English a very well-deserved compliment. He says that they never commit a useless crime. When they hire a man to assassinate an Irish patriot, when they blow a Sepoy from the mouth of a cannon, when they produce a famine in one of their dependencies, they do not have an ulterior motive. (Pearse, 1952, p.5)

In *Ulysses Annotated* Gifford suggests that Tomkin-Maxwell was a 'fictional name that suggests extraordinary pretension to 'good family' backgrounds' (Gifford, 1974, p.337). Coincidentally, Maxwell was the name of the commander who presided over the executions of the participants of the Easter Rising. Pearse wrote before his execution:

I desire in the first place to repeat what I have already said in letters to General Sir John Maxwell and to Brigadier General Lowe. My object in agreeing to an unconditional surrender was to prevent the further slaughter of our gallant followers who, having made for six days a stand unparalleled in military history, were now surrounded and (in the case of those under the immediate command of Headquarters) without food. (O Buachalla, 1980, p.379)

Although Joyce may not have been aware of Pearse's final missive he would have known, as would his readership, who the military representative in charge at the time of the Easter Rising executions was. Pearse's references to the Sepoys in his *The Murder Machine*, published originally between June 1913 and January 1914, also prove that the Sepoy rebellion was an issue of the day at the time Joyce was writing *Ulysses*.[8]

---

[7] Robert Emmet (1778-1803) was executed as an Irish revolutionary. (See Welch, 2000, p.105.

[8] Pearse discusses the original publication of his articles in *Irish Freedom* in the preface to *Political Writings*.

The Easter Rising had occurred by the time *Ulysses* was ready for publication and this hindsight enabled Joyce to consider the language of provocation that had contributed to the eruption of violence in Ireland.

Pearse's pamphlet certainly demonstrates that Joyce was not isolated in his interest in the history of India. In fact, even though the drinkers in Barney Kiernan's bar in 1904 may not have had access to the eyewitness accounts of events in India, incidents in other parts of the colonial globe were regularly reported in Irish newspapers. An Irish nationalist newspaper set up by Thomas Davis, an individual frequently alluded to in this chapter of *Ulysses*, goes into great detail regarding military events in India.[9] Davis' writings were and remain influential for nationalists and there are examples of the reportage of Indian events in Irish newspapers. For example, in the very first issue of Davis' *The Nation* on October 15, 1842 the various troop movements of the British forces in India are recounted in great detail under the heading 'The Overland Mail'. Alongside the journeys of troops, cattle and guns an account is given of 'A Suttee in Nusserbad':

> We have just heard of the death of the Maha Rana of Oudipore, in his 45th year; he was the highest Hindoo in the country. You will be glad to hear that none of his wives committed suttee owing to the great exertions used by the Politicals to dissuade them from it. A concubine, however, ascended the pile, a most beautiful young woman; she was paraded on horseback, magnificently caparisoned; the corpse followed in a sitting position, borne by several men on a gold litter; the wretched woman appeared quite unconcerned, and was dressing her hair by a glass, and eating paun the whole way; on arrival at the pile she walked calmly up to the throne, the body was then placed in her lap, and amid deafening music and shouts of the spectators, the torch was applied. The victim could not have suffered much, as the place on which she sat was charged with powdered rosin, cotton and tow, well saturated with oil. (Davis, 1842, p.6)

Even though detailed British troop movements in India were reported in newspapers, the passage above demonstrates that the Irish were fascinated with death and more particularly the funereal customs of India. In fact, the sacrifice of the concubine presents an uncanny echo of the later fate of the defeated Sepoys. It raises the following disturbing question: could the British have executed the Sepoy Indians in a manner

---

[9] Joyce, *Ulysses*, p.410.

designed to parody Indian religious practices? The dialogic links evidenced in 'Cyclops' that unite the Sepoy Mutiny, Irish nationalism and hurling form part of the complex relationship between Imperial dominance and colonial resistance. The Indian cultural spaces that are present in Irish texts form part of the complex discourses relating to the aspirations of Ireland for independence.

The Sepoy Mutiny remains a source for fiction written in English; and this examination of the Sepoy Mutiny, as a representation of South Asian culture, will draw to a conclusion by examining an example of a more recent fictional account of the Sepoy Mutiny. J.G. Farrell, an Anglo-Irish author, has also used the Sepoy Mutiny as a context for his Booker Prize-winning novel entitled *The Siege of Krishnapur*. Published in 1973 it tells the story of the Sepoy Mutiny through the experience of British held at siege in Krishnapur during the 1857 Mutiny. The bravery of the English survivors is explored, their trials and resilience under extreme conditions is related in detail. Farrell uses a combination of irony and realism to evoke a real sense of the experiences of the British during the Mutiny. Skirmishes between doctors and the women folk form part of an interesting tapestry of the British experience of the Sepoy mutiny. As a precursor to the siege itself, some discussion is made of the Sepoy objection to the Enfield rifle. But no attempt is made, even in retrospect, by any character including the third person narrator to examine the causes of the Sepoys' outrage and eventual mutiny. The Sepoys' objections to British dominance may have precipitated into mutiny when they were ordered to use the Enfield rifle, but their way of life had been undermined by British missionary activities as well as other forced changes in the internal matrix of their society.

Farrell's text combines an in-depth characterisation of British individuals with a total absence of character development of 'Jack Sepoy.' The lower classes of Indians are represented as servants who bear a form of feudal loyalty towards their more 'civilised' masters and they are demonstrably treated with disrespect, Mr Rayne, for example has given his Indian servants new names: 'Ram', 'Ant', and 'Monkey' (Farrell, 1973, p.56). This disregard for the feelings of these servants is represented without irony. The aristocratic Indians in their turn are treated as belching overweight comic characters (Ibid. p.77). The Indian spectators of the siege taunt the starving occupants of the Residency by dancing and gorging themselves on banquets (Ibid. p.174). Not a single Sepoy is actually individuated and there is no mention of their experiences of the Mutiny, *The Siege of Krishnapur* is a truly one-sided tale. In fact, more was said regarding the Sepoys in the House of Lords in 1858, an establishment which could hardly be said to have looked on the

Sepoys with favour, than in Farrell's historical/fictional account. In a 1999 publication of critical works concerning Farrell, *J.G. Farrell The Critical Grip*, it is suggested by Judie Newman that *The Siege of Krishnapur* does more than simply consign the Indians 'to the status of figurative or metaphorical existence' (Crane, 1999, p.82). In her article, Newman argues that the 'metaphorical method' employed by Farrell exposes his anti-imperialist leanings. This explanation of Farrell's anti-imperialist agenda is not convincing. The aftermath of the Mutiny and the 'blowing' of the Sepoys from cannon are omitted from Farrell's text and, even though the British are treated with an ironic admiration, the absence of the Sepoy narrative provides an overwhelming imbalance to the events that take place in a text which has aspirations to historic accuracy. Farrell's book does demonstrate that the Sepoy Mutiny maintains a textual presence in western popular culture but the aftermath of the Mutiny still remains too distasteful a subject to be broached in a work of fiction.

Bibliography

Bakhtin, M. (1994) *The Dialogic Imagination,* University of Texas Press, Austin.

Bourchier, G. (1858) Eight Months Campaign Against the Bengal Sepoy Army, During the Mutiny of 1857, Smith, Elder and Co, London.

Cheng, V. (1995a) *James Joyce and the Question of History*, Cambridge University Press.

Cheng, Vincent (1995b) *Joyce, Race and Empire*, Cambridge University Press, Cambridge.

Connolly, S.J. (1998) *Oxford Companion to Irish History*, Oxford University Press, Oxford.

Crane, Ralph, J. (1999) *J.G. Farrell The Critical Grip*, Four Courts Press, Dublin.

Davis, T. (ed.) (1842) *The Nation*, Trinity Street, Dublin.

Ellmann, R. (1982) *James Joyce.* Oxford University Press, London.

Encyclopaedia Britannica, (1998) CD Multimedia edition.

Fairhall, J. (1995) *James Joyce and the Question of History*, Cambridge. University Press, Cambridge.

Farrell, J.G. (1973) *The Siege of Krishnapur*, Orion Books Limited, London.

Gifford, D. and Seidman, R. (1989) *Ulysses Annotated. Notes For James Joyce's Ulysses,* University of California Press, Berkeley.

Hansard's Parliamentary Debates, (1857) Third Series vols. CXLV-CXLVIIICornelius Buck, London.

Hewitt, J. (ed.) (1972) *Eye-Witnesses to the Indian Mutiny*, Osprey, London.

---

[10] Hansard's Parliamentary Debates for the years 1857-1858, for example Volume CXLVIII pp.1359-1363, contains frequent discussions of the reasons for the mutiny of the Indians as well as references to their caste system and heroism in death.

Hobsbawm, E. (1995) *The Age of Capital* [1965], Weidenfield and Nicholson, London.

Homer, (1991) *The Odyssey*, Penguin, London.

Irish Archaeological Society, (1842) *Tracts Relating to Ireland,* vols. I-II, Dublin.

Joyce, J. (1993) *A Portrait of the Artist as a Young Man* [1916] Chancellor Press, London,

Joyce, J. (1992) *Finnegans Wake* [1939] Penguin, London.

Joyce, J. (1992) *Ulysses* [1922] Penguin, London.

Kay, J.W. () *A History of the Sepoy War in India*, W.H. Allen & Co., London, 1880.

Knollys, H. (ed.) (1873) *Incidents in the Sepoy War 1857-8*, William Blackwood and Sons, Edinburgh.

McCormack, W.J. (2001) *Modern Irish Culture*, Blackwell, Oxford.

O'Buachalla, S. (1980) *The Letters of P.H.Pearse*, Colin Smythe, London.

Parliamentary Debates, Fourth Series, (1914) vol. CXXXVI, Wyman and Sons Ltd., London.

Pearse, P. (1913) *Political Writings and Speeches*, Talbot Press, Dublin.

Ram, S. (1970) *From Sepoy to Subedar*, [1873] 2nd edn, Routledge & Keegan, London.

Welch, R. (2000) *The Concise Oxford Companion to Irish Literature*, Oxford University Press, Oxford.

Part 2: Revisiting Colonialism: The Persistence of the Raj

Finding Ceylon in 1693: Remembering Gamini Salgado

John Simons

This is not a scholarly article. Rather it is a personal memoir, an act of homage, perhaps even an anecdote. Whether this essay will penetrate the complexities of South Asian culture or the relationship of that culture with other cultures is doubtful. What I hope it will do, however, is to remind readers of a man who was an important figure in the English and Sri Lankan literary and academic establishments but who was never sufficiently prominent to be generally remembered. I also hope that this little paper will illuminate at least one possible way of understanding the manner in which the memory and experience of growing up in colonial south Asia could become inextricably linked with mastery and partial adoption of the colonising culture.

Gamini Salgado was born in Ceylon in 1929 and died suddenly and tragically in England in 1985.[1] Between those two dates he achieved the signal distinction of being the first Sri Lankan to become a Professor of English in a British university (Exeter) and, very probably, certainly as far as I am aware, the first South Asian of any nationality to achieve this rank. Gamini came to England in 1947 where he took a first in English at the University of Nottingham and followed this up with a doctorate at the same university. Thereafter, with the exception of a brief period back home in Ceylon working for Unilever and another as a lecturer at the University of Singapore, Gamini made his home in the UK and posts at Belfast and Sussex preceded his appointment to the chair at Exeter in 1977. At the end of his life he spent a brief period teaching in Saudi

---

[1] All information is taken from his own, posthumously published, autobiographical work, *The True Paradise* (Carcanet, Manchester, 1993) and especially from the Afterword contributed by his widow, Fenella Copplestone (pp.173-181) In some cases I have also drawn on details that Gamini had mentioned in conversation with me and with others. Gamini is mentioned in D.C.R.A. Goonetilleke's survey of Sri Lankan criticism as the 'most successful' of the group of scholars who came under the influence of the dominant Cambridge English approach propounded in Ceylon by E. F. C. Ludowyk, the first Sri Lankan to be appointed to the chair of English at the University of Ceylon (E. Benson and L.W. Conolly (eds) *The Routledge Encyclopedia of Post-Colonial Literatures in English*, Routledge, London, 1994)

Arabia before returning to England and an intended early retirement that was cut short by the early death that had been predicted for him by the astrologer who cast his chart when he was born.

These are the bare bones of Gamini's professional life. His academic achievements were many and various. His early research on D. H. Lawrence has been the basis of later work on the establishment of the Lawrence canon.[2] He also wrote critically on Lawrence and on British theatre – he was an enthusiastic actor and also an imaginative director.[3] But Gamini's greatest scholarly achievements lay in his address to Elizabethan and Jacobean culture. He was an editor and commentator on the dramatic works of Shakespeare and his contemporaries and on the Restoration – his student cast production of Aphra Behn's *The Rover* in 1981 must have been one of the first to revive the works of an author who is now all but canonical.[4] He also edited a selection of pamphlets (by Robert Greene and others) on life in the Elizabethan criminal underworld and, in 1977, published an excellent monograph (still in print) on Elizabethan low culture.[5]

It is at this point that I enter the story. I went to Exeter to take up a teaching post in 1980 and took with me a mostly completed doctorate on Elizabethan popular prose. I took up the offer of finishing this degree under staff regulations at Exeter as the £100 I would have had to pay to stay registered at my previous institution was, in those days, a lot of money to the most junior species of university teacher. Gamini was the natural choice to act as my supervisor and he kindly agreed to take on this role. I also had the privilege of teaching with him and, in 1981, we jointly designed a special option course on Elizabethan popular literature.

---

[2] This was his doctoral thesis.

[3] Among other things Gamini wrote *The Everyman Companion to the Theatre* (Dent, London, 1985) (with Peter Thomson) *A Preface to Lawrence* (Longman, London, 1982) *English Drama: a Critical Introduction* (Arnold, London, 1980)

[4] This work was published as *Three Jacobean Tragedies* (Penguin, Harmondsworth, 1965) *Three Restoration Comedies* (Penguin, Harmondsworth, 1968) and *Three Jacobean City Comedies* (Penguin, Harmondsworth, 1975) He also edited *Othello* (Longman, London, 1976) and the 'Text and Performance' volume on *King Lear* (Macmillan, London, 1984) He provided introductions to the facsimiles of George Saville's *Miscellanies* (Gregg International, Farnborough, 1971) and *An Account of the Growth of Popery and Arbitrary Power in England* (Gregg International, Farnborough, 1971) His *Eyewitnesses of Shakespeare* (Chatto and Windus, London, 1975) remains an invaluable source.

[5] The edition of the works of Greene and other commentators on Elizabeth low life was published as *Cony-Catchers and Bawdy Baskets* (Penguin, Harmondsworth, 1972) the monograph was *The Elizabethan Underworld* (Dent, London, 1977)

Gamini had a very distinctive teaching style. His work appeared unstructured and casual but as the hour unfolded he would take the students through unfamiliar texts and we would always end on time and with a sense of a closed argument that offered further reading and more to say. My role was as a kind of straight man and occasional provider of dates of publication. Gamini would begin most classes by lighting a cigarette (in those days everyone still smoked) – he would always strike the match on the wall of the classroom - and then leaning back and exhaling a series of perfect smoke rings – one of his great skills – he would start a kind of meditation on the text in hand punctuated by disconcertingly direct questions to the students.

It would be possible to continue in this vein with tales of Gamini but I have a different purpose. I want to suggest that in his research and teaching of material drawn from the street cultures of Elizabethan England Gamini was, with various degrees of explicit acknowledgement, reproducing and representing to himself and his British students, some aspects of the cultures of his native Ceylon.

This first became apparent to me when we were teaching a class on Elizabethan broadside ballads and particularly ballads concerned with crime. These texts led Gamini to reminisce about a story teller/ballad singer that he had heard when he was a child in Ceylon. The story went that a man had broken into a house with the intent to rob it but discovered the householder's beautiful daughter asleep in bed. Overcome with lust he advanced on her but at that moment the roof, heavy with monsoon rain, collapsed and the ensuing deluge not only woke the household but also, quite literally, cooled the would-be rapist's ardour. As Gamini observed, this kind of story is very typical of the sort of thing one finds in the various cautionary ballads that were popular in pre-industrial England and in recounting this memory to his students he was showing them how traditions can survive and mutate around a common core of material which is, to some extent, impervious to specific cultural influences. He was also placing himself not only back in the market place near Colombo but also, in a very real fashion, in the street outside the Globe Theatre waiting to see Mr Shakespeare's latest and passing the time by listening to an itinerant hawker. And this, of course, is what makes good scholars and teachers. It is that ability to make the subject real to the students not by sitting them in front of screens so that teaching in higher education becomes a simulation of television watching but by showing them personal investment in the subject and commitment to the material. But Gamini's investment and commitment had a double nature. It linked him not only to the great traditions of English literature but also to the smaller traditions of Sinhalese popular culture. In studying the Elizabethan underworld he brought these two things together for himself and for his colleagues and students.

However, it would not be true to say that these two traditions are strictly separated either in Gamini's case or in the cases of the generations of South Asians who have lived, to varying degrees, under the influence of British Colonial rule since the middle of the eighteenth century. I think it would be true to say that, for Gamini, British literature and English formed just as important a part of his childhood and formative influences as South Asian literatures and Sinhalese and that, in common with many of his generation, his early education was carried out in a context which appears to have been 'more English than the English'. Certainly, the memories of schooldays recorded in his posthumous book of autobiographical sketches show a picture of a very British schooling under the supervision of an English Headmaster.[6] The journey to school was punctuated by English advertisements (Robin starch, Sunlight soap, Wills Goldflake tobacco) beside the railway and the propaganda posters (this was during the Second World War) showing pink handed gardeners digging for victory in suburban plots. The young Gamini noted that it was 'funny to think of gardening with trousers and shoes on'.[7]

In addition to the cultural mix of his schooling, there was the influence of English literature at home. His father's small library was mostly in English and comprised the major Romantic poets, Burns, Dickens, Wodehouse, Stevenson, Arnold, Edgar Wallace, Macaulay, Emerson, Kingsley, Shakespeare, Longfellow and Conan Doyle. This all constitutes, I would argue, a fairly typical example of the collection of any lower middle-class Englishman with social aspirations at this time. In addition, there were the English translations of Tagore, and the Ramayana and Mahabarata.[8] Gamini's earliest important exposure to English seems to have come through his father and he records how his father's conversations with him were 'in Sinhalese, but using the English words 'snow', 'robin', 'daffodil''.[9] Growing up in colonial Ceylon was, then, an experience in which the rhythms of local language interacted with those of English and in which much of the imaginative furniture of the young Gamini was being provided through the medium of the colonising language.

However, Gamini's access to literary culture at home was not wholly Anglicised and he remembers the large stock of stories told by his great

---

[6] See *The True Paradise*, op. cit. especially pp.75-97

[7] ibid. p.76

[8] ibid. p.25 and p.56

[9] ibid. p.61

aunt. These stories opened up the life of Gamini's ancestors at a time before the full colonisation of the island. I remember Gamini himself telling me that his great aunt had, in fact, claimed to have access to direct eye-witness stories (passed down through the oral tradition) of the Dutch fortifying the walls of Colombo. In addition to these stories Gamini also had access to the ballads and chapbooks performed and sold by street vendors. These were of both a secular and a religious nature. The secular ones were often romantic love stories, the religious ones recounted tales of the many incarnations of Lord Buddha. The peddler would carry these books to market and then, spreading them out, would proceed to chant the stories from some of his wares. In his attention to these traditional media and his pleasure in them Gamini was not only participating in the traditional cultures of Ceylon, he was also becoming part of a transnational communicative web that had been active since the development of printing and which does not depend on any particular local materials for its sustenance.

It is worth, at this point, observing that what Gamini found in the Ceylon of the late 1930s and early 1940s was a situation not so very different from the way in which popular reading material was transmitted in the Britain and Ireland between the the seventeenth century and the middle of the nineteenth century - although I have seen a picture of an itinerant bookseller working in the village of Brenchley, Kent, as late as 1890.[10] A similar situation obtained in France during much the same period. Itinerant booksellers worked in the United States too and chapbook reading materials may be found in most European countries up to the middle of the nineteenth century and, in some cases, slightly beyond. In the early twentieth century Judaeo-Spanish chapbooks were being produced for the Sephardic Jewish community of Salonika.[11] In the present day there are vibrant chapbook industries in Brazil and Nigeria (associated especially with the market at Onitsha).[12] Arabic chapbooks are still produced in Egypt and Punjabi and Pashto chapbooks still circulate in

---

[10] On this John Simons, *Guy of Warwick and Other Chapbook Romances* (Exeter University Press, Exeter, 1998) and John Simons, 'Romance in the Eighteenth-Century Chapbook' in John Simons (ed.) *From Medieval to Medievalism* (Macmillan, London, 1992) pp.122-143

[11] See G. Armistead and J. Silverman (eds.) *The Judaeo-Spanish Chapbooks of Yacob Abraham Yona* (University of California Press, Berkeley, 1971)

[12] On Brazilian *folhetos* see Peter Burke, 'Chivalry in the New World' in Sidney Anglo (ed.) *Chivalry in the Renaissance* (Boydell and Brewer, Woodbridge, 1990) pp.253-262; on Nigerian chapbooks see E. N. Obiechina, *Onitsha Market Literature* (Heinemann, London, 1972) and B. Lindfors, 'Heroes and Hero-Worship in Nigerian Chapbooks', *Journal of Popular Culture*, 1 (1967) pp.1-22

Pakistan.[13] I would expect that the kinds of thing Gamini saw as a boy in the 1940s still exist in Sri Lanka today. So the experience of street-based popular reading and performance was not one that was distinctive to Ceylon. But, at the same time, the experience did have a specificity. This was bounded on the one side by the Buddhist content of many of the books and, on the other, by the interplay between vernacular and English language and culture which increasingly defined the lives of young people at this period in south Asia. It is in this interplay and its negotiation as either conflict or resolution that forms the heart of the post-colonial experience.

Gamini himself addressed this issue in his inaugural lecture 'Shakespeare and Myself' which he delivered on taking up his chair at Exeter.[14] In this extraordinary piece he considered not only his own encounter with Shakespeare and the linguistic challenges this posed for him but also brought to bear consideration of the transcultural value of his study of English. He points out, for example, that although the Sanskrit poet Kalidasa sets enormous problems for the translator, as the flora and fauna of India are not familiar to most western readers, this is no different from his encounter with the daffodils, primroses and oxlips of Shakespeare. But for Gamini this kind of difficulty and its overcoming not by recourse to works of reference but by imaginative and emotional effort is precisely what constitutes literary understanding. For him then, the act of reading in a foreign language was not an act of translation but an act of spiritual reconstruction, a recognition of value in Otherness. This Otherness exists, of course, not only between cultures but also across time. When he reminds us of the Buddhist wheel of life Gamini brings together not only his recognition of the ways in which his own Sinhalese

---

[13] See W. L. Hanaway, 'Chapbooks in Pakistan', Wilma Heston, 'Pashto Chapbooks, Gendered Imagery and Cross-cultural Contact' and Ulrich Marzolph, 'Still the Same Old Jokes; The Continuity of Jocular Tradition in Early Twentieth-Century Egyptian Chapbooks' in Cathy Lynn Preston and Michael J. Preston, *The Other Print Tradition*, (Garland Publishing, Inc. New York, 1995) pp.127-143, 144-160, 161-179. There are also Pakistani chapbooks written in Urdu, Siraiki, Baluchi, Brahui, Khowar, Persian, Arabic, Hindko, Sindhi and English but the main industries serve the Pashto and Punjabi speaking communities. The range of Pakistani chapbooks is much the same as those which circulated in Ceylon in the 1930s and 1940s (see *The True Paradise*, p.3 for a brief list) and include traditional tales and wisdom, modern stories, religious materials, books of jokes, books of film songs, small anthologies of classical poetry. This range is pretty much identical with the spectrum of chapbook subject matter in Britain from the 17th to the 19th century.

[14] *Shakespeare and Myself: an Inaugural Lecture delivered in the University of Exeter on 27 May, 1977* (Exeter University Press, Exeter, 1977) reprinted in *The True Paradise*, op. cit. pp.151-172

culture made Shakespeare understandable but also his view of the transcultural, transhistorical cores that appear to characterise great art.[15]

But in spite of this idealised view of literary study – an idealised view of which Gamini was well aware and which fitted paradoxically with his rigorous historical scholarship (as, perhaps, his father's membership of the Rationalist Press fitted paradoxically with his firm belief in astronomy) - Gamini was also engaged, consciously or not in a systematic bringing together of his early cultural experience with his mature academic study. At a very trivial level this could be signified by his vigorous efforts to collect the first thousand Penguins. How much of this interest was inspired by a desire to meet again the old favourites of his boyhood, to reproduce the collection his father had developed from the habit of 'bringing home a new Penguin each day when he came from his office in Colombo'?[16] I am not here, by the way, presuming to attempt anything like a psychoanalytic approach to Gamini's engagement with literature merely recording what would appear to be a perfectly straightforward motivation.

More subtly I think that Gamini's attention to the Elizabethan underworld and to the small books and pamphlets that recorded the language, subterfuges and adventures of armies of forgotten rogues and vagabonds was stimulated, consciously or unconsciously by his early life experiences in Ceylon. Gamini was one of the first modern scholars to take more than a passing interest in these works and this world and when we read his accounts of the peddlers, beggars, itinerant performers and snake charmers that passed down the road outside his family home in Ceylon it is not difficult to see how when he encountered the Elizabethan underworld, he saw connections between it and his own lived experience. Indeed, in his autobiographical sketches he actually provides a descriptive typology of the beggars of Ceylon in the 1930s which is not so very different from the sort of thing produced by Robert Greene and others in England in the second half of the sixteenth century.[17] Here, of course, we may also see an influence travelling in the other direction. Gamini became

---

[15] The True Paradise, p.171

[16] ibid. p.25

[17] Compare, for example, the list of rogues given in John Awdeley's *The Fraternity of Vagabonds* (1565) or Thomas Harman's *A Caveat for Common Cursitors* (1567) – both edited by Gamini in *Cony-Catchers and Bawdy Baskets* – with the list of itinerants and beggars given in *The True Paradise*, pp.21-32. Gamini also mentions (*The True Paradise*, p.31) the Sinhalese traditional song-dance drama to which he was rarely taken as a child – his parents preferred the classical operatic drama based on history of Buddhist legend – and had to sneak out of bed to 'listen in the darkness'. This early attachment also clearly relates to Gamini's specialised interests in Renaissance drama in England.

interested in Elizabethan beggars because of his experience of Ceylon but when he came to write about that experience after many years of success in England he used the tools of literary scholarship and his reading in English literature to structure his thoughts. One minor sign of this is his reference to the motor car as 'a nine days wonder' in pre-war Ceylon. This phrase has important resonance in the Elizabethan theatre and alerts the reader immediately to the complex and multiply focused cultural network that begins to spread in Gamini's writings.[18]

I was once advised (on setting out to study pre-industrial popular culture in England) that if I wanted to understand the nature of street culture in Elizabethan London I would do well to start with Lane's description of street culture in nineteenth-century Cairo.[19] I am still unsure as to whether this was good advice or not (though it led me down some interesting tracks). But the point is that it was based in the not entirely accurate but not entirely false perception that there are analogies between the pre-industrial west and parts of the developing world. I would rather look at this as an issue which is best understood in terms of traditional cultures where production is still a function of localised and particularised needs and belief as against mediated cultures where culture is entirely reified and commodified and has become a function of consumerism. However, from this perspective it might be possible to study – in the sense of understanding - the age of Queen Elizabeth I by considering later periods in south Asia.

What Gamini did was, I think, somewhat similar. In addressing the problems of underworld literature in Elizabethan England he was not seeking to understand them through his experience of beggars in colonial Ceylon. Rather he was bringing together first hand experience of one culture with the imaginative and intellectual realisation of the other. In London of 1603 he found rural Ceylon of 1943 but, at the same time, he seems to have found that this discovery – a post-colonial encounter of a rare kind – enabled a language for the description of both. If his early encounter with English culture was complicated by the curious politics of language learning in a colonial environment, his later mastery of that culture was structured by his experience outside of the dominant language and offered a new way of understanding Ceylon.

---

[18] The original 'nine days' wonder' was Thomas Middleton's play *A Game at Chesse*. This was so called because it was staged for nine consecutive days: a run of Mousetrap proportions in the world of Jacobean theatre.

[19] Edward William Lane, *The Manners and Customs of the Modern Egyptians* (Charles Knight, London, 1836)

When I came to write this piece and to think about Gamini it came as a shock to realise that he died as long ago as 1985. His conversation and ideas are still fresh to me and his scholarship still resonates in my own work on popular culture. When I knew Gamini I did not really consider the role of his upbringing and the fact that he came from Ceylon as significant to his work. Certainly, with the exceptions of the odd anecdote Gamini never really made much of his Sinhalese background and I am not sure how interested he would be in my view that his work articulates this in subtle ways. But with hindsight and re-reading of his autobiography I have seen determinate patterns at work that were not clear to me at an earlier point. I would like to claim that Gamini's work does, in fact, offer an interesting insight in the modulations of the post-colonial experience. However, even if my very brief account of some features of this work is not convincing I am glad to have been able to say a few words about Gamini who deserves to be remembered not only as a scholar but also as an important figure in the history of the South Asian community in the UK.

Gamini usually had the last word so I'll leave him with it again:

Since it was not one of my youthful ambitions to be a Professor of English, I look forward to my tenure with no more than the usual apprehension of one who knows he has been fortunate beyond his deserts. What I really wanted to be was a snake-charmer.[20]

Bibliography

Anglo, Sidney (ed) (1990) *Chivalry in the Renaissance,* Boydell and Brewer, Woodbridge.

Armistead, G. and Silverman J. (eds) (1971) *The Judaeo-Spanish Chapbooks of Yacob Abraham Yona*, University of California Press, Berkeley.

Benson, E and Conolly, L. W. (eds) (1994) *The Routledge Encyclopedia of Post-Colonial Literatures in English*, Routledge, London.

Burke, Peter, 'Chivalry in the New World' in Anglo, pp.253-262

Hanaway, W. L. 'Chapbooks in Pakistan' in Preston & Preston, pp.127-143

Wilma Heston, 'Pashto Chapbooks, Gendered Imagery and Cross-cultural Contact' in Preston & Preston, pp.144-160

Lane, Edward William, (1836) *The Manners and Customs of the Modern Egyptians,* Charles Knight, London.

Lindfors, B. (1967) 'Heroes and Hero-Worship in Nigerian Chapbooks', *Journal of Popular Culture*, 1, pp.1-22

---

[20] From 'Shakespeare and Myself' in *The True Paradise*, p.172

Marzolph, Ulrich, 'Still the Same Old Jokes; The Continuity of Jocular Tradition in Early Twentieth-Century Egyptian Chapbooks' in Preston & Preston, pp.161-179

Obiechina, E. N. (1972) *Onitsha Market Literature,* Heinemann, London.

Preston, Cathy Lynn and Preston Michael J. (1995) *The Other Print Tradition,* Garland Publishing Inc. New York.

Salgado, Gamini, (ed) (1965) *Three Jacobean Tragedies,* Penguin, Harmondsworth.

Salgado, Gamini, (ed) (1968) *Three Restoration Comedies,* Penguin, Harmondsworth.

Salgado, Gamini, (ed) (1971) George Saville's *Miscellanies,* Gregg International, Farnborough.

Salgado, Gamini, (ed) (1971) *An Account of the Growth of Popery and Abitrary Power in England,* Gregg International, Farnborough.

Salgado, Gamini, (ed) *Cony-Catchers and Bawdy Baskets,* Penguin, Harmondsworth.

Salgado, Gamini, (1975) *Eyewitnesses of Shakespeare,* Chatto and Windus, London.

Salgado, Gamini, (ed) (1975) *Three Jacobean City Comedies,* Penguin, Harmondsworth.

Salgado, Gamini, (ed) (1976) *Othello,* Longman, London.

Salgado, Gamini, (1977) *The Elizabethan Underworld,* Dent, London.

Salgado, Gamini, (1977) Shakespeare and Myself: an Inaugural Lecture delivered in the University of Exeter on 27 May 1977, Exeter University Press, Exeter.

Salgado, Gamini, (1980) *English Drama: a Critical Introduction,* Arnold, London.

Salgado, Gamini, (1982) *A Preface to Lawrence,* Longman, London.

Salgado, Gamini, (1984) *King Lear Text and Performance,* Macmillan, London.

Salgado, Gamini, (1985) (with Peter Thomson) *The Everyman Companion to the Theatre,* Dent, London.

Salgado, Gamini, (1993)*The True Paradise,* Carcanet, Manchester.

Simons, John, (1998) *Guy of Warwick and Other Chapbook Romances,* Exeter University Press, Exeter.

Simons, John, (1992) 'Romance in the Eighteenth-Century Chapbook' in Simons, John, (ed) *From Medieval to Medievalism,* Macmillan, London, pp.122-143

Picturing 'India' from M.M. Kaye's *The Far Pavilions*

Sylvia Woodhead

Introduction

This study seeks to examine the role of a historical novel in the formation of images of culture, from the perspective of acquisition of personal knowledge of south Asia. In examining the representation of place images in a novel, it also seeks to question whether a Western outsider view can be of value in debates about South Asian culture. The arguments are situated within the literature of place images in cultural geography.

Personal knowledge acquisition of India[1]

Knowledge of places is gained most reliably from first hand experiences: field visits, holidays, places lived (Haynes 1981), and by its nature first hand place knowledge is more usually limited to local scale encounters. Place knowledge derived from secondary sources, brought by the plethora of mass media, and from education, is generally regarded as less reliable than first hand experiences, because of inherent bias. Representation is not neutral (Whatmore in Cloke et al 1999 p.7). When asked to contribute to a study of representations of south Asia, my first reaction was that, having never visited, and thus having no direct knowledge, I could make no useful contribution, when my sole source of information was having read, in the 1990's, and enjoyed a second hand copy of the 1984 edition of the novel The Far Pavilions.[2] What follows is an introspective exploration of the role of M.M. Kaye's novel The Far Pavilions in forming personal knowledge. Parallels to this Western view of oriental culture may be seen in some of the views expressed by older generations in recent South Asian films, such as *East is East.*

My upbringing in suburban Birmingham, insulated and isolated from the rest of Britain, let alone the rest of the world, contrasts strongly with

---

[1] Note that the term India is intended here to imply the India (of 1855-78) of M.M. Kaye's *The Far Pavilions*. Similarly Anglicised versions of Indian names, such as those used in the novel are employed here.

[2] The book is currently still in print : M.M. Kaye, *The Far Pavilions,* St Martins Press, 1997

the globalisation influences experienced by many Eastern people. Gurnah (2002 p.347) growing up in Zanzibar[3], reflects that he was lucky from the outset to experience 'cultural confluence'. He heard foreign radio, saw films of many nationalities, read Enid Blyton, and knew English literature and Shakespeare, but also had competence in Arabic and Kiswahili. Only by a fluent grasp of French can I begin to understand Gurnah's 'linguistic plurality'. Further contrasts exist in terms of food: in Zanzibar Indian, Arabic, African and Chinese foods were readily available.

Gurnah concludes that African children in Zanzibar in the 1950's were able to acquire other cultures from a very wide range of sources, and while that these foreign experiences were 'all partial but never superficial' (ibid. p.350) 'engagement with foreign cultures introduced us to arguments...' 'It gave us the language with which to promote those elements in our culture we recognised as unique' (ibid. p.351). Gurnah comments that European culture profoundly affected his life, and influenced his tastes. Looking back it is difficult to realise how restricted my upbringing in Birmingham's suburbs was. My British cultural experiences of literature, film, fashion, food and music were all narrow and parochial, though I was unaware of this at the time. There was no cultural diversity in my upbringing. This discussion of different backgrounds and experiences of growing up highlights the different mind set, knowledge and assumptions in which place knowledge was acquired at similar times, but in different parts of the globe. It sets the scene for discussions of difference, and for recognising the 'cognition' which filters perceptions of different places (Downs in Pepper 1994). This analysis of cultural place meanings of *The Far Pavilions* is based solely on the novel.

Textbook pictures of India

In the next section I compare knowledge of India derived from school to the influence of novels, using the work of Ploszajska (1999) to challenge my initial recollection that I have no relevant memories of learning about India at school. Ploszajska's exploration of the ways in which geographical ideas are forged and passed on triggered memories that my schooling was dominantly 'verbal imagery' (ibid. p.27) where the views of teachers and texts were not questioned. Her comments that education 'stressed mechanical commitment to memory' (ibid. p.69) is supported by my recollections. Her analysis places my education in an era influenced by implicit stories of empire. I was certainly exposed to 'imperial propaganda' (ibid. p.17) through membership of the Girl

---

[3] It is interesting to note that Zanzibar is the focus of another of M. M. Kaye's historical novels, the equally evocatively named *Trade Wind*.

Guides, 'that exemplar of popular imperialism' (ibid. p.254). I was educated in the legacy of imperialism, when geographical knowledge was a tool of empire enabling acquisition of territory and exploration of resources (Driver, 1992, p.27).

The influence of school textbooks upon my imagination varies somewhat from Ploszajska's (op.cit. p.29) assertion that 'textbooks provided visual images of people and places which conveyed powerful messages'. My subconscious view of India derived from schooling was based more on text than on visual images, finding resonance with the following representations of Indian culture in textbooks of 1937-1949:

Native people of India 'were a chaotic mixture of peoples whose characteristics ranged from mystical exoticism to total barbarism and were unified solely by a complete inability to govern themselves peaceably'. (ibid. p.37)

The overwhelming vision of India which textbooks created was of a chaotic and confusing kaleidoscope of innumerable religious, linguistic and cultural groups. (ibid. p.156)

Textbooks are held to be powerful vehicles for transmission of ideologies; Ploszajska (ibid. p.46) notes that still today their views are accepted without question. I must have swallowed unquestioningly the climatic determinism of the time, that the humidity of the lowland climate of India was said to adversely affect the health and spirits of even natives: 'the Indian climate was particularly damaging to the health and morale of British children' (ibid.). Textbooks risk oversimplification in their treatment of distant and large areas. H.J. Fleure's comment in Ploszajska (ibid. p.56) that that we should not just think of 'India as providing tea or jute for our benefit' is precisely the simplified view I can remember from my schooling.

By contrast, fictional worlds provide training in forming vivid mental images of fantastic landscapes, such as can be seen on the book covers of the many editions of *The Far Pavilions*. Ploszajska notes (ibid. p.85) that India was depicted, in pre-war texts, as a kind of 'fairyland', 'an evocative means of conjuring to children's imagination vivid ...images of unknown places'. Like the fairy stories which Ploszajska refers to (ibid. p.100) I have repeatedly read *The Far Pavilions*. Experiences from 1950's novels could be said to represent images of fantasy worlds.

While little knowledge of south Asia was derived from my personal education, some developed from preparation of teaching materials.

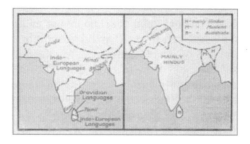

Figure 1 : Language and Religions Maps from a 1966 school textbook
Chaturvedi (2002) regards this simple representation of Hindus and Muslims as imperial mapping of British India aimed at transforming a highly pluralistic and diverse civilisation into a controllable colonial object.
Source : Honeybone, R.C. & Graves, N.J. *Geography for Schools Book Three, North America and Asia,* Heinemann Educational, London, 1966.

Figure 2 : South Asia as depicted in a 1968 atlas[4]
The triangular shape has what Lynch (1960) called high 'imageability'.
Source : *Phillips Modern School Atlas,* George Philip and Son Ltd, London, 1968.

---

[4] Phillips (in Cloke et al. 1999, p.277) comments that maps show power rather than straightforward description. Place names are in English, thus asserting an English way of seeing the world. Brayshay & Cleary, (2002, p.6) consider that maps allowed the British to conceive of and possess their overseas domains.

Figure 3 : M.M. Kaye and her husband, Geoffrey Hamilton
Above: M.M. Kaye on her 90th birthday.
Below: Goff (Geoffrey) Hamilton on active Frontier service wearing the same headgear as his men to avoid becoming a target for enemy snipers: he appears the epitome of the hero Ashton Pelham-Martyn in *The Far Pavilions*
Sources: www.kourtoulou.freeserve.co.uk, Kaye, M.M. *Enchanted Evening*[5], third part of *Share of Summer*, her autobiography, Viking, 1999.

---

[5] M.M. Kaye's third book of her autobiography ends, in true romantic novel style, on her first meeting her husband Geoffrey Hamilton, *Enchanted Evening,* 1999.

Analysis of a 1966 textbook[6] still in my possession leaves people hazy. The fuzzy black and white photographs are largely devoid of people; its focus was on physical geography. Very simple maps show languages and religions (Figure 1). Depiction in the text is impersonal and cold, without people:

The sub-continent of India, although it was once unified under British administration, is really a very varied area. It is possible to travel from the lofty peaks of the Himalayas to the low level plains of the Ganges in just over a hundred miles; to move from the hot sticky atmosphere of the coastlands around Bombay to the much drier plateau of peninsular India in about a hundred and fifty miles; to leave a rural settlement in Bihar state where oxen are pulling primitive ploughs and suddenly come upon the huge modern iron and steel works at Jamshedpur. It is an area not only split by religion, but divided by languages. Thus, although Hindi is the official language of India, substantial minorities of Indians in southern India neither speak it nor understand it. In Pakistan all languages spoken are Indo-European languages, but Urdu, spoken in West Pakistan, is incomprehensible to the Bengali-speaking inhabitants of East Pakistan. Only English, spoken by many educated people as a second language, can serve as a common language. Thus, the task of educating in the universities is often complicated by the necessity for students to learn a second language which in most case is English' (Tuan, 1991, p.688).

'In India, Pakistan and Ceylon, the problem which requires an urgent solution is that of the fast-growing population.' (Honeybone and Graves, op.cit. p.341)

In comparison to texts, maps provided more potent visual imagery:[7] the triangular shape of India in an atlas (Figure 2) is one of my clearest memories. Knowledge derived from geographical educational texts, of such a large 'place' as India is, as Gustafson (2001, p.12) suggests, dominated by natural environmental themes. The strongly Euro-centric (or Anglo-centric) filter through which I examine the role of *The Far*Pavilions in picturing South Asian culture, contrasts with the background and life path (ibid. p.9) of M.M. Kaye, its author.

---

[6] Presumably I used this text for secondary school teaching in the 1970's. It illustrates the 'Western' site of production of geographical knowledge (McEwen, 1998, p.373)

[7] Radcliffe (1996, p.27) comments on the powerful symbolic effect of the immediate recognisability of atlas maps of places.

Meticulous background - a hybrid eye?

M.M. Kaye (Mary Margaret (Mollie) Kaye) was born in India in 1908, in Simla, the hill station in the Himalayas where British families escaped from summer heat. Biographical details given on the inside covers of her books note the following:

M.M. Kaye was born in India, and spent most of her childhood and much of her early married life in India. Her ties with India are strong: her grand father, father, brother and husband all served the Raj, and her grandfather's first cousin, Sir John Kaye, wrote standard accounts of the Indian Mutiny and the first Afghan War. When India achieved independence her husband joined the British Army and for the next nineteen years she followed the drum to all sorts of exciting places she would not otherwise have seen.

In the three books of her autobiography, M.M. Kaye (Figure 3) details the life of the British Raj in 1920's India; constant parties, dances, banquets, with painting, amateur dramatic productions and visits to pass the time. Her family had several Indian servants and travelled widely within India. Like Ash, the hero of *The Far Pavilions*, M.M. Kaye considers herself Indian, loving India as home, and finding its scents and sounds, sights and faces, names of railway stations familiar and reassuring. She writes from a thorough knowledge of India, and shows empathy and understanding for its people and culture. *The Far Pavilions* was first published in the UK in 1978, and made into a film in 1984. The novel has been a million seller, with editions in many languages. The background is meticulously researched,[8] a wealth of detail of India provides the backcloth for the development of the characters. The M.M. Kaye fan club web site[9] features 50 cover illustrations, which picture romantic portrayals of the landscape and chief characters. These book cover images convey the idea of far-flung places and the lives of exotically different people: they find resonance with Said's comment (in Cloke et al 1999 p.49) that representation of the romantic mystical Orient acts as a container for Western desires and fantasies. Most of the book

---

[8] M.M. Kaye travelled to India in 1963 to research the book, (Kaye M.M. ed. (1980) *The Golden Calm: An English Lady's Life in Moghul Delhi,* Webb & Bower, Exeter, England). Despite being neither a geographer nor a travel writer, as discussed by Morin (1998) and McEwen (1998) M.M. Kaye is certain in the placing of her characters; her accounts are geographically accurate.

[9] Run by Michael Kourtoulou, see www.kourtoulou.freeserve.co.uk

covers repeat the theme of distant mountain peaks, fantasy palace in mid-ground and romantic pair on horseback or embracing, and are based on an original watercolour by M.M. Kaye. The front cover of the 1984 edition (958 pages, with additional notes[10] and glossary) announces 'the famous story of love and war in nineteenth century India, now made into a sumptuous screen production'. The Times Review on the novel's back cover claims '*A Gone With the Wind* of the North-West Frontier', and continues:

> *The Far Pavilions* is the story of an Englishman - Ashton Pelham-Martyn - brought up as Hindu. It is the story of his passionate but dangerous love for Juli, an Indian princess. It is the story of divided loyalties, of friendship that endures till death, of high adventure and of the clash between east and west. To the burning plains and snow capped mountains of this great, humming continent, M.M. Kaye brings her exceptional gifts of storytelling and meticulous historical accuracy, plus her insight into the human heart, [capturing] the very presence of India.

The Italian cover featuring an elephant is reminiscent of Rudyard Kipling, M.M. Kaye's favourite author.

The film version book covers focus on the love story. The UK version depicts dark-haired, Anglicised characters, while the Spanish cover shows Ash in Army uniform with Juli as a princess. The Norwegian paperback cover renames the book *Ashton and Anjuli*, while the characters have an indefinable 'northern' look. The Swedish hardback, with a title of *Valley Beyond the Mountains*, volume 2 *Marriage at Bhithor* features a split cover : Ash as an Afghan tribesman in mountains to the left, with Ash and Juli on the right. Other book covers show similar nationalistic traits.

The lure of a love story : an eternal (cultural ?) relationship

In this section, the love story element of *The Far Pavilions* is extracted from the complexity of sub plots and a multitude of characters and scenes, and analysed to reveal the social spaces of relationships in a South Asian context. *The Far Pavilions* is a romance, rooted in the reality of India: the title is romantic, as are the book covers. A handsome Englishman, born in India and believing himself Indian for his early life,

---

[10] M.M. Kaye notes that although the main characters of Ash, Zarin and Awal Shar are fictional, and that the suttee described was fictional but based on fact, all other events in the book are based on fact.

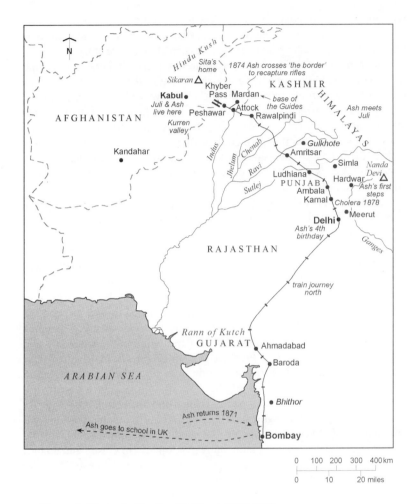

Figure 4: Places in The Far Pavilions, 1855-1878
Places become familiar after reading *The Far Pavilions,* forming a reminder
of geography lessons of the Punjab, The Land-of-the-Five-Rivers
Source: Created by Ann Chapman from Sylvia Woodhead's mental map
after reading *The Far Pavilions.*

wins his Indian princess after an increasingly exciting series of adventures which cross and re-cross the north west of the Indian sub continent; they may or may not live happily ever after. It is an eternal love story.

The romantic pair first meet as children, when Ash, believing himself to be Ashok a Hindu, becomes a valued servant of the young Prince of the mountain kingdom of *Gulkote*: Juli, a skinny 4 year old, is an undervalued and frightened princess, who takes a childish fancy to Ash. Both are lonely, kept virtually prisoner in a palace full of intrigues and murder plots, and seeking comfort, which they find in a ruined tower where Ash makes offerings to his sacred mountains, the *Dur Khaima* or Far Pavilions. Ash is forced to flee, leaving Juli disconsolate, but clutching one half of a pearl token of their childish love.

Ash next encounters Juli when he rescues her carriage from overturning in a river crossing, while escorting two princesses south to their wedding. Juli on her part has to overcome her initial horror and disbelief that Ashok, the Hindu servant she once knew is now Ashton Pelham-Martyn, as English officer. Only in the exceptional circumstances of the travelling camp are they able to continue to meet, and to consummate their love in a cave in a dust storm.[11] Ash leaves Juli, determined to do her duty, and her sister to be married in *Bhithor*; until he hears of the death of their husband, and that the widows are to become suttee, that is burnt on their husband's funeral pyre. Ash rescues Juli, and is hotly pursued. They live together first in secret, disapproval of their 'unsuitable' relationship being shown on both sides, before fleeing north into the mountains in search of their Far Pavilions and a secure life together. The love story thus paints British-Indian, commoner-Royalty, Hindu-Christian relationships: it has the enduring appeal of eternal relationships between two people, set against the romantic and exotic backdrop of India's northern mountains. As Agnew (in Gustafson, op.cit.) argues, meaningful places emerge from the novel through social relationships which are clearly geographically located, and set in cultural and historic surroundings.

Pictures of India: vivid place backdrop

Throughout *The Far Pavilions,* Relph's (in ibid.) three components of place; physical setting, activities and meanings play a recurrent pattern in an upland-lowland theme. The love of mountains and the familiarity of home places are repeatedly contrasted with fear and apprehension in the

---

[11] In book 2 of her autobiography, M.M. Kaye recounts her familiarity with Rajputana dust storms.

hot flat plains of the south. The geographical description of India is vivid and can be accurately followed on the map.[12] (Figure 4) Of the many places mentioned in the novel, only three, Gulkote, Dur Khaima and Bhithor are invented. Quotations illustrate the narrative-description approach of linguistic place-construction (Tuan, op.cit. p.686). The lyrical evocation of mountains starts in 1855, romantically 'in a camp near the crest of a peak,' in 'the cold air'of the Himalayas, with 'the clean scent of snow,' where Ash is born of British parents and took his first steps within sight of the towering peaks of *Nanda Devi*[13]. Sita, a hill woman from the *Hindu Kush*,[14] who becomes Ash's mother, continues the theme by telling him stories of a hidden valley in the mountains, where they can both live safely. Thus the themes of safety and belonging become associated with mountains. In a tall tower in *Gulkote*, the views of the distant mountains, the Far Pavilions or *Dur Khaima*, 'the highest mountain in the range you can see from *Gulkote*: a great crown of snow peaks' (p.213) become Ash's idol, 'beautiful and mysterious, robed in forest of rhododendron and deodar and crowned with snow' (p.68). Following his expulsion from *Gulkote* Ash and Sita journey north towards the *Jhelum* river 'within sight of the Kashmir snows' (p.102). The mountains become less attainable as Ash, after consigning Sita's body to the river, is sent to school in England, which he hates.

On his return to India in the late summer of 1871 as a young British Army officer, Ash's first sight of the Himalayas is portrayed as a moving experience. He saw above the far horizon to the north a long jagged line of pale rose glowing bright against the cool green of the sky, and he knew he was looking at the snow peaks of the Himalayas (p.144).

Later when crossing the Salt Ranges between *Jhelum* and *Rawalpindi*:

The hills were nearer now, and the horizon no longer limited but bounded by bleak folds and ridges of rock that changed colour with every hour of the day... behind them the Border hills... rose

---

[12] For example when cholera, brought by pilgrims from *Hardwar,* where the river Ganges meets the plain, kills the camp, Ash and Sita travel to Delhi, entering by the *Meerut* road, crossing the *Jumna* ford, but discover that an uprising has killed the ruling English. After Sita's death from exhaustion, Ash takes the road that leads from *Attock* (on the River Indus) to *Peshawar,* crossing the *Kabul* River to the British troops stationed at *Mardan*,

[13] Weinbaum (1981, p.249) describes M.M. Kaye as 'drunk with the beauty of India', and comments that she captivates readers with her descriptions, which emphasise the 'gorgeousness of mountains': a sense of mystic beauty of the Himalayan mountains permeates the book,

[14] The *Hindu Kush* mountains lie in Afghanistan.

up in ridge after ridge like frozen waves breaking on the rim of the plain, guardians of a harsh land inhabited by a score of turbulent tribes who recognised no law save that of force, lived in fortified villages and indulged in blood-feuds, and waged perpetual war either on each other or the British. (p.150)

Ash explains his devotion to the Dur Khaima to his friend Wally:[15]

I used to think of the *Dur Khaima* every time we sang in chapel. He turned to face the foothills and faraway line of mountains that rose up behind them, dark against the stars, and quoted in an undertone and 'I will lift up mine eyes unto the hills from whence cometh my help.' (p.215)

Wally says of his first view of the hills, in a comment redolent of M.M. Kaye's own love for the Dal Lake in Kashmir:[16]

The whole country seemed extravagantly beautiful to him, from the lotus-strewn lakes and the winding, willow-fringed river, to the vast forests of deodar and chestnut that swept upwards to meet the shale and the great glaciers that lay above the snow line. (pp.217-218)

The 3-day train journey north from Bombay to the North West Frontier, to Delhi, then on to the Punjab, through *Karnal, Ambala, Ludhiana, Amritsa*, and crossing the *Sutlej* and *Ravi* rivers, allows Ash to voice similar feelings to M.M. Kaye, of joy in return to familiar sights and smells of India. 'He knew them all... for this was the country across which he and Sita had wandered in the months that followed their escape from *Gulkote*.' (p.125)

Tree clad gorges and lush greenness of the south gave place to the parched emptiness of rock and sand. The rich spicy food tasted ambrosial after a diet of boiled beef and carrots, watery cabbage and suet puddings, while the heat and smell and noise of the city was an intoxication and a deep delight. (p.142)

Familiarity with a home place is also the theme on Ash's return to *Mardan*, with its: 'familiar scents and sounds' (p.154) of the Punjab, the

---

[15] Wally Hamilton was a true character who arrived at Rawapindi in the autumn of 1874 and joined the Corps of Guides in 1876 (end note to *The Far Pavilions*)

[16] Recounted in *Golden Afternoon*, 1997.

Land-of-the-Five-Rivers, formerly a Sikh province, when 'the only British troops within its borders were East India Company regiments[17] (p.153).

Ash quickly falls into disgrace by taking unofficial leave in 1874 'across the border' for 2 years to capture stolen rifles, and is banished from his beloved mountain area. As a punishment for his unreliability and preference for Indian companions, he is ordered to accompany two princesses south to their wedding[18] in *Bhithor*, after which he is stationed, in effective exile, in *Gujarat,* returning to rescue Juli from suttee in *Bhithor*.

The Far Pavilions brings alive the north west of south Asia; its place names, rivers and scenes are deep with meaning. Apart from *Gulkote* and *Bhithor*, where important parts of the story occur, the places are real. In these invented places M.M. Kaye chooses names redolent with meaning: *Bhithor*, in its enclosed valley, portrays malignant threat, of physical and mental discomfort of the unfamiliar. Gulkote, on its mountain top location giving warning of attack, reflects an upland landscape preference. It is also in these invented places that the geography becomes vague. While *Gulkote* lies in northern Punjab, *Bhithor* is less clearly situated. It is not clear if it lies north or south of Ahmahabad, except that it is described as lying south of Bombay and Baroda: other places are firmly rooted in reality.

Later in the book, as Ash and Juli move north to *Mardan*, fear from the plains of *Bhithor* seems to follow them. They seek, ironically in Kabul[19], a home place, recognition of their pairing, security from fear and freedom to live their lives. Their mixed marriage makes them both misfits. As Ash is able to pass as Pathan, speaking Pushtu and to live as an Afghan tribesman, he resigns from the Army and becomes an intelligence agent, Akbar. His horror, redolent of the present day, mounts in considering a possible Afghan war 'appalling problems posed by supply and transport,' there being no maps of Afghanistan. Harsh conditions prevailed; in 1878 the monsoon failed, resulting in famine and cholera:

---

[17] The role of the East India Company in controlling trade is vividly told by Moxham, R. (2001) *The Great Hedge of India,* Constable, London, in his quest for the Customs Hedge laid across India until 1879 to tax salt imports.

[18] A single officer (not in the Guides) was deputed to accompany a wedding party, of larger scale, involving 2000 elephants and 3000 camels, and on arrival the ruler behaved much as the fictional Rana of *Bhithor*. (Endnote to *The Far Pavilions*).

[19] A stark contrast is illustrated in Deborah Ellis's story of the confinement and terror of family life in Kabul under Taliban rule in 2001.

There was frost on the higher hills, and behind them, very far away, Wigram[20] could see the gleam of snow, and the white soaring peak of Sikaram, queen of the Safed Koh. It would be winter soon, he thought; the nights would be bitterly cold, and once the snow began to fall the northern passes would be blocked. He wouldn't have said, himself, it was a good time to start a war in Afghanistan' (p.748). However 'there were butterflies on the hillside: familiar English-looking butterflies, fritillaries, brimstones, meadow-browns, and tiny common blues that reminded him of summer holidays long ago' (p.750).

In the autumn, in spite of the first Afghan war, Wally saw Kabul and its setting 'beautiful with a wild, spectacular beauty that took his breath away' (p.869). Ash and Juli finally flee north to their valley in the mountains they call *Dur Khaima* or their Far Pavilions.

Representation of Culture

It is perhaps timely to examine South Asian culture through the eyes of a romantic novel:[21] Driver (1995) notes that geographers have neglected popular forms of production and consumption of imaginative geographies. The novel is still popular; a West End musical is planned for 2003. The evocative writing of The Far Pavilions opens up a different world, providing a glimpse of understanding of a very different culture; of complexity, immensity of distance and dangers of simplification. The creative power of the words defines places, they impart emotion and personality (Tuan, op. cit. p.685). The view is complete with scents and sounds. The reader can see the hillsides and mountain views, can taste the flinty soil of the dry air, can feel the freshness of the mountain winds, can touch the cold rock in the mountain camp where Ash was born. The novel describes sensory experiences not just of eyes, but also of ears, and senses of smell and touch, senses which define place and provide a vivid 'way of seeing' (Rodaway, 1994, p.4). Places come alive in all senses through the many traditions and festivals. Ideas of difference (Nash, 2002, p.22) such as of mountain people, with their lighter skin, different religion, food, preferences and language emerge. In the personal interactions and restless travelling over India place identity is formed (Massey, 1999, p.262). The many languages, like Pushtu, Hindustani, become clearer, and the frequent occurrence of cholera, and troubled times. The story

---

[20] Wigram Battye was also a real character.

[21] Weinbaum (1981) p.247, notes that the novel provides an immersion into culture and customs such as purdah, arranged marriages and suttee. She calls it an 'intensely visual novel'

encapsulates both British and Indian perspectives. It is possible to see both how the English colonists 'uninterested in the country or its people' lived and behaved in India, and how complex, vast and vibrant was the life of native peoples, with their many castes, religions and festivals.

Ash clearly shows 'place attachment,' (Gustafson, op.cit. p.10) to India as opposed to England which he hated, to *Mardan,* his home base, and to the mountains. His views correspond to those expressed by people in Sweden interviewed by Gustafson (ibid. p.10) about their feelings for places. Ash has mixed feelings on what is home: the search for security and belonging are recurrent themes. Massey (op.cit. p.264) argues that new geographical imaginations are needed to understand how to belong, and that places and cultures are being challenged. *The Far Pavilions* represent Ash's semi-religious search for the mountains of his youth; a mystical world where he could be safe. It is a representation of mountains as sacred, the home of gods; a view held both by British Romantics (Brown in Silvertown & Sarre, 1991) following the Wordsworth tradition, and in South Asian religions. The novel illustrates all three of Gustafson's (op.cit. p.9) themes in the meanings of place: self, others and environment. The 'life-path' of 'self' is illustrated by the hybrid life of Ash, his identification with India as home, his roots, where a continuity of family life[22] can be observed. His 'self-identification,' (Ash sees himself as Indian) sense of home, and search for security are described in the places. Place becomes meaningful because of the 'others,' the local community, be it Hindu, Pathan or British. Environment features strongly in the contrast of cool, rainy mountains and hot arid plains.

The Far Pavilions is a memorable story, populated with a wealth of realistic characters. It is imaginative literature, where the places are inextricably part of the experiences of love or tragedy (Pocock, 1986, p.56). The romantic descriptions of the landscape put into the mouth of Ash's poetic friend Wally counterpoint the horror of the Afghan War. Much of the end of the story takes place in Kabul: the novel asserts the importance of the border, which was repeatedly crossed at that time.

Mind's eye distortions

This analysis of The Far Pavilions is presented here as an examination from a consumer of one form of popular culture (Driver, 1992, p.34). There are imperfections; it seems unlikely that the cholera outbreaks, at the beginning and end of the novel, were both spread by pilgrims from Hardwar. Secondary sources are bound to be limited. A romantic novel

---

[22] Neither Ash nor Juli are encumbered by parents in *The Far Pavilions:* family life is demonstrated by the loyal supporters of both characters.

cannot be regarded as an authentic, trustworthy and objective source of 'what is really happening out there,' as Banks (2001) claims for the news, in his analysis of the role of TV news in constructing realities of other places. It differs from the 'image region' based on the imagined landscape of Catherine Cookson, where Pocock (1992) notes that visitors could 'see the inhabitants in my mind's eye,' even when looking at the site of demolished buildings. A romantic novel concentrates on developing believable characters, and it is through these that pictures of India are made. From the frequent references in The Far Pavilions to the noisy battles, bazaars and festivals, it is clear that sound is part of the Indian environment for M.M. Kaye. The vivid picture of the sounds of south Asia contributes to the processes by which place-affinity is built up (Pocock, 1989, p.194). In relying solely on the novel compared to a film source, the sensory losses include accents, language and pronunciation of names of places and people. An imperfect vision filtered by UK experience and knowledge may be unaware of making false assumptions, which may unwittingly cause offence.

Modern Relevance of *The Far Pavilions* story

At first sight the historical nature of the novel; the action occurs at the end of the nineteenth century, must limit knowledge of present day South Asian culture. However, as Massey claims (in Gustafson, op. cit.) that an understanding of place is based on its history and tradition, south Asia needs to be interpreted in relation to the outside world, in this case British colonists, Gustafson's significant 'others.' India's place characteristics are made special by the past activities of the British Raj and their relationships with local people. Massey also comments that place meanings can change with time, as the balance of power shifts, as is seen now. It is interesting, in the light of the frequency in which characters in The Far Pavilions think nothing of crossing the (India–Afghanistan) 'border,' to note Massey's comment that the definition of a place may mean drawing a boundary around it. The drawing of political boundaries has certainly been an important part of India's past. The novel clearly considers Pathans and Afghanistan to be part of India. Re-reading the ending of the novel around Kabul presents an encounter with newly familiar names of places in the news in spring 2002; the Khyber Pass, Jalalabad, Kandahar. The rich descriptions of the beautiful harsh scenery, and the savagery of the battles, give background to war in Afghanistan, and engender a deeper understanding of the land and its people. History and maps of the area can perhaps help explain current tensions. Given the eternal nature of stories of personal relationships, and the enduring appeal of love stories, this novel still has relevance to a modern audience in making cultural background accessible. What emerges is a cultural landscape, the home of real people: M.M. Kaye paints a personality of India.

Conclusion

Through a reading of The Far Pavilions, South Asian culture emerges as exciting, vibrant and noisy. Images recur of colourful clothes, tasty food, hot dusty plains contrasting with cool, fresh mountain air. It brings me close to characters I may never meet in real life; people with strong religious beliefs, which impose constraints on behaviour, activities and food; with taboos often greater than the power of personal friendships with people of other race; people who celebrate joyous festivals, whose languages I cannot understand. I experience the love and familiarity of India as home, and see England, pale and cold, through Eastern eyes. The Orient is painted as a desirable, fantasy world, exotic and dangerous, a place of love and war. The novel portrays an evocative picture of traditions, complexity and difference. 'India,' vast and vibrant, emerges as part of self-identification.

Acknowledgement

I am very grateful to Michael Koutoulou for his help in providing high quality versions of the book covers from his Web site.

Bibliography

Banks, M. (2001) 'Representing regional life: the place discourse of *Granada Tonight.*' *North West Geography*, 1, pp.2-10.

Brayshay, M. & Cleary, M. (2002) 'Shaping Colonial and Imperial Landscapes,' editorial. *Landscape Research* 27 (1), pp.5-10.

Brown, S. (1991) in Silvertown, J & Sarre, P *Environment and Society.* Open University / Hodder & Stoughton.

Chaturvedi, S. (2002) Process of Othering in the Case of India and Pakistan, *Tijdschrift voor Economische en Sociale Geografie,* 93(2) pp.149-159.

Cloke, P, Crang, P. & Goodwin, M. (1999) *Introducing Human Geographies,* Arnold.

Driver, F. (1995) 'Sub-merged identities: familiar and unfamiliar histories,' *Transactions of the Institute of British Geographers*, 20, pp.410-413.

Driver, F. (1992) 'Geography's Empire : histories of geographical knowledge,' *Environment and Planning D: Society and Space* 10, 1992, pp.23-40.

Ellis, D. (2001) *The Breadwinner.* Oxford University Press.

Gurnah, A. (2002) 'Elvis in Zanzibar,' in Dear, M. & Flusty, S. *Spaces of Postmodernity: Readings in Human Geography,* Blackwell.

Gustafson, P. (2001) 'Meanings of Place: Everyday Experience and Theoretical Conceptualizations,' *Journal of Environmental Psychology*, 21, pp.5-16.

Haynes, R. M. (1981) Geographical Images and Mental Maps, Pelican.

Honeybone, R.C. & Graves, N.J. (1966) *Geography for Schools Book Three, North America and Asia,* Heinemann Educational, London.

Kaye, M.M. (1999) *Enchanted Evening,* third part of *Share of Summer,* her autobiography. Viking.

Kaye, M.M. (1997) *Golden Afternoon,* second part of *Share of Summer,* her autobiography, Viking.

Kaye M.M. (ed) (1980) The Golden Calm: An English Lady's Life in Moghul Delhi, Webb & Bower, Exeter, England.

Kaye, M.M. (1978) The Far Pavilions, Penguin.

Kaye, M.M. (1978) *The Sun in the Morning,* first part of *Share of Summer,* her autobiography. Viking.

Kaye, M.M. (1963) *Trade Wind,* Penguin.

Kaye, M.M. www.kourtoulou.freeserve.co.uk

Massey, D. (1999) 'Geography Matters in a Globalised World,' *Geography,* 84(3), pp.261-5.

McEwen, C. (1998) 'Cutting the power lines within the place? Countering paternity and eurocentrism in the geographical tradition,' *Transactions of the Institute of British Geographers,* 23.3, pp.371-384.

Morin, K. (1998) 'British Women Travel Writers and their construction of racial difference across nineteenth century American West,' *Transactions of the Institute of British Geographers,* 23.3, 1998, pp.311-330.

Lych, K. (1960) Images of the City.

Moxham, R. (2001) *The Great Hedge of India.* Constable, London.

Nash, C. 'Cultural Geography: post-colonial cultural geographies,' *Progress in Human Geography* 262, 2002, pp.219-230.

Pepper, D. (1994) *Modern Environmentalism,* Routledge.

Phillips Modern School Atlas, (1968) George Philip and Son Ltd, London.

Ploszajska, T. (1999) 'Geographical Education, Empire and Citizenship: Geographical Teaching and Learning in English Schools 1870-1944,' *Historical Geography Research Series No. 35.*

Pocock, D. (1992) 'Catherine Cookson Country: Tourist Expectation and Experience,' *Geography,* pp.236-243.

Pocock, D. (1989) 'Sound and the Geographer,' *Geography,* 74(3), pp.193-200.

Pocock, D. (1986) 'Literature and Humanist Geography,' *Area,* 181, pp.55-56.

Radcliffe, S. (1996) 'Imaginative Geographies, Postcolonialism and National Identities; Contemporary Discourses of the Nation in Ecuador' *Ecumene* 3 (1), pp.23-42.

Rodaway, P. (1994) Sensuous Geographies: Body, Sense and Place, Routledge, London.

The M.M. Kaye page at.www.geocities.com/mmkayefan/

Tuan, Y-F. (1991) 'Language and the Making of Place : A Narrative-Descriptive Approach,' *Annals of the Association of American Geographers,* 81(4), pp.684-696.

Weinbaum, F. (1981) '*The Far Pavilions,* M.M. Kaye,' *Journal of South Asia Literature* 16 (1) (book review) pp..247-249.

From *Heat and Dust* to *East is East*: Journey from the Colonial to Post-colonial South Asian Cultural Space

Karen D'Souza and Tasleem Shakur

Urdu – language of the court in days of royalty – now languishes in the back lanes and gutters of the city…We have no future. There is no future. There is only past. (Desai, 1984, p.204)

This investigation of South Asian culture pictured in English examines a range of literature and film produced in the postcolonial period, identifying differences in representation which emanate from the location of author, genre and assumed reader or audience. Our study takes us on a spatial and temporal journey from images of British colonialism, through the postcolonial space of contemporary India, to the South Asian diaspora experience of northern England. The criteria for the selection of material under review was determined by reasons exterior to the texts, rather than from any shared thematic or stylistic characteristics. Rather they were chosen for the particular author's individual cultural positioning, and the targeting of a mainstream, British or western audience, rather than one of cultural or ethnic specificity. The three texts under review are Heat and Dust (1975) by Ruth Prawer Jhabvala, Anita Desai's In Custody, published in 1984, and East is East by the playwright Ayub Khan-Din, 1996. Each text has been produced as a film version, two of which were directed by Ismail Merchant (Heat and Dust, 1982 and In Custody, 1994). East is East was directed by Damien O'Donnell and released in 2000.

Throughout our exploration we have found it illuminating to examine, with respect to cultural representation, the nature of the changes made in the translation from written text to film. In this respect we find that E.M. Forster's *A Passage to India* (1924) in the novel and the film, becomes an inevitable benchmark. Where we find Forster echoing through the pages of *Heat and Dust*, in terms of the changes made in cinematic depiction of India for commercial and personally motivated reasons we need only look to David Lean's comments on his making of the film of *A Passage to India (1984)*. The film versions of such texts as *A Passage to India* and *Heat and Dust* are readily hijacked by those who wish to read only the personal and romantic dimensions, and are often heavily injected with the sort of 'end of empire' nostalgia that is to be found in popular novels of colonial discourse. Salman Rushdie (1991) writing on the false popularity of such 'Raj novels' in his essay *'Imaginary Homelands'* has already quoted David Lean to make his point with regard to the appropriation of such literature:

> Forster was a bit anti-English, anti-Raj and so on. I suppose it's a tricky thing to say, but I'm not so much. I intend to keep the balance more. I don't believe all the English were a lot of idiots. Forster rather made them so. He came down hard against them. (David Lean, quoted in Rushdie, p.128)

Anita Desai has also condemned Lean's manipulation of Forster's text, in particular she takes issue with the changes made by the film director to the ending of the novel, in the belief that he is improving upon Forster. Desai's claim that what "he is admitting is that he feels he has improved history as well" (New Republic, 1985, p.28) draws attention to a continuing imperialist urge to control and censor the images of India. Also, in David Lean's claim to 'keep the balance more' it is easy to identify the change in emphasis that emerges in the film, and encourages the popular view that such novels as *A Passage to India* sit generically alongside Paul Scott's *The Jewel in the Crown* (1966) and M.M. Kaye's *The Far Pavilions* (1978) in which the focus is on the personal experiences of the British during the decline of empire.[1]

Heat and Dust published in 1975 charts the story of Olivia, who married civil servant Douglas Rivers and came to live in India in the 1920s, and subsequently scandalised British society by eloping with an Indian prince. This narrative of cultural engagement between South Asians and the British involves the reconstruction of Olivia's story by her step-granddaughter Anna fifty years later, who also becomes personally involved with India. Exploring the space of post-independence, trade liberated India, Anita Desai's *In Custody* charts the aspirations and inadequacies of Deven, impoverished Hindu scholar in an insignificant college. In an attempt to escape his mediocrity he accepts a request by his old friend Murad to interview the once celebrated but now degenerated Urdu poet, Nur. The novel's engagement with a sophisticated but now decaying Muslim Urdu literary culture is set against an aggressive materialistic global Indian culture. A further cultural tension is identified in *East is East,* as it engages with some of the issues of modern diaspora

---

[1] A range of literature of this type is available, but see particularly Paul Scott's *The Jewel in the Crown,* 1966, and M.M. Kaye's *The Far Pavilions,* Penguin, 1978, as illuminating examples.

communities and generational differences in the play's dramatisation of inherent cultural conflicts raised by a Pakistani father's insistence on tradition and an easygoing English mother. Ayub Khan-Din's comic portrayal of this Salford family enunciates the mixed values experienced by second generation Asian communities. Taken together these three texts suggest varied terms of 'cultural engagement'.

With regard to the examination of cultural engagement, Homi Bhabha provides an important pointer towards a more holistic understanding of culture in his introduction to the *Location of Culture*:

The move away from the singularities of 'class' or 'gender' as primary conceptual and organizational categories, has resulted in an awareness of the subject positions - of race, gender, generation, institutional location, geopolitical locale, sexual orientation - that inhabit any claim to identity in the modern world. What is theoretically innovative, and politically crucial, is the need to think beyond narratives of originary and initial subjectivities and the focus on those moments or processes that are produced in the articulation of cultural differences. (Bhaba, 1994, p.1)

Under such pretext *Heat and Dust*, *In Custody* and *East is East* provide tapestries of 'in-between spaces' suggesting some interesting identities of South Asian subcultures whether being singular or communal.

Heat and Dust offers an image of imperialism viewed through the lens of the post-imperial age and goes some way to re-examining this period of colonial history. In terms of picturing South Asian culture Jhabvala's representation of the imperialist period displays an elegant past which is at once seductive and nostalgic, and which clearly functions as a veil over the reality of India. This visualisation of the imperial period is not unique – as mentioned above it echoes *A Passage to India*: the British civil service is there in all its stereotyped glory; the dutiful, conscientious British administrator, and the insularity of the British women are typical representations found in Anglo-Indian fiction.

What does emerge from the historical scenes in *Heat and Dust* is that British identity is relatively self-assured. It reverberates with the Victorian civilising mission of British imperialism and with attitudes inherited from Kiplingesque depictions of India. Douglas is cast in the mould of Forster's (op. cit.) Ronnie Heaslop – he greatly admires his peers, the 'old India hands'; he emulates his parents' lifestyle impressing upon Olivia the 'traditions' of colonial India. However Jhabvala is more sympathetic in her portrayal and certainly less satirical. Above all, this representation of the colonial period demonstrates the imposition of 'order' by the British and their unwillingness to comprehend the cultural forms of India.

There are considerable differences in emphasis between the novel and film versions, which underpins Rushdie's point noted above. While the novel pays significant attention to setting and costume, the emphasis rests on a process of cultural interaction, misapprehension and difference. Whereas the film luxuriates in atmospheric, tranquil colonial settings, foregrounding the conventional theme of love transcending social and cultural boundaries, which begs comparison with one of David Lean's earlier works. Lean's directing of Pasternak's *Dr Zhivago* (1958) sidelines the novel's pervasive backdrop of the Russian Revolution and elevates the romantic interest.

Yet underneath the elegant veil of the creamy-white linens and lace of colonial life, the text hints at native subversion rupturing the surface order, challenging British authority, and this is further underpinned by the juxtapositioning of the contemporary story of Anna: the two narratives combine to project and foreground Indian culture. Thus, Jhabvala's work can be distanced from Forster and the Anglo-Indian genre through her strategy of prioritising issues of Indian identity in a narrative of Englishness. Certainly Englishness in *Heat and Dust* is once again under review, but in terms of the legacy of imperialism.

Jhabvala's character, Olivia, in comparison with Forster's Fielding, and Adela Quested,[2] is apolitical, as she does not arrive in India armed with liberal pretensions or aspirations of discovering the 'real' India. Boredom and romance provide Olivia with the impulse to make the leap, to 'cross over', in the language of Major Minnies, and to take up the scandalous position of lover to the Nawab. Here Jhabvala presents us with a controversial reversal of previous cultural traffic. As Singh (1996) discusses in a chapter entitled 'The gendering of empire' (pp.79-119) prior to the arrival of British women in India during the 19th Century it was not unusual for officers of the Raj to establish relationships with Indian women, and although this became increasingly discouraged, it did not disappear altogether. Yet there was very little contact between British women and Indian men on a social or cultural basis. This lack of cultural interchange between these two sections of Indian society during Imperialism is borne out by absences and gaps within the novel, which are then foregrounded by the contrasting but enigmatic relationship which emerges between Anna and Inder Lal. The strategy deployed in the film is however more direct in its attempt to demonstrate this cultural void.

---

[2] Fielding has a developed interest in and experience of India, while Adela Quested has arrived in India with a determined, but naïve notion, with regard to social and cultural engagement with the 'real' India.

Olivia's intrusion into the conventionally male-only after dinner cultural entertainment at the Nawab's palace, emphasizes the barriers of race and gender. Cultural engagement, wherever it did take place, was a pragmatic activity to be endured by the men. Again the ease and freedom with which Anna travels through India and enthusiastically engages with the people and customs of India offers a judgement on these former British attitudes.

Jhabvala writes about the colonial period with a freedom and insight that would not seem possible in earlier times. As Singh (ibid. p.91) notes, European women were perceived by the British as repositories of morality, in contrast to the Indian mistresses they had replaced. Denied an active role in the Raj, the British women seemingly contribute to civilisation merely by their presence. That they are also significant in bringing about the separation of the races is a continuing stereotype borne out in both Forster's and Jhabvala's novels as they reiterate this generic convention, but with a different purpose. As literary convention seems to dictate the British women are depicted as a disruptive and alienating presence, although represented more sympathetically by Jhabvala, the void between the two cultures is symbolised by the lack of interest and understanding shown by the two groups of women dramatized in the historical sections of the novel. Yet in the contemporary narrative of Anna, it is the women although initially wary of each other, who seem able to make connections, despite the physical relationship which takes place between Anna and Inder Lal. Yet despite the symbolic inferences in the birth of Anna's baby, whereas Olivia's pregnancy was terminated, the relationship between Anna and Inder Lal seems more symptomatic of the social and cultural liberation of sexual attitudes in the 1970s, and depicts a native curiosity in western women.

What is acknowledged by Jhabvala, in contrast with Forster, is a greater societal role played by the Indian women. The novel identifies clearly the assertive presence of the cigar-smoking Begum, a depiction which reiterates images seen in the work of indigenous artists such as in Satayjit Ray's film *The Chess Player* (1977) based on an Urdu novel, *Shatranj Ke khiladi,* by renowned writer Prem Chand. In *Heat and Dust* the Begum is a beguiling and dominating force, but also behind the scenes at the palace there is a world of feminine indulgence and pleasurable activity where we gain insights into rituals of popular culture such as the performance of Hijra.[3] For Jhabvala these women are not merely background characters surfacing only as a pious presence, or to be revered in the role of mother, daughter, wife. Where South Asian women were

---

[3] Part of the popular culture of South Asia; a theatrical performance of male cross-dressing, originating with the custom of eunuchs.

often kept very much in the closet in Anglo-Indian fiction (Kipling, Forster etc), Jhabvala opens the door ajar onto a previously misunderstood and ignored world of South Asian women. Interestingly in Jhabvala's depiction of women, British and Indian, they seem equally confident with their identity and role within their respective societies. However in terms of depiction of South Asian culture these insights into the women at the palace very much stand as a microcosm of the hierarchical nature of a class structured society in India, and in this respect demonstrate a mutual understanding between the British and Indian elite. Yet reciprocity is limited and is on the whole one-sided as the restricted communication between the two groups of women takes place in English and under the cloak of western manners and affectations. The Muslim women depicted here are of the social elite and are sufficiently Europeanised to be affable and interactive, demonstrating an intriguing and uninhibited degree of hybridity in their ability to dance the Cha Cha wearing a sari, as depicted in the film version. Implicit in this representation of social interaction is the impact of the British Raj on Indian nobility which is not well documented in works of fiction. A comparable characterisation is to be found Ray's film *The Chess Player* (1977) in which the Nawab's mother politically strong-minded, and communicates with the British on equal terms.

In this representation of the colonial period it is South Asian native masculinity, in the figure of the Nawab, which is confused and unstable in its relationship with the socio-cultural milieu. Here we detect a line of South Asian male characters with mixed loyalties contesting the cultural space in which they live, from Forster's (*Passage to India*) Dr Aziz as our prototype, through the Nawab (*Heat and Dust*) the poet Nur of *In Custody* and George Khan in *East is East*. Like Dr Aziz, the Nawab has professional connections with the British, but his social position demands a greater degree of political and cultural interaction which culminates in a sense of ruptured identity. Metaphors of potency run through this narrative and the Nawab, a token figurehead of his province, is rendered impotent by the British in their negation of his historical role of tribal leader, actually encouraging the subversive forces of the Nawab.

The film especially depicts with some poignancy the extravagant splendour with which the Nawab panders to western codes and conventions of hospitality. The novel, with greater emphasis in the film, investigates the stance of the Nawab's liberal attitude towards both South Asian and English culture. He exercises his charisma but also his shrewdness in charming the English, being adept at presenting a polished veneer, attuned to British sensibilities. The subtext of the novel however demonstrates how at the same time he accommodates the socio-political demands of his native tribesmen, with which he ultimately identifies. The duality of the Nawab is reflected in his adoption of western dress usually accompanied with native cultural trimmings, and in his apparent equal interest in both Nawabi and English culture, embracing cultural hybridity and multiculturalism. This would be perceived as outwardly a sign of progress, and from the British point of view goes some way to vindicating their civilising mission. As noted above Jhabvala subtly demonstrates the rupturing of this polished surface, fragments of frustration with the British are glimpsed, revealing his discontent and the cultural contest which seems to recur.

Within the novel native culture is constantly pitted against British law: administrators are unable to eradicate the traditional Hindi custom of Sati;[4] the ineffectiveness of the British is signified in the continual unrest between the Hindus and Muslims triggered by the annual festival of The Husband's Wedding Day (encouraged by the Nawab). This episode is a subtle representation of the cultural tensions raised by the ancient Hindu/Muslim conflict but is also indicative of the seething anti-English feeling evident in the novel's subtext. The explorations of such controversial cultural issues are only sketchily outlined in the film diminishing the potential for cultural understanding.

A contrasting description of the festival is related through Anna's experience of contemporary India.

> Typical of the way things get mixed up in India is the story of Baba Firdaus' shrine. As the Nawab had explained to Olivia, this had originally been built by his ancestor Amanullah Khan in thanksgiving to a Muslim faqir who had given him shelter. It is now sacred to Hindu women because it is thought that offerings at this shrine will cure childlessness. But it is sacred to them for only day a year. (Jhabvala, 1975, pp.65-66)

She recognizes the festival as an example of India's ability to absorb and intertwine competing cultures, as she acknowledges the Hindu appropriation of the Muslim shrine of Baba Firdaus (ancestor of the Nawab). The shrine has become the place of pilgrimage and a picnic site, illustrative of the continuity of the Sufi tradition of 'shrine ritual culture' shared by both religious groups. Although Anna perceives the shrine as an example of the positive cultural integration of India, it is in fact suggestive of the cultural tension raised by the dominance and marginalisation of competing cultures in the modern period (a theme

---

[4] Sati - the ancient Hindu custom of women joining their dead husbands on the funeral pyre and which was formally outlawed by the British.

which is further explored by Anita Desai in *In Custody*). It is however also indicative of continuing western misunderstanding, that homogenised perception of the oriental space identified by Said (1978), or as in Spivak's more specific remark about 'India' as an identity.

'India', for people like me, is not really a place with which they can form a national identity because it has always been an artificial construct. 'India' is a bit like saying 'Europe.' (Spivak, 1990, p.39)

Such issues of cultural tension and suppression are further identified through the characterisation of the Nawab and his relationship with the British. The Nawab's traditional authority and leadership is constantly undermined and restricted by the political situation. A recurring motif in the texts examined here is the impulse to retreat into a cultural past, real or imaginary. The Nawab, like Dr Aziz in *A Passage to India*, turns to Urdu poetry as means of expressing frustration with the British. This impulse is also evident in *In Custody* and *East is East*. In the former, it is a dominant strategy of expressing the themes of social and cultural dissatisfaction with contemporary India experienced by male protagonists; whereas in the latter, working class George is not sufficiently versed in the purity of Urdu poetry, but the impulse manifests itself in his deep desire to engage his sons with the noble language of their inheritance and therefore enforce a retreat into the incumbent traditions. Interestingly, the film versions of these texts omit or sideline such small, but insightful details, devoting energies to the 'universal' passions of the main plot.

Jhabvala's writing acknowledges Edward Said's identification of the 'culturally sanctioned habit of deploying large generalisations' (Said, E. 1978, [rpt 1993] p.227) within colonial discourse. This is reflected throughout the historical sections of the novel, but is also delineated in the contemporary episodes, indicative of this concept as a continuing process. Anna's experiences of India dramatize the continuing practice of England defining itself against India (the East), as the 'other'. The European travellers that Anna meets are representative of the superficially enlightened attitude of 1970s back-packers, signifying a reversal of conventional positions. Where Victorian imperialists considered themselves 'lightbearers', the 'hippies' identified India as an immaterial opposite to Western consumer society and went in search of spiritual enlightenment. Jhabvala's resists a western urge to romanticise India, and invariably the realities of modern India are overwhelming and assault the stereotyped pre-conceptions mired in the popular consciousness of the west, historically exacerbated by fiction and western readings of such narratives, as commented upon above by Rushdie (op. cit.) The contemporary travellers are deceived by India, and Europe is identified by Jhabvala as a continuing place of illusion with regard to the 'other'.

Cultural conflict is subtly represented in *Heat and Dust*, and the film especially appears to focus on the romantic plot played out between Olivia and the Nawab, which has the effect of diluting the sense of anti-English feeling that seethes underneath. However the 'Laura Ashleyfication' of the colonial setting does seem to have the effect of deliberately perpetuating the orientalist attitude of the western audience, which Jhabvala then seeks to undermine in her dramatisation of contemporary India.

In Anita Desai's work the post-colonial space is not immediately apparent as she explores the cultural particularities and diversities of India. Within these novels of colonial consciousness her focus is on the renewal and renegotiation of Indian culture and shows a departure from strategies of binary codes of recognition and categorisation so much a part of colonial discourse.

Jan Mohamed's discussion of the two phases of colonialism seem relevant here. He identifies these as the 'dominant' phase and the 'hegemonic' (Jan Mohamed, 1985). The dominant phase begins with the establishment of a colony and is in force until independence. In this phase the colonized remain passive and are directly controlled, but paradoxically remain interactive with their native culture as both are condemned as primitive by the colonizer. In contradistinction the hegemonic phase is more insidious as the colonized adopt and accept 'a version of the colonizers' entire system of values, attitudes, morality, institutions, and more important, mode of production' (ibid. p.62). It is this aspect of the 'legacy of imperialism' which surfaces in Desai's novel, such as in the workings of the college, its internal politics and hierarchical system.

Although Desai claims not to write 'social document' novels and describes her work in 'universalist' terms (Srivastava, 1984) she is identified by Juneja (1995) as one of few Indian postcolonial writers whose work is sociological, rather than mythological in its detail (p.116). Indeed her claim that:

> By writing novels that have been catalogued by critics as psychological, and that are purely subjective, I have been left free to employ, simply, the language of the interior. (Desai quoted in Srivastava, op. cit. p.3)

may be examined in light of Jameson's (1981) arguments which negate the aesthetic of universalism, and in which he relates text to context noting that intellectual disciplines (such as novel writing) are discursive practices which are always historically and socially positioned. In such a context Desai's novel with its blend of social realism and modernism, provokes interest with regard to the images of India presented in the novel. The novel's polyphonic, competing voices, and disrupting devices of modernism placed within a narrative firmly rooted in accurate social detail, provides an appropriate strategy with which to convey and interrogate the problematic landscape of a specific postcolonial space and the particularities of the cultural contexts of post-independence India.

It is through the characterisation of Deven with which Desai dramatizes the problem of reclaiming and renegotiating the experience of India. The textual representation of India is one of cultural assimilation of discrete centres, thereby challenging that colonial construction of India as a homogenous unit commented on earlier. Deven is a typical character within Desai's narratives as an outsider or marginalized figure, undermining the validity of the post-independence utopian attempts to construct a socially harmonious pan-India with fully integrated Muslim and Hindu communities. As a character Deven is doubly marginalized as he negotiates his way through a marginalized culture which exists in an increasingly Hindu dominant society which usurps the space relinquished by colonial authority, and also finds himself alienated by the growing consumer society of the modern progressive world. His ability to transcend his dominant Hindi culture and embrace Urdu seems to some extent reminiscent of Nehruite liberalism of the 1950s and 60s, but it actually indicates his disavowal of popular culture generally, as he desires a return to an imagined purer, refined past vaguely located somewhere other than the here and now. Again this motif of the frustrated or dissatisfied character with a desire to engage with the discourses of the pre-colonial time emerges. Deven's love of the Urdu language and culture reveals his desire to reach his perceived pre-colonial roots and turn away from the social change and the influences of outside forces brought about the trade liberalisation of the late 1970s.

Deven feels more oppressed by the circumstances of modernity rather than the need to assert a modern identity in the absence of the British; in contrast his wife yearns for the trappings of capitalism which hold the promise of real and tangible life improvement. The differences in their aspirations are quite revealing: Deven like Nur looks to the past as a means of escape from failure and decline; while Sarla, and Nur's younger wife are far more ready to accept changing social circumstances, identifying in their individual ways, the benefits of modernity. The novel produces images which are reflective of changing social values as India moves towards a more capitalist, materialist ethos.

The poet Nur embodies the pre-colonial, Moghal ideal for Deven, as he embarks on the pursuit of trying to preserve the image and reputation of the aging, fading poet, ignoring evidence of decline and apathy. Nur in fact signifies not just a form of cultural decay, but how competing cultures within India continue to strive for dominance and attempt to marginalise others within the post-colonial space. This is reflected through Desai's writing strategies which echo the multiplicity and hybridity of the cultural space. Bakhtin developed the concept of 'heteroglossia' as a means of explaining and understanding notions of competing languages and discourses in texts which are imbued with 'verbal-ideological belief systems'. In Stam's interpretation of Bakhtin, the role of the artistic text 'is not to represent real life "existents", but rather to stage the conflicts inherent in heteroglossia, i.e. the coincidences and competitions of languages and discourses' (Stam, 1988, pp.122-3). Desai's novel depicts a variety of intersecting discourses (gender, religion, language) but essentially the conflict being staged here is the clash of a dying, feudal, Mughal Urdu culture with that of a rising European mercantile ideology.

The plurality of voices which defy fusion into a single dominant consciousness in Desai's novel exist on various levels. Most significantly the competing, oppositional cultures of Urdu and Hindi are foregrounded, but other competing voices within the modern society of India are also charted: competing college departments; the naivety of Deven's scholarly activity and Murad's commercial pragmatism; competing voices of men and women, the differing aspirations of Deven and his wife Sarla in particular. Consequently the conflict between tradition and modernity is diversely reflected within a context of changing economic conditions which specifically result from policy changes which brought about trade liberalisation. Deven and Nur are resistant to the influence of capitalism and material culture, but each is representative of a complex and differing response to the decay of a once thriving cultural and linguistic community.

The representation of women in the novel requires more discussion than there is room for here, but briefly we might detect motifs of modernity in the actions of the various wives, indicative of undercurrents and discontent within Indian society. The silence of Deven's wife speaks loudly, and although she communicates only through the culturally sanctioned methods of expression, her discontent is articulated within the gaps. From a Western perspective the insight into South Asian culture gained through Deven's treatment of Sarla, in his unwillingness, or culturally inherited inability, to confide or discuss anything of significance with his wife demonstrates an inpenetratable gender divide resulting from the patriarchal society, and diminishes sympathy for his sense of isolation and failure. Nur's wives are more vocal than Sarla. The older wife is assertive on behalf of her husband, which displays like Sarla, the loyalty of both Hindu and Muslim women in the patriarchal hierarchy of South Asian culture. The junior wife seeks personal recognition. In what seems to Deven and Nur a travesty of the traditional form of classical Urdu poetry recital, Nur's wife is a great success both earning popularity and an income. Learning her craft from Nur, she ransacks her husband's poetry but with it produces something that seems both vital and relevant. However Desai's characterisation is sufficiently ambiguous as to allow various readings and variable positionings regarding cultural representation. Often perceived as ruthless, selfish, careerist, and disrespectful towards her husband, she does possess a genuine creative talent, as Deven reluctantly notes:

> The elegance and floridity of her Urdu entered Deven's ears like a flourish of trumpets and beat at his temples while he read. The essential, unsuspected spirit of the woman appeared to step free of its covering, all the tinsel and gauze and tawdriness, and reveal a face from which the pain and powder had been washed... (Desai, op. cit. p.215)

One of the most important images in the novel is the coincidence of Deven's acknowledgement of his failure and sense of relief in the continuing entrapment in his mean life, with his symbolic failure to acknowledge the poetry of Nur's wife as a means of upholding the traditions of Urdu poetry.

> ...Deven did not have the courage. He did not have the time. He did not have the will or the wherewithal to deal with this new presence... (ibid. p.217)

Whilst this inevitably raises questions regarding the positioning of the author, it is interesting to note the changes made by Ismail Merchant in his film.[5] The novel explores the imprisonment of insignificance and failure felt by Deven, compounded in the conclusion by the continuing financial burden placed upon him by Nur. This is poignantly underpinned by his tragic inability to grasp a real opportunity to preserve Urdu literary culture offered by the young wife. Yet in the film the sense of being 'in custody' is re-positioned as Deven being the custodian of the dead poet

---

[5] Film version of *In Custody* was directed by Ismail Merchant in conjunction with Film Four, 1994.

Nur's final manuscripts and body of work sent to him by his wife. Such changes greatly affect responses to the narrative, while one version is perhaps more provocative it raises the question of validity, do the changes made by Merchant diminish or change the reader's understanding of South Asian culture?

Ayub Khan-Din's *East is East* brings us back to a more tangible colonial collision as the play explores South Asian culture and its relationship with that of the host nation. George Khan's experience of Britain as a first generation immigrant activates a sense of confusion and alienation which leads to a questioning of cultural identity. This theme emerges in several writers of South Asian origins, including V.S. Naipul, identifiable in their depiction of the common experience of 'double exile', the struggle to come to terms with the present, and to resist dehumanising definitions of their otherness by the host culture.

George Khan, (we note the English name, English wife, chip shop) left his first wife in Pakistan, seems to have ruptured his ties with his homeland, but the play identifies in George an increasing urge to reconstruct his former cultural connections. There is constant conflict with his family to forge and consolidate these links with visits to the Bradford Asian community, enforcement of sibling visits to the mosque, arguments over the issues of circumcision, arranged marriages and so on. These are often desperate attempts by George to impose his cultural past on his children, who themselves represent a range of responses to their hybrid identity and possess mixed cultural loyalties.

The play (and film) of *East is East* dramatizes issues addressed by Homi Bhabha's discourse on the tensions within hybrid cultures (op. cit.) The play undoubtedly has some powerfully moving scenes, but there is a great deal of comedy in the presentation of the conflict between the popular culture of South Asian Muslims and resistance to the dominant western value systems. Ultimately within the family George remains an isolated, alienated figure, the least able to accept his duality, becoming violent as he feels his identity slipping away and his traditional authority undermined by the adoption of western values. In this respect comparisons are found with the Nawab of *Heat and Dust,* with regard to issues of masculinity and the undermining of the role of the male figure. In fact the character of George resonates with Forster's Dr Aziz, the Nawab and Deven – the same impulse to seek solace and identity by turning to the Urdu language and cultural forms in a world where they feel increasingly marginal. This impulse in George further manifests itself in his ineffectual attempts to acculturate his children.

In Khan-Din's depiction of the South Asian migrant community his writing displays parallels with work of Kureishi.[6] Significantly the drama is written about the 1970s retrospectively. George is a first generation immigrant living in Salford and is consequently comparatively isolated from his community, which is further compounded by having an English wife and mixed race children. The effectiveness of the comedy is also questionable: in an obvious over-simplification (but based on anecdote and observation) we might contend that white English audiences enjoy the humour in the film enjoying the stereotypical characterisation of Islamic culture, whereas Asian reactions to the film comment on the apparent demonising of George in his attempts at resistance. In Kureishi's screenplay of *My Son the Fanatic* (Udayan Prasad, 1999) similar themes emerge, a generation on, but here it is the father figure Parvez, liberal and tolerant taxi driver who is resistant to, but also disturbed by, the fundamentalism of his disillusioned son. In explanation of his liaison with local prostitute that friendships are good, but they are found in strange places he attempts to explain his resistance to cultural boundaries Islamic fundamentalism attempts to place on him. The film, inevitably champions the cause of Parvez rather than his zealous son, despite illustrating the tensions experienced by the migrant community.

In his exploitation of the comic genre Khan-Din is positioned alongside an increasing list of British Asian artists such as Kureishi and Meera Syal who are successful beyond the Asian community, and *East is East* is part of the growing list of popular film and TV credits which includes *Goodness Gracious Me! My Son the Fanatic, Bhaji on the Beach,* and *Bend It Like Beckham*.[7] How far can these comic cultural portrayals which seem constructed to the sensibility of mainstream British audiences offer a social critique, or are they merely a pragmatic strategy? Why are such films hugely popular with Western audiences but not necessarily with the British South Asian community?

Implicit in this question is a wider concern regarding the creation and reception of images of South Asian culture pictured in English. In terms of Edward Said's influential critical stance of 'the orient being an integral part of European material civilization and culture' (Said, 1993, op.cit. p.42) probably comes to life in the cultural landscape of *Heat and Dust.* Both the nostalgic colonial and the optimistic post-colonial cultural spaces are evocatively described in the novel and mystically re-created in

---

[6] Compare Hanif Kureishi's screenplay *My Beautiful Laundrette*, (1985) director: Stephen Frears, and the novel *The Buddha of Surburbia,* Faber (1990) or the TV adaptation, (BBC TV, 1993)

[7] *Goodness Gracious Me!* – BBC TV. 1998-2000, *Bhaji on the Beach,* director: Gurinder Chadha, 1992, *Bend it Like Beckham*, director: Gurinder Chadha, 2002.

the film version. Said's reference to and endorsement of Gramsci's analytic distinction between civil and cultural society and the production of 'cultural hegemony' is also worth revisiting through the representation of the 'colonial and 'post-colonial' cultural spaces in *Heat and Dust*. In a deconstruction of the novel and possibly more obviously so of the film, the neo-Marxist critics may have a sound grounding on which to uphold the aspects of the 'hegemony of European ideas about the Orient, themselves reiterating European superiority over Oriental backwardness, usually overriding the possibility that a more independent, or more sceptical thinker, might have had different views on the matter' (ibid. p.48). The perceived subtle 'superior moral grounds' of Olivia and Anna over the Nawab and Inder Lal may reinforce the hegemony of European ideas.

A similar analogy may be applied to *East is East*. Although the play and its film version attempts to provide a sympathetic portrayal of working class South Asian diaspora culture, ultimately George Khan's English wife and the northern English community (with whom the audience identifies) emerges as more tolerant, sympathetic and sagacious. However, such analysis is perhaps not applicable to *In Custody* as there is not an obvious encounter with the West. The notion of 'cultural hybridity' and 'cultural diversity' appears to be more prominent than cultural hegemony. The collaboration of Anita Desai and Ismail Merchant for the film version of *In Custody* provides a unique production of an authentic post-colonial third space, as suggested by Bhabha (Soja, 1996, p.139). To some extent *In Custody* is a third cinema providing an alternative space successfully illustrating 'social marginality' of the decaying Sufi culture which originally developed from a cultural hybridity of Persian and Indian culture. However, from a more critical stance one may interrogate whether the novel and the film version have artificially constructed a popular culture and negotiated its identity (Gillespie, 1995, pp.76-108).

On the determination of social action in space and time in a capitalist society Nigel Thrift's assertion of the major contradictions between socialized production and private appropriation could be well illustrated in all three films (Thrift, 2002, pp.110). *Heat and Dust* oscillates between colonial and post-colonial space and time while *East is East* attempts to capture the emerging South Asian diaspora in the north of England during the early 1970s. The three films deal with a series of binary relationships between coloniser/colonised, core/periphery, East/West, or North/South. However distinctions should be made between the perceived 'time and space' of the characters within the play/novels/films, and the production and conceived spaces by the writers, directors, readers and the audience. Such notions should take us to the postmodern concepts of 'social' and 'representational' space (Lefebvre, 2002, pp.131-141). In *Heat and Dust* the focus is on the relationship between the upper class society of the British Raj with an Indian princely state in the colonial period, and the brief encounter between a liberated middle class English woman with a middle class neo-liberal Indian male. The presence of the overwhelming working class/peasant society of India is kept firmly in the distance.

The time and space of *In Custody* is located in the advanced capitalist society of India of the 1980s and is engaged in a binary relationship between someone who exists in the 'core' but has his heart in the 'periphery' (Deven) and some in the margin (Nur). The plot remains within the middle/lower middle class society within the context of trade liberalisation. Again the urban lower classes are only a somewhat distant backdrop, therefore the representational aspect of *Heat and Dust* and *In Custody* is limited to the portrayal of a tiny minority of the upper and middle classes of India. *East is East* makes an interesting departure from such middle class representations of south Asia through its focus on a working class Pakistani living in the North West city of Salford. Both the play and the film foreground two sets of binary relationships: the intergenerational (first and second generation South Asians living in Britain) and the power relationship between a diaspora population and the dominant host culture.

The range of images of south Asia depicted in these three texts and films offers a microcosm of characters and portrayals canonised in narratives which focus on South Asian culture. How far are such images authentic or representative? *Heat and Dust* and *East is East* attain a degree of authenticity through the localized images and descriptions of the cultural practices, however the effect of such picturing of South Asian culture within the particular narrative development actually comments more upon the Western engagement with the culture. In *Heat and Dust* the contemporary Western sensibility appears the more potentially tolerant and liberal in its interaction with Indian society. The purpose of picturing India here is pre-dominantly to foreground the liberalising, or the humanizing of the Western consciousness. Similarly with East is East, as Ella Khan displays a self-reflexiveness of which George seems incapable, and she wins the moral battle and audience sympathy with her balance of tolerance and seemingly appropriate contempt for George's excessive demands. Of the three narratives, *In Custody* offers the greater insight into South Asian culture, as it less concerned with mapping out aspects of ethnicity in order to authenticate the text, and partly as it is uninhibited by a Western presence or character, the cultural conflict is therefore more subtle, but also more complex.

The film version of each of the three texts takes a cue from David Lean's work by changing either plot lines, or shifting emphasis which ensures that political or controversial elements are buried deep within the stories of the personal or sentimental. In doing so such film directors avoid the problematic, inhibit wider understanding of South Asian culture, and further contribute to the practice of censoring images of south Asia, for reasons which result from pragmatism or a continuing ideological imperialism.

Bibliography

Ahmad, Aijaz. (1992) *In Theory: Classes, Nations, Literatures*, Verso, London, New York.

Bhabha, Homi K. (1994) *The Location of Culture*, Routledge.

Childs, Peter & Williams, Patrick (1997) *An Introduction to Post-Colonial Theory*, Prentice Hall, Hemel Hempstead.

Desai, Anita (1985) 'The Rage for the Raj,' *New Republic*, 25 November 1985.

Desai, Anita (1984) *In Custody*, Heinemann, London.

Forster, E.M. (1989) *A Passage to India*, Penguin (first published 1924)

Gillespie, Maries (1995) Television, Ethnicity and Cultural Change, Routledge, London.

Jacobs, J N. (2002) '(Post) Colonial Spaces' in Dear, M.J. and Flusty, S. (eds) *The Spaces of Postmodernity,* Blackwell, Oxford.

Jameson, F (1981) The Political Unconscious: Narrative as a Socially Symbolic Act 1981, Cornell University Press.

Jan Mohamed, Abdul R. (1985) 'The Economy of Manichean Allegory: The Function of Racial Difference in Colonialist Literature,' *Critical Inquiry.* 12,1, Autumn.

Jhabvala, Ruth Prawer, (1975) *Heat and Dust*, Futura, London.

Juneja, Om P. (1995) *Post Colonial Novel, Narratives of Colonial Consciousness,* Creative Books, Delhi.

Kaye, M.M. (1978) *The Far Pavilions*, Penguin, London.

Khan-Din, Ayub. (1986) *East is East,* NHB, London.

Kureishi, H. (1990) *The Buddha of Suburbia*, Faber and Faber, London.

Lefebvre, H. (2002) 'The production of Space' in Dear, M.J. and Flusty, S. (eds) *The Spaces of Postmodernity,* Blackwell, Oxford.

Pasternak, B. (1958) *Dr Zhivago*, Collins, London.

Rushdie, S. (1991) *Imaginary Homelands* Granta Penguin, London.

Said, Edward, (1993) *Orientalism* - From his Orientalism (Routledge and Kegan Paul, 1978, Penguin, 1985) in Ann Gray and Jim McGuigan (eds)_Studying Culture: An_Introductory Reader, Edward Arnold.

Scott, P. (1966) The Jewel in the Crown, Penguin, London.

Singh, Jyotsna G. (1996) Colonial Narratives/Cultural Dialogues 'Discoveries' of India in the language of Colonialism, Routledge, London.

Soja, Edward W. (1996) *Thirdspace: Journeys to Los Angeles and other real-and-imagined places,* Blackwell publishers, Oxford

Spivak, Gayatri. (1990) *The Post-Colonial Critic: Interviews, Strategies, Dialogues*, ed. Sarah Harasym, Routledge, London, New York.

Srivastava, Ramesh K. ed. (1984) *Perspectives on Anita Desai,* Ghaziabad.

Stam, R. (1988) 'Mikhail Bakhtin and Left Cultural Critique, ed. Al Kaplan, *Postmodernism and its Discontents: Theories and Practices*, Verso, London/New York.

Thrift, N.J (2002) in On the Determination of Social Action ad Time in in Dear, M.J. and Flusty, S. (eds) The Spaces of Postmodernity, Blackwell.

Filmography

A Passage to India (1984) Director: David Lean.

Bend It Like Beckhan (2002) Director: Gurinder Chadha.

Bhaji on the Beach (1992) Director: Gurinder Chadha.

Dr Zhivago (1965) Director: David Lean.

East is East (1999) Director: Damien O'Donnell.

Goodness Gracious Me!! (1998-2000) BBC TV

Heat and Dust, (1982) Director: Ismail Merchant.

In Custody (1994) Director: Ismail Merchant.

My Beautiful Laundrette (1985) Director: Stephen Frears.

My Son the Fanatic (1999) Director: Udayan Prasad.

The Chess Player (1977) Director: Satayjit Ray.

The Buddha of Suburbia (1993) BBC TV

Part 3: Communicating Identity: Language and the Popular Cultures

Confronting Attitudes towards English in Britain and South Asia: Language as an Expression of Identity in South Asian Contexts.

Clive Grey

Introduction

In December 2001, in the midst of the moral panic and media frenzy about asylum seekers waiting in France to cross to Britain apparently in their hundreds David Blunkett, British Home Secretary stated publicly that people wanting to become British citizens should take part in programmes in which they are taught some English:

> We want to make becoming a British citizen more attractive and ensure there are light-touch programmes to obtain naturalisation. One of these would be a modest grasp of the English tongue, so they can feel and become British. (*The Times,* 10 Dec. 2001)

Members of ethnic minority communities should abide by British *'norms of acceptability'* when they become citizens. His view that acquiring a modest grasp of the English language would mean that they could *'feel and become English'* is entirely questionable in that it suggests that they will no longer feel outsiders if they *do* learn some English well enough, and, more subtly, that they would be better off discarding their first language in favour of an acquiring an English identity, as if the issue was a simple one about choice of language. That people speaking a South Asian language, or any other language, could be capable of being competent bilinguals and being fully British at the same time is not entertained.

Examining popular expectations about what being and speaking English actually means requires us *also* to consider what being South Asian means, and what speaking a South Asian language, or any other first language, actually involves as well, otherwise we fail to understand the linguistic issues that confront the immigrant properly. If language is the key to acquiring an identity at all, let alone improving one's English identity, then a proper consideration of linguistic issues confronting speakers of South Asian languages might well explain the difficulty many Asians apparently have in acquiring English in the first place.

But for that to take place the complexity of language usage in south Asia has to be understood first. Blunkett's remarks are at least timely in that they allow us to focus in on parallel debates about the continuing widespread use of English in south Asia itself, 56 years after partition, especially as a language of instruction. Nobody in India is saying that to be Indian you should give up speaking English. Attitudes towards the value of multilingualism in Britain and south Asia are clearly very different, but attitudes towards the value of local languages are surprisingly similar.

Blunkett on integration and knowledge of English

While immigration policy has been a prominent theme for much of New Labour's period in office since 1997, responding to popular misgivings over the scenes at Sangatte refugee camp across the Channel on the French coast as necessary, his Home Secretary's words were undoubtedly triggered by the summer of urban discontent that was a feature of several northern towns and cities in 2001, towns such as Burnley and Oldham and Bradford. It was fairly clear which groups Blunkett had in mind when he voiced his concerns over groups of long-established residents unable to speak English competently.

Blunkett's views are not new. Fifteen years ago an article appeared that the writer uses with students on and off entitled 'Cheat gets Plain English' (*The Guardian,* 5 May 1988) where a Birmingham judge is reported to have sentenced an Asian man, found guilty of fraud, to a term of English lessons as the judge considered it 'plain stupid' that the defendant could not speak English after 25 years residence in the city. Almost all students who read the article conclude after reading it that it is quite impossible that a person could not understand English well enough after 25 years of residence to get by without an interpreter in court. People seem quite unable to countenance the possibility that under certain social conditions a person could live in an Asian-speaking community over a long period and not pick up enough English to fill in forms.

Even more recently Home Secretary Blunkett has again provoked controversy by using the word 'swamping' in a parliamentary debate on immigration, echoing Thatcherite days, leading to much discussion in the media about what is appropriate language in relation to debating immigration and policy and settlement of asylum-seekers in high places. Set against the context of the Damilola Taylor court cases going on elsewhere in London one *Sunday Times* reporter felt moved to inform readers:

> When David Blunkett, the Home Secretary, stood up in parliament last week to debate the immigration and asylum bill and courageously spoke of swamping, he made it very clear that he was

thinking only of certain schools and medical practices which are overwhelmed by asylum seekers needing interpreters and special services. I immediately thought of the estate where Damilola Taylor was killed. That estate is extremely mixed; according to estimates from the Peckham Partnership, the ethnic composition of north Peckham is 43.4% white, 15.9% Black Caribbean, 26.6% black African, 4.1% black other, 7.9% Asian and 2.2% other.

To throw together a group of such hugely disparate people in a deprived part of London and on very low involves is obviously to invite community breakdown. To speak of swamping in such a context is hardly racist; it is only to suggest that the usual ties of community and understanding must be stretched almost to breaking.

Community needs a critical mass of familiarity, shared language, shared tradition and shared moral attitudes; a strong community can accept outsiders and is often enriched by them, as children, too; racism is not restricted to white people, here or anywhere else, and my own view is that white people generally are less racist than some other ethnic groups. What you get in places like Peckham is antagonism between more or less every group; it is quite incredible folly to dump a whole lot of minorities together in a poor estate and leave them to get on with it... In such an atmosphere of educational deprivation, it is hardly surprising that children resent clever, hard-working English speakers such as Damilola. (Marrin 2002)

While we may note how in this apologia for Blunkett's use of the word 'swamping', and we now find terms such as 'dump' used without a thought, that the murder of a young black boy could be explained as an almost inevitable consequence of being bright but living in the wrong district is not excusable at all.

Blunkett's invitation to reflect on what makes people more British surely invites the parallel question of what might make people more Asian, or at least Asian-'aware': learning Bengali perhaps? Should English-speakers be required to learn Urdu so they fit in more with the Asian communities if they live in Bradford? In any case where do British people get their awareness of South Asian culture from? What aspects of South Asian culture present a problem for British ministers? Is it behaviour, language or customs or what? It is useful to consider what images of South Asian popular culture are presented to the white British public for them to form a view, which we come to shortly.

I would argue that we cannot really understand the nature of the link between language and South Asian identity unless we recognise the complexity of the link even in south Asia. If we attempt to construct identity around speaking a particular language we need to be clear what kind of language South Asians have available to them in the first place. Estimates put English speakers in India at 120 million, and people are as different from each other in south Asia in terms of knowledge of languages and ability to speak languages as much as people are different from each other in Britain. Large numbers of people use English everyday in south Asia.

Acquiring images of South Asian culture

Ask English people for the images they have of India (which they probably derive through reading newspapers, or literature by people like Kipling and Forster), or just experiences in their local take-aways, rather than actual visits to south Asia), and people will trot out list things like food words such as *tandoori, curries, chapattis*, activities such as playing polo or dipping in the Ganges, and images such as painted elephants and cows walking through massively overcrowded streets in intense heat, full of maniacal drivers, or images of great monuments like the Taj Mahal, with or without a princess sitting in front, (see the front cover) or the great monuments such as the Victoria Memorial or the Red Fort. They may have seen *Passage to India* at the movies or seen Douglas Fairbanks in the screen version of Kipling's *Gunga Din*. They may know expressions like the 'black hole of Calcutta' and may use words like thug and bungalows on and off, or drink punch or occasionally *kick someone in the goolies*, or get a plumber to have a *dekko* occasionally, or know people who have *cushy* jobs, and we can *add juggernaut, guru, fakir, pyjama, sahib* and *wallah* to our list, but the true origins and significance of these words and images may remain obscure at best. The British no longer rule India and national service no longer requires a tour of duty there, because there is no longer national service.

Non-Asian British TV viewers get edited glimpses of apparent British Asian lifestyles in comedies such as *Goodness Gracious Me!* itself a catchphrase developed by the late Peter Sellers in one of his South Asian characterisations. Occasionally we are treated to seeing British politicians adopting South Asian patterns of behaviour in gestures such as hand-clasping to appear 'normal' in a South Asian context. One could easily come away from these regularly appearing cartoons with the impression that Britain's Asian communities are full of Gandhi look-alikes or quasi-Mujjahedin or Taleban fighters. What is interesting is that people thinking about Indian and South Asian culture automatically plug into the geographical south Asia, not the cultural south Asia alive and well in

Britain. They do not immediately plug into a South Asian culture that exists within present-day Britain, often just round the corner.

Where once English words flowed on the tongues of India's elite, it is now Indian words that seem to flow off the tongues of millions of ordinary English speakers in Britain. Indeed it has become fashionable to think of curry and rice as the national dish replacing time-honoured fish and chips. Quite a few food programmes have helped promote South Asian cooking, and a recent TV series hosted by Floyd on regional Indian cooking showing delicacies such as skinned rabbits cooked in banana leaves on cow dung on a hot Rajasthan day contributes in part to that peculiarly skewed image of south Asia's culture constructed for the viewer who might well think this was normal cuisine in Oldham or Bradford. Similar images in newspapers construct a view of India for British readers as either an exotic tourist haven for foreigners, or a place of grinding poverty and injustice. It's quite easy to identify visual representations of south Asia - they tend to be perceived as exotic and exciting in geographical South Asian perspective, but as alien in relation to lifestyles that are non-English in Britain.

English is, however, a feature of south Asian-ness anyway, even in south Asia. English as a language belongs as much to India as anywhere else. To cite a parallel case, Spanish is now the dominant language of much of Latin America. Spanish is no longer considered a foreign language there as such, nor is it considered the preserve of Spaniards any more. Blunkett's statements about the need to speak English to be English offers a good opportunity to reflect on attitudes towards the English language in south Asia where the situation is the other way round: in many areas people are being asked to give up, or at least think about, their use of English over Indian languages, but there is resistance even there. The difference however is that nobody in south Asia is saying that giving up English will make you more Indian or Pakistani or whatever, because English as a South Asian language is now well established as an economic and social necessity for many. We cannot define ethnicity in terms of language use among South Asians if we do not understand the linguistic realities and politics of language, and the politics of English in south Asia itself. Alladina (1981) is a good source of information on the nature of language survival in various South Asian language communities in Britain of late.

Linguistic realities in present-day South Asia

It is interesting to compare the different attitudes to English that are around in India at present. In Pakistan the national language is Urdu yet only 8% of it speak it as a first language. Urdu is the fifth language in Pakistan's linguistic pecking order in terms of speakers, but it is the favoured language for education in the early years. After then it is English. In India an estimated 15% of the population use English, but it is the only language of higher education instruction, and many middle class parents insist their children receive all their education from as early as possible through English. When we come to language usage by communities there are a whole series of dimensions that are often forgotten by English audiences. An old Welsh saying has it that 'a nation without a language is a nation without a heart.' And in Irish too people say that a nation without a language is a nation without a soul. In both countries the indigenous language has been or is being replaced by English. Both were, or are still part of what is left of the British Empire. In Ireland, independence from Britain came at about the same time as independence came to India. In both cases however, the English language is very much alive, long after the last British troops left, and is spoken by more people than ever. In Ireland native speakers of the indigenous language have all but vanished, while in south Asia English has a long way to go to overtake local languages in terms of numbers of speakers yet. Nevertheless its role is well established and, controversial as it may sound, English belongs as much to India as any other country these days. English is very much a language of India. The soul of India is not under threat.

Blunkett's statement that immigrants need to start speaking English and give up their Asian languages as a first step to becoming British therefore has a certain curiosity about it. In a sense many people in south Asia see ability to use English as an essential part of their identity as Indians. Many bring with them a regional South Asian variety of English to Britain. Are they to replace this with a more British version of English? Would they be considered more British if they gave up their South Asian English? One can conclude that viewing language selection as expressing an identity in such a simplistic way disregards the linguistic facts. People in south Asia have massively different linguistic backgrounds and linguistic abilities. It is clear that they variable exposure to English as a first or second language and their lifestyles differ as much as anyone's in Britain. Linking identity with whichever language you speak even in a South Asian context is itself highly problematic and certainly controversial.

Blunkett's views have not gone unnoticed on the Internet. The BBC Asian Network web pages show how the issue has provoked considerable debate. There is some support for Blunkett, but on the whole contributors to the website were against his suggestion.

If we consider the role of English in present-day India we highlight points such as the following:

- English is the language of instruction in all universities

- English is the language of administration and interstate communication in India

- English is the language of business communication in India

- the language of the judiciary is predominantly English

- the language of instruction of teacher training programmes is English. You cannot become a teacher unless you can understand English and pass the course in English.[1]

This all points to a language that, while non-indigenous, is well entrenched in modern South Asian society.

English and Indian languages in competition in South Asia: social class, multilingualism and diglossia.

The rise and role of English as a living language in India and Pakistan is easily traced and well documented by contemporary observers e.g. Agnihotri & Khana (1994), Baumgardner (1994), Dasgupta (1993), Fernando (1986) and Rahman (1997). The period of British rule in India can be traced back to 1611 with the establishment of the East India Company at Masulipatam. The English language could be argued to have established itself as an important language only after 1780 with the appearance of English newspapers on the streets. After 1817 English began to appear on school curricula in Agra and Calcutta. After 1833 district schools in Delhi and Benares were offering English at the request of some Indians. The establishment of universities served to strengthen the awareness of English among the higher classes. By 1902 even though Indians dominated the educational system in India English was the medium of instruction at secondary and college level, often at the expense of the mother tongue. Even 10 years after independence in 1947 it was still thought important that all university students should study English literature in order to promote critical thinking and writing in Indian languages (Krishnaswamy & Burde, 1998, p.186). Unlike the Irish situation, differences in the numbers of English and non-English speakers never forced non-English speakers westwards to more economically barren areas. Also, English has had to compete with a whole host of solid regional vernaculars with well-established literary histories in many cases. Then there is the situation of Hindi being increasingly used by politicians as a vehicle for creating a Pan-Indian identity, a quasi-national language at least in the north. Many far-right politicians would prefer to see Hindi, not English as the language for internal communication across all of India, both south as well as north. Indeed the Draft National Policy on Education of 1979 makes it a requirement at secondary level that Hindi is studied through the whole of India, along with the regional language, while English at secondary level is

---

[1] http://www.indiapolicy.org/lists/india_policy/2000/Dec/msg00008.html.

only compulsory in the south. Yet just as in Ireland two centuries ago, speaking and writing English is now seen as an essential tool for social improvement, a way out of poverty, especially among the middle classes, many of whom send their children to all-English schools where the language of instruction is only English, not Hindi, the language of the home.

India, in other words, represents a country where the nation is in no danger of losing its heart or its soul, unlike Ireland or Wales, but where there are in fact too many hearts beating away, sometimes out of sync, and often irregularly, sometimes stronger, sometimes weaker. If it were possible for souls to be schizophrenic then we could talk of a state of schizophrenia over the future status of English as a means of communicating in the India of the 21st century. Many third world countries have used language as a way of creating a sense of nationhood. A single language promoted at the expense of others, despite being little used can serve as a unifying force. Urdu in Pakistan is a good example. Despite being the official language it is only spoken by 8% of the population as a first language, and is only number 5 in the order of speakers after Punjabi, Pashto, Sindhi and Saraiki.

Sociolinguistically, India represents a real source of interest for linguists interested in looking at language conflict, mass multilingualism, and the links between mass diglossia and residual caste structure. Khubchandani (1991), Aggarwal (1988), and Dimock (1992) provide greater coverage of these issues than here.

The range of linguistic conflicts is huge, from ones involving national vs. regional languages, (Hindi vs. Marathi), or regional vs. local and tribal languages (as well as issues to do with regional languages in conflict (Tamil vs. Telugu) in the south, and the issue of what is the appropriate languages for international communication across and beyond south Asia (English vs. Hindi). Then there is the link between social class and language use, and the situation of support for those language internal migrants seeking better lives in other parts of India. Then there is also the question of Hindi as opposed to Urdu. Are they in fact the same language, and how are they developing in India as opposed to Pakistan? Are they really the same language, simply disguised by different writing systems (Muslims refer to the language as Urdu, and use a Persian-Arabic script, while Hindus and others refer to it as Hindi and use the Nagari script).

As the middle classes are concerned English plays an essential role in everyday communication and maintaining social status. Melvyn Bragg, in his *Routes of English* radio programme (BBC Radio 4, 13 September 2001) recently interviewed some schoolchildren at the all-English La Martiniere private school in Calcutta, and came across comments from the children such as:

English is our main means of communication. None of us, we rarely converse in Hindi, sometimes at home. It's very essential to know your roots and regional language because if you want to actually work in India and if you want to reach out to the people you must know the regional language, because that is very important, but at the same time, you must know English, because that is how you are going to communicate with people at your level and maybe at the international level. So both are very important. When we go to south India we don't converse in Hindi at all. We either converse in either Tamil or in English. So English is the only binding language through which we can converse with local people... We have just embraced English like we have embraced so many foreign things over the years. Our culture is an amalgamation of foreign things... English has also taken so many things from our language and we have also taken the positive (things) in English. Indian culture is such a melting pot. India is a mixture of so many cultures. That is the beauty of India. Everyone comes together, lives together and is able to mingle with each other.

S. Chaudhuri, a linguist based at Jadaphur University, Calcutta, on the same programme is heard to come out with a similar comment on the high status of English for middle class people in relation to the local Bengali:

In certain rather elite contexts of Indian life, and air travel in India does count as one such context, you are expected to talk in English, even if you and the other person share a common Indian language. On an Air India flight I would normally talk to the cabin crew in English. I might conceivably talk in Hindi, even if I happen to know that the stewardess was a Bengali like myself. I would not talk to them in Bengali. The educated Indian has traditionally been for the last hundred years or more one of the most bilingual creatures on earth and we move in and out of two languages quite freely, even three sometimes, but deplorably to the detriment of the culture we are getting a thin layer who have lost their mother tongue and who only speak English and it is English of a very distinctive nature. It's enough for daily business transactions and office transactions and geared to certain kinds of globalized pop culture. But there are whole sectors of experience and sectors of Indian experience which English cannot accommodate at all. It can only be accommodated by weaving the occasional Indian word into it.

A contributor (MV) to the *IndiaPolicy.org* website lists other registers where use of English comes with money attached, e.g. the setting up of local schools:

> If the Venture Capitalists, dot com companies, cell phone wallahs and umpteen software companies who are investing millions will invest a couple of million reach in every village to set up English medium schools they will be able to reap rich profits in a few years. Think about it... [2]

He continues:

> Regarding [the] suggestion to encourage venture capitalists to come forward to develop good English medium schools, let us not delude ourselves: there is simply no profit in going to villages for teaching poor villagers' children as they cannot pay any user charges. When there is no profit, no venture capitalist will ever care to venture. Of course individuals with good charity motives can help, as they have all along been doing, within their limitations, on a small scale in a few villages. [3]

A more interesting comment is one that relates to different ethnic groups in India being more tolerant of English in everyday communication than others. It is claimed that Hindi, Bengali and Tamil speakers seem less apologetic about speaking their own language than English. [4]

Another commentator (Komagiri) remarks that it is impossible to learn south Indian languages in Delhi: there is no provision at all. On the other hand lessons in European foreign languages are easily obtainable:

> The other day I was in Delhi and interacted with a north Indian social worker, who asked me a simple question. He said, 'I want to learn Telugu. I can devote three hours in a week. Can you tell me where I can learn Telugu?' I searched around in Delhi and found that AP Bhawan does not have such programme. There is a Telugu samajam, but they just meet once at Ugadi or organize some kuchipudi dance once in a while, but they do not have wherewithal to organize this kind of effort. (I shall be more than glad if somebody can prove me wrong, as my friend over there is still waiting to learn Telugu). New Delhi is a lovely city, where you can learn German,

---

[2] http://www.indiapolicy.org/india_policy/2000/Dec/msg00001.html
[3] http://www.indiapolicy.org/india_policy/2000/Dec/msg00011.html
[4] http://www.indiapolicy.org/india_policy/2000/Dec/msg00000.html

French, Russian and so many languages. All languages in the world are good and have beautiful literature, no doubt. But here the point is that in New Delhi, there is no place where somebody can learn a south Indian language. There are more than a thousand places in Delhi where you can learn computer languages. And may be about 500 places where you can learn spoken English. This illustrates that there is no market in Indian languages. It does not pay to learn an Indian language.[5]

Some people point out that nation building might well rest upon the selection of one language nationally, but not necessarily English. A particular view of the role of youth in this enterprise comes through in the next quote (RV again):

The need of the hour is to see how the youth in villages do not flock to cities and towns in search of flashy lifestyles and end up in slums, but to see how they can work for themselves and for the upliftment of their villages in a number of ways. Merely teaching English language as a medium of instruction would not address the issue of their livelihoods at all. That would alienate the youth further from nation-building and make them even more useless for the society. [6]

English as a continuing medium of instruction in schools

There are other processes that hinder what might be termed the 'dis-Englishing' of India. While the language of internal television programmes is generally Hindi, not English, the situation over printed media is rather different. About one third of all published books and one fifth of all periodicals are published in English according to a 1988 survey. English easily outstrips Hindi in terms of language of monthlies, quarterlies and annuals. Of 36% who are literate in India at all, one sixth (17%) of these people were literate in English (1956 census). Figures likely to have increased considerably 50 years on. Three million students were studying English at higher education institutions in 1987. In recent years India has experienced a period in which the survival of English has come into question on several fronts. Language issues provoke controversy at several levels; the level of the individual and the level of the state. The attempted imposition of Hindi, the major language of northern India as the language for all India, south and north; the survival of English as the main medium of

---

[5] http://www.indiapolicy.org/india_policy/2000/Dec/msg00002.html
[6] http://www.indiapolicy.org/india_policy/2000/Dec/msg00011.html

instruction in secondary and higher education; the perceived link between improved social status and knowledge of English.

The comments of some children attending a private school in India above have not gone uncriticised. The Indian language debate in relation to schools excites a great deal of controversy. David Crystal (1995, p.360) has identified two key questions in relation to the maintenance of English in India:

i.   in education should teachers choose standard English as a model in class, or allow the use of the regional features [of Indian English] which the children hear around them?

ii. in literature, should authors opt for Standard English, which will guarantee them a readership throughout the world, or write according to regional norms which will give them a more authentic and personal voice?

It is possible to assemble the main arguments for and against continued use of English in south Asia as follows:

(i) Arguments for English as a medium of instruction in schools

- English enables India to come together. India would not have secured independence if Gandhi had used Gujarati rather than English to speak to the masses.

- English is good for communicating with people outside India and across different states within India.

- Teaching English in schools does not preclude the teaching of local languages. We are not training English teachers to have perfect English pronunciations. Perfect pronunciation is not necessary, as long as people are able to communicate.

(ii) Arguments against English as a medium of instruction in schools

- just going to an English school does not mean people speak good English - many speak a kind of 'butler English' reminiscent of the colonial days

- not the case that knowledge of English will eradicate caste system and social division - indeed it seems to be creating new social divisions in terms of jobs

- people can perform perfectly well in Indian Civil Service exams without having attended English schools

- the growth of English or 'Hinglish' is allowing public services to become available to many, while excluding them to others.

- the teaching of English is promoting widening inequality

- the teaching of English is ridiculous when there is so still so much illiteracy in local Indian Languages.

- Jobs in IT sector requiring good competence in English do nothing for improving prosperity of villages

Some contributors to the *'Indiapolicy.org'* website e.g. Komagiri emphasise the illusion that speaking English means a candidate for a job is better qualified than one who does not:

[The] reason we have all around [us] convent schools is the obsession everybody has with English. Their misplaced notion that one who speaks English has higher knowledge or marketability.[7]

The next quote takes us back to the notion that a person who speaks English is someone who is entitled to better service:

If I request something from a clerk across the counter in a government office and speak to him in an Indian language there is sometimes reluctance to part with information. But if I use English, the guy thinks I am great, or that I could put him to trouble and does the job without much hassle.[8]

There are those however who point out that outside towns English still has little relevance to ordinary people's lives:

There is also a question, in the first place, of why at all one should attempt it... Let me reiterate that if one goes beyond cities and towns, English is almost irrelevant to the major chunk of the Indian people. You can go to any village to check this out. All their cropping practices, all names of various stages of agricultural practices, names of crop diseases or pest attacks, names of weeds, names of common plants and trees which are useful in village life, the kinds of fuel, names of instruments which the artisans use, the land matters, various nallas and bunds over small streams, different types of soil in

---

[7] http://www.indiapolicy.org/india_policy/2000/Dec/msg00002.html
[8] http://www.indiapolicy.org/india_policy/2000/Dec/msg00002.html

the village, the folklore and history of that area, the festivals which need to be celebrated, kind of discussions that take place in the villages, the arguments , quarrels and attempted solutions or debates in the village over different matters, are all in Indian languages. For most of these words, it is difficult to find English equivalents readily. If you were to really take up teaching everything in English language to everybody, just think how you would actually get the teachers in the first place.[9]

We are living in times when very few doctors like to work in villages and commercialization of education is taking place in small towns. There are already two worlds in India and these two worlds are becoming more and more divergent while the talk of globalization goes on... Today a lot of doctors are people from towns/cites, we cannot expect them to go and serve in villages. If we have more doctors from the villages, then a few of them may move to cites but some of them will stay back. This is exactly what we want isn't it? ...The son of our black smith joined engineering in a reservation quota, he was a brilliant student had first class in X std from vernacular high school of the village, but without reservation he wouldn't have got admission to engineering if he had studied in English medium school i am sure he would have got into engineering without reservation. He didn't have any problem in working alongside his father till he got job and left [the] village.[10]

MV continues:

Why do we ignore basic institutional factors and say, 'Hey, kid! Concentrate on learning physics in English language!' when what the person in the village requires is a basic security over the land which he has been tilling over generations but for which no record of right exists and he can be thrown out at will? How can one say that prosperity comes by merely learning academic matters in English language, when what is required at a basic level is a whole new paradigm of empowerment through participation of people? If what you mean is development of skills which are required in day to day lives of the villagers, I am all with it and that can be certainly done most efficiently in [a] local Indian language.

---

[9] http://www.indiapolicy.org/india_policy/2000/Dec/msg00011.html
[10] http://www.indiapolicy.org/india_policy/2000/Dec/msg00011.html

Legal challenges to the continued use of English

In relation to the continuing use of English India in schools at least one recent legal case is instructive: in 2000 the Madras High Court struck down an order by the Government of Tamil Nadu in the south that the local regional language should be the sole medium of instruction at primary level in the state. A group of associations representing English medium schools in Tamil Nadu successfully challenged the ruling on the basis that it was a fundamental right under the UN charter that parents have the right to choose which education was right for their child, and what kind of education their child could be exposed to. Despite the intentions of those who wrote the Indian constitution in 1947 that children should get their education in their mother tongue various flexibilities were built into the rules, and it these that are regularly exploited by people who wish to preserve the use of English as a vehicle of transmission for primary education. Recent research e.g. Ramasamy (2001) and Iype (1999), suggests that people in lower social class groups do better at school when their education is offered through their mother tongue where contexts for the use of English is limited. However, many parents especially in the middle classes see use of English in schools as essential for certain career paths, otherwise blocked to people who are unable to communicate well in English.

Conclusion

It is not possible to address all the different sources of linguistic tension in such a short article as this. One area to watch is place name revision, e.g. the replacement of city names, e.g. Calcutta becoming Kolkata, reflecting an earlier name and rejecting later colonial versions of it, and the proposed Karnavati for Ahmedabad, much to the distaste of local Muslims, (Mallik 2001) along with attempts to replace English street names. In south Asia, language is often manipulated to heighten ethnic tension or emphasise division, even single words, let alone the selection of a whole code such as English. That English survives in strength in south Asia at all is extraordinary, but then south Asia is part of a rapidly expanding global economy serviced by knowledge of English. The widespread use of English in south Asia can be interpreted in various ways: a response to the necessity of India's position in the global marketplace, a reflection of the solidity of a style and system of government and social order, or a consequence of economic policy. Politicians in Britain need to recognise that English is as much a language of India and south Asia as much as any other country. Increasingly spoken as a second language by younger South Asians, even as a first language, it is arguably no longer a foreign language in India, having developed well-established regional forms and idioms, a variety in its own right on the global scale. By asking immigrants to improve their competence in English, Blunkett may well be paradoxically encouraging them to use a well-established South Asian language.

Bibliography

Aggarwal, K.S. (1988) 'English and India's 3-language formula: an empirical perspective', *World Englishes*, pp. 289-293.

Agnihotri, R.K. & Khana, A.L. eds. (1994,) *English in India*, Research in Applied Linguistics Series. Vol. 7. Sage, London.

Alladina, S. ed. (1991), *Multilingualism in the British Isles*. Vol. 2. Longman, London.

Baumgardner, R.J. ed. (1994) *English language in Pakistan*. Oxford University Press (Pakistan)

Crystal, D. (1995) *Encyclopaedia of the English Language*, Cambridge University Press, Cambridge.

Dalrymple, W. (2001) *The Age of Kali*. Flamingo, London.

Dasgupta, P. (1993) *Otherness of English: India's Auntie Tongue Syndrome*, Language and Development Series. Vol.1. Sage, London.

Dimock, E. (1992) *Dimensions of Sociolinguistics in South Asia*. Oxford University Press, Oxford.

Fernando, L. (1986) Culture in Conflict: Essays on Literature and the English Language in SE Asia. Graham Brash, Singapore.

Iype, G. (1999) 'Imposition of Tamil angers students, teachers in Tamil Nadu'. *ReDiff on the Net*. [Online], Available:

http://www.rediff.com/news/1999/dec/14iype.htm [accessed 19 Dec. 1999].

Khubchandani, L.M. (1991) 'India as a Sociolinguistic Area', *Language Sciences*, vol. 13, no. 2, pp. 265-288.

Krishnaswamy, N. & Burde, A.S. (1998) Politics of Indians' English. Linguistic Colonialism and the Expanding English Empire. Oxford University Press (India) New Delhi.

Mallik, P. (2001) 'Will Ahmedabad be named after Hindu, tribal or Muslim ruler?' [Online], Available:

http://news.indiainfo.com/2001/01/06/06ahmedabad.html.

Marrin, M. (2002) 'Swamping isn't a racist term – it reflects reality'. *Sunday Times*, 28 April, 2002.

Rahman, T. (1997), *Language and Politics in Pakistan*. Oxford University Press, Pakistan, Karachi.

Ramasamy, K. (2001) 'Mother Tongue and medium of Instruction – A Continuing Battle', *Language in India*, vol. 1. [Online], Available: http://www.languageinindia.com/oct2001/ramasamyk1.html [accessed 6 Oct, 2001]

Popular Culture of Himalayan Women in English Writing

Annie Montaut

It is sometimes thought that the sense of history which has been granted to India as part of the colonial legacy, is still very much lacking in the popular expression of the local culture[1]. Myths and stories are systematically opposed to history in the shaping of Indian culture, and history, as a way of looking at one's past and present, is thought to be only available in the forms of 'westernised' writing, whether it consists in the scholarly studies of historians or in the fictional work of modern creative writers. Understanding the past and the present as separate and linked requires the ability of discriminating causes and consequences, isolating things and events from each other, disentangling real facts from mental constructions, contingent events from eternity, looking at facts from an 'objective' position. That is, first, having some notion of the border separating inner and outer world, subject and object, extracting oneself from the moving and otherwise ungraspable sea of events: taking an external, objective stand. To sum up: rationality. Without such rationality, a gift from the Western Enlightenment[2], it is thought impossible to reach democracy, which is grounded on the recognition of subject as an individual responsible entity, susceptible to knowledge as power of discrimination. The question of myth or history as the salient feature of the present Indian 'way of thinking' is then far reaching.

---

[1] Hence resulting in a split between the intellectual elite and the popular mass, as stated in Nandy (2001: pp.41-2): 'Fonder une identité historique dans une société historique entraîne une complexité de second ordre quand cette identité n'obtient pas l'adhésion consensuelle de la communauté ou de la culture au sens plus large (...); l'Inde compte encore de très nombreuses communautés ou personnes qui vivent avec des idéologies fondées sur des modes non historiques de reconstruction du passé.' For a more developped discussion of this 'assumption that cultures living by myths are ahistorical and thus representative of an earlier, second-rate social consciousness,' see Nandy 1998 (2: pp.60-63).

[2] Eighteenth century 'lights' originally stemmed out from the French 'philosophers', around Voltaire and Diderot, who started questioning the fundamental legitimacy of faith in matters of scientific knowledge and political government, eventually leading to the French Revolution.

A culture of the self-with-the-gods and without history?

A very striking description of this state of affairs is given in Naipaul's first look at the land of his ancestors. Let us first look at this exemplary view of the Indian way of thinking, which typically confirms the danger of the non historical stand imputed to it, before contrasting it with a woman writing in English on her local culture and its relevance to the question of history and democracy.

In *An Area of Darkness* (1964) written at the end of the Nehruvian period, as well as in *A Wounded Civilization* (1977) written during the Emergency State,[3] Naipaul repeatedly stigmatises what he calls 'a defect of vision,'[4] responsible in his eyes for the general failure of modernization and democracy. The root of the disease of this 'diseased society' which he analyses, according to him, lies in the failure to see, in correlation with the inner retrieval, denial, quest for mystical escape and obsession of purity and caste. An example oft repeated of this defect of vision, which he borrows from a mysterious observer is the squatting figures of defecating Indians on river banks or railway tracks.

> These squatting figures are never spoken of; they are never written about; they are not mentioned in novels or in stories; they do not appear in feature films or documentaries. This might be regarded as a part of a permissible prettifying intention. But the truth is that Indians do not see these squatters and might even, with complete sincerity, deny that they exist: a collective blindness arising out of the Indian fear of pollution and the resulting conviction that Indians are the cleanest people in the world'. (Naipaul, 1977 p.70)

Not being seen, being denied as every disturbing object, the existence of such figures, or of other 'unbearable' images of poverty and beggars, need no explication and no attempt to change conditions which made them as they appear.[5] The same observer then is confronted in the train with a smiling upper-caste traveller who agrees to shift berth but appears totally

---

[3] Imposed in 1975 by the then Prime Minister Indira Gandhi, an authoritative gesture against liberal trends which cost her the power at the next elections won by the opposing party (Janata).

[4] Chapters 'The Colonial' is in the first book, 'A Defect of Vision' in the second, first one in a section entitled 'no ideas, but Obsessions.'

[5] The second book, written in the time of the official slogan '*garibi hatao*, "remove poverty,"' lengthily explains that the way this motto is emphasized throughout the country does not echo a real attempt to remedy social evils but a passionate love for images, symbols and empty slogans.

unwilling and unable to lift his bedding and suitcase himself, and reflects on the typical Indian reluctance towards physical labour and on the 'Indian callousness', revealing 'a sad want of consideration for others', both derived from cast consciousness. At this point it appears that the mysterious observer, who 'is seeing what no Indian sees' is no other than Gandhi. Gandhi's power to change India into a really social democracy originates from his ability to see. But the interesting correlation Naipaul repeatedly emphasizes[6] is the colonial modernity in Gandhi's look and his ability to criticize, analyse, contrast, act. 'He saw India so clearly because he was in part a colonial. ... Gandhi never loses the critical, comparing South African eye; he never rhapsodises, except in the vague Indian way, about the glories of ancient India'. His emphasis on defecation and sanitation is deemed 'correct', because 'sanitation was linked to caste, caste to callousness, inefficiency and a hopelessly divided country, division to weakness, weakness to foreign rule' (Naipaul, 1964, p.74). Gandhi's obsessions (the spirit of service, excrement, bread-labour, the dignity of scavenging) hang together... they answer the directness of his colonial vision'. They oppose the 'Indian' vision, which does not recognize the value of labour or the spirit of service[7]. They also oppose the 'medieval mentality' which refuses to see disturbing historical facts and clings to a vision of homogeneity and continuity, integrating new facts into traditional schemes which neutralize them, creating 'a world, which, with all its ups and downs, remained harmoniously ordered and could be taken for granted', a world which, for this very reason, 'failed to develop a sense of history, which is a sense of loss.' (ibid. p.144)

Now, if the defect of vision is so crucial in the Indian 'social disease', resulting in a general denial of reality and lack of the sense of history, how to account for it? Naipaul does so by exploring the genesis of the subject, with the help of the Indian psychoanalyst Kakar.[8] What Naipaul quotes from personal communication can be found in a more detailed fashion in

---

[6] Which is now not so original, a number of historians having interpreted part of the Gandhian political ethos as foreign.

[7] Even the great classical texts which form the bulk of the Hindu culture, even the 'selfless action' advocated in the Gita is analysed by Naipaul as an encouragement to selfishness : see the example of the picnic on the banks of a river, someone is drowning in front of the people and nobody will rescue him because it is not in the prescribed dharma (each cast has its dharma, each individual his function, no action outside this function is expected from him, and each has his private *contract* with God). Needless to say, Nandy (for instance) has a totally different vision of Gandhi's pragmatism (1998-2: p.62)

[8] Who at the time of his meetings with Naipaul in preparation of the book, was himself preparing his first book *The Inner World* (1978). See on this point particularly the section in Kakar (1978: pp.108-112) and Lannoy (1975: 111sq, p.210)

The Inner World (1978) The denial of reality and inner retrieval, both observed in different ways is to be correlated with an 'underdevelopment of the self': for the Indian ego, reality has a very tenuous existence, real objects in the outside world are not clearly distinguished from the inner experience. Such a stage, normal in childhood, is typical in adult life of what Freud called the primary narcissism, encouraged in India by the extended family pattern: the fusion with the mother as internalised object, maintained far longer than in the West, and the diversity and inter-changeability of authority figures (father identification figures), profusion of deities and human figures on the same level of reality, make the child unwilling to separate and perceive himself as a separate subject confronting a separate object, and also unfit for responsible attitudes, hence further prone to submissiveness (renouncement: inward retrieval and authority of the guru). The analysis of children's drawings, full up to the brim with various human and divine figures with no centre identifiable, leads Lannoy (1975), after Erikson (1970), to similar interpretations of a psychologically immature ego in the Indian self.[9] Kakar concludes that such a behaviour and 'underdeveloped ego', if is not socially sanctioned as neurotic behaviour as it would be in the West, is a 'dangerous luxury' for a new modern country in changing times like independent India. A conclusion which goes largely unquestioned, and emphasized in Naipaul (1977, p. 111).[10] However, it is not the danger, but the benefits which are enhanced in some of the popular creative narratives in contemporary India.

Story-telling, myth creative interpretation, and history

Although reaching similar interpretations which point to the Indian 'primary narcissism', Erikson and Lannoy do not emphasize the danger of it in the same way as Kakar. Kakar's viewpoint regarding the influence of folklore and myth on the Indian psyche has indeed been proved to voice a typically male brahmanic viewpoint (Raheja and Gold, 1996, pp.32-38). The ideal

---

[9] Among which the inability of the object-subject adult relation (Lannoy 1975, p.111). Children drawings inspired Erikson (1970, p.40) the following: 'If one finally asks what (and, indeed, *where*) is the "exciting scene," one finds it embedded somewhere where nobody could have discerned it and certainly not as a central one. (...) significant moments embedded in a moving sea of unfathomable multiformity (...). One moves in a space-time so filled with visual and auditory occurrences that it is very difficult to lift an episode out of the flux of events, a fact out of the stream of feelings, a circumscribed relationship out of a fusion of multiple encounters. If, in all this, I should endow one word with a meaning which unites it all, the word is fusion.'

[10] Who quotes from personal communications with the psychoanalyst in the late seventies. The feudal mentality and lack of sense of history generated by such an 'underdeveloped ego' is according to him responsible from the deviation of democratic tools into mere symbols and empty images to be worshipped.

submissive woman modelled after Sita, as well as the split image of women's sexuality (when uncontrolled, a threat for men, when under control, denied) is only one possible way of reading the mythology that permeates every day life and thought. Although this way of reading is quite typical of the dominant elite, both traditional and westernised. Besides, such a view is based on a notion of culture as 'a mode of thought that incarcerates the native in a fixed and definite way of thinking' strongly criticized by Appadurai (1988, pp.37-8). Using the same referential literary frame (classical mythology) as Kakar, but extending to the more popular and local lore of Himalayan goddesses, Mrinal Pandey, writing in English produces a half fictional, half auto-biographical report on local culture. She unveils the woman's viewpoint regarding their own self ideal, as drawn from their own interpretation of the myths. In this rather strange narrative, which interweaves adaptations in English of the major classical myths from the epics and puranas, popular stories from the local lore, the family saga centred on the figure of the Grand Mother Bari Amma, and reports of social workers fighting for the rights of women, the novelist and journalist advocates a very different vision.[11] Although she provides her own interpretation by rephrasing and commenting on the stories, and by arranging the fragments of myth or lore and the sequences of social action within a global narrative structure which clearly shows how the first generates the latter, the bulk of her material is in itself a first-hand interpretation quite illustrative of the women-folk's point of view on their own agency.

Telling the story of the hungry daughter-in-law ('once there was this woman who had a real shrew for a mother-in-law...') Mrinal Pandey in *Devi* wants to illustrate a cultural state where human beings and goddesses were the same stuff, and women lived their '*kanyahood*' on par with the goddesses, perceived themselves as part of the same world and at the same level of reality and dignity. She also illustrates the legacy of courage and rebellion infused by a certain reading of classical and popular Hindu mythology, through the character of major and minor goddesses, a source of inspiration for many women, simple housewives and social workers. This daughter-in-law was, of course, exploited and starved by the shrew until the day when, deprived of a single morsel of bitter gourds, her favourite dish, she steals some and flies to the temple of the village goddess to eat happily the curry and rice far from indiscreet looks before hurrying back home. The goddess is amazed and cups her hands under her chin in a sign of

---

[11] *Devi. Tales of the Goddess in Our Time*, was published by Penguins India in 1996. Bracketted page numbers with no other mention of name and date refer to this edition. Mrinal Pandey, daughter of the Hindi writer Shivani, started writing Hindi fiction before shifting to English.

disapproval. Later, when the villagers come, they find the idol in this strange position, the whole village trembles and the old priests start looking for the culprit who has angered the goddess. The young woman flies back to the temple, crosses her arms and says to the goddess:

> Who do you think you are? Where you never a wife and a daughter-in-law? Do you not know how many ruses a daughter-in-law must employ in order to survive in her mother-in-law's house? What kind of a woman are you, pretending to be shocked I stole in and ate a bit of curry and rice in front of you? Have you no shame? Put your hand down now, or I will hit you on the head with my pot'. (Pandey, 1996, p.123)

The goddess came back to her initial position and the young woman went to tell the old priests that they must have had hallucinations.

If older listeners to the story would 'praise the young woman's cleverness and modesty in keeping her defiance of oppression and successful challenge a secret', identifying with her as survivors to an unfair system, many in the younger generation would see only a sad example of the oppressive patriarchal society and condemn the goddess's anger; religion being women's enemy. Pandey does not interpret this variance as a decline in faith among educated urban youth, but as a 'basic change' in relating to the Devi. For elders and those who made up such legends, goddesses were familiar figures with literal meaning, people who shared the same transcendent principle of being *kanyas*, and as such, were to be addressed as sisters, with whom one could 'share a sari or a pod of tamarind or a flower garland'. And who should commit herself to protect her sister in a mutual bond? Such a view of kanyahood is obviously at variance with the male concept of *kanya* and *kanyadan*, according to which women are passive objects to be given away for ritual purpose and the welfare of the whole community: the daughter-in-law of the story drives a rebellious energy from her kanyahood which subverts the patriarchal hierarchy and mocks the pandits. What is obvious from both the story and its comment is the ironical ambivalence of the girl's protest, an irony which always acted as a sideways glance towards emancipation (Ramanujan, 1989). This ambivalence, which allows her to subvert the patriarchal law, may well be considered as a true manifestation of subaltern consciousness, once we assume that the subaltern voice should not be essentialised into a 'self-originating self-determining individual who is at once a subject in his possession of a sovereign consciousness whose defining quality is reason, and an agent in his power of freedom (O'Hanlon, 1988, p.191).[12] There is no doubt Pandey's actors are subaltern voices and that they voice a specific link between legend and history, radically distinct from the sociologist or modern historian for whom there can be no continuity between them. But nowadays there is no longer room for 'such happy affinity' among modern urban intellectuals, the strength derived by listening to and believing in such tales is lost, a strength which made women efficient agents, assertive even if not openly confronting religious laws, still defiling in their way the brahmanical ethos and village customs. Moreover, Pandey goes on, by leaving the lore to backward rural masses, and ignoring story and legend, we deprive ourselves from history.

This is a provocative conclusion, very much opposed to the sociologists, anthropologists, philosophers or historians for whom there is an irretrievable lakshman-rekha separating history and myth.[13]

I will not dwell on the exact meaning of 'history' in Mrinal Pandey's view here. What is certain is that this notion of hers is consistently illustrated throughout the book by examples of social protest, both individual and collective, aiming at building a participative democracy. So there is a relation between the popular way of living in and with lore and myth as the basic mental frame, and the building of social justice in a democratic state like India. Many such connections are explicitly drawn in the book, many implicitly, always relating a particular interpretation of the religious tradition and lore with its contemporary relevance. A particular interpretation: as suggested about the 'five memorable ones' - Ahilya, Kunti, Draupadi, Tara and Mandodari. These five rebellious women created by the 'drop-outs' Vyasa and Valmiki 'out of their own wayward life' may be judged very differently according to one's view-point: from the prevailing popular conformism as well as from the bourgeois stand, and the right wing interpretation, such women have gone into trouble because of their wish to claim their rights and their desire for freedom, instead of being submissive. Accordigly they have destroyed themselves, their men and their clan, like Draupadi, who caused the cataclysmic great war of Mahabharat. Already shared between five husbands, the Pandava brothers, after the

---

[12] This essentialisation has been criticized by Spivak (1985a) who emphasizes the non continuity, absence of self determination of actually heterogeneous and discontinuous discourses. But she also says that women's "self abasement" makes them unable to represent themselves and to "speak in a language other than patriarchal authority", a " repeated emptying of her meaning as instrument" (Spivak 1985b, p.362). Guha too, in his famous paper on dominance without hegemony (1989), acknowledges the contradictory and fragmented nature of the subaltern consciousness.

[13] Even Ashish Nandy who is not ready to suppress the cultural value of myth accepts its opposition to history when he states that most people even now in India are living in a myth-like cultural frame and untouched by the historical mentality.

inadvertent word of the mother-in-law, Draupadi was sold to the other clan in a dice game, then publicly humiliated by being dragged naked by her hair. She was ultimately saved by the god Krishna[14], leaving so much hatred and rage between both clans that the most terrible war started, because of her lack of submissiveness. But 'myths breathe different secrets for story-tellers as they forage for them in damp family vaults', they show that such female rebels 'may be victimized, stifled and oppressed but never silenced' (Pandey, 1996, p.167).As such a story-teller, Pandey intertwines stories from the myth, here Draupadi's or Kunti's story, to relations of modern combative women who fought for their rights when unjustly beaten, gang-raped, unheared by the police, like the story of Banwari Bai. Banwari was a potter's wife and social worker who was gang-raped by a village lobby after the shop has been ransacked, and who finally managed to win her cause by involving other social workers and women's groups; the story of Draupadi Bai, elected as *sarpanch* (village head) and gang-raped by the other members of the village council in November 1995, who symbolically refused to do her hair like the other Draupadi and started roaming the whole State in quest for justice, to such a point that she gathers popular support and people stand with her calling her molesters Dushasana and Duryodhana (names of the villains in the *Mahabharat*). The heroines of the great myths and popular legends still infuse their strength and spirit of justice to the present actors, and the dark *shakti* (a word which means strength, and divinities associated with shaivaism and Kali the Goddess of destruction) are still visible in the 'fibrous wrists' and 'corded necks' of the innumerable female labourers struggling for their life whenever they stand up against injustice, exploited but not silenced. Such goddesses as Ahilya or Draupadi, even now, especially now, concludes Pandey,

> must be asked to lend us their tenacity and their rage, so we may comment on our travesty of democracy, on globalisation and labour laws all of which burn women alive on funeral pyres and then look beyond the flame and chant: '*Sati Mata ki jai!*' may our glorious, self-negating mothers live long!'. (Pandey, 1996 p.167)[15]

The story of the earth (mother earth) bears a similar lesson: rudely exploited and betrayed by her children (settlers and nomads) first, then by Prajapati (the creator) harassing her for giving more and more, the gentle and bountiful Medini (that was her first name: made of fat) then became enraged and resolves to become infertile. When Prithu tries to settle the

---

[14] At this point of despair and rage in front of the passivity of her legitimate protectors, she invokes Krishna and he makes the sari infinite, so that the more it unfolds the more numerous new folds appear to veil her body.

matters in a harsh way she turns into a cow to escape his arrows and asks him to turn into a calf and gently milk her, a metaphor of earthy love as the need for kindness and the rage at being sold piece-meal, as well as suggesting that generosity (in wives and mothers) should not be wrongly mistaken for passivity. Prithu bows to this legitimate claim, then adopts her as his daughter, hence her name Prithvi.[15] (op.cit. p.90)

Those are some of the 'different secrets' that myths 'breathe to story-tellers' and their listeners. And they promote the understanding of action in a modern changing world, because they all show that the continuity of legend and social consciousness, voiced and heard from the non dominant viewpoint, does not rule out the sense for democratic action.

English writing of the lore: a special brew

The art of story-telling has developed in Badi Amma's family (narrator's grand-mother, who provides the frame of the narrative[16]) in a way that both continues the traditional art of passing down the bulk of popular lore and myths and articulates this tradition with modernity and English. Badi Amma herself, once a young rebellious girl educated in the Sanskrit scriptures and astrology by her grandfather since her absent father, doing his 'service' in far away places, could not be a proper recipient of the grand paternal knowledge. Kept outside family bounds until her thirties she then married a medical doctor who had returned from abroad, 'the good doctor', the 'celebrated dandy in the Edwardian tradition', an embodiment of western rationality[17] and totally indifferent to popular worship. The new story-telling tradition emerges when she discovers that her usually taciturn husband agrees to answer if talked to in English. Starting from this

---

[15] Medini, from *meda*, the fat from twin monsters killed by Vishnu-Narayana, is otherwise named *bhumi*, 'a land that yielded a steady supply of nourishing and rejuvenating food' (p.89)

[16] And inspirator of the writer: near the fire-place in her home, in winter 'the stories thawed and flowed, in summer they blossomed and blossomed. Badi Amma is the Mahadevi enthroned in the very heart of the literary no-man's land where women roam as goddesses. She is the Gangotri from which all my tales flow, gurgling, happy and wayward, or unhappy and sullen' (p.182)

[17] The circumstances of the first encounter and love at first sight are such: the westernised dandy, a frail and refined man, condemned to come back in his Himalayan birth place because of climatic reasons (a lung disease) arrives in a palanquin and sees the massive young lady on the side of the path, busy painting flowers. The very next moment she starts painting the Kumarasambhava décor and dreaming of love and speaking birds. Her devotion is intense, yet very 'personal,' and for instance to get her first son, she operates a fantastic puja with a thousand dung *shivalingam* decorated with a thousand and one white flowers and grains of rice, such an extraordinary sight that even the unbeliever husband agrees to enter the puja room and bow to them.

discovery, the passion for stories gets mixed up with the passion for gossip, political information and popular lore, in a mixture of three languages: 'she wove Sanskrit with Hindi with the deftness of a master weaver, handling several shuttles at once. Words came alive at her touch, mysterious stories took shape in intricate patterns', and with the English / Hindi mixture (Hindi translation for the children in the initial stages) 'new and innovative types of verbal foreplay' took place, a 'strange mixture of smooth English seasoned with pungent phrases in Hindi'[18]. In this way the children themselves quickly became master story-tellers, nurtured in this art by both parents according to whom thought and circulated stories are the only way to get youngsters (and adults) understanding right from wrong[19]. They 'discovered a most interesting new world through three languages, all of them laced with chillies and garlic. Their skins soaked up the words, their blood the garlic sauce. Their minds further stored away this heady mixture as a preservative for tales' (op.cit. p.105). Chilly and garlic do not only refer to the pungency of the style which makes the stories alive and juicy, it concretely refers to the conviviality of eating together while elaborating on the stories, making the art of story-telling part of an art of living together. This living-together is seen as a holistic creation with no partition between mental and physical frames, and with spices mattering as much as the objective information provided by a rational, objective, aseptic observation. As for the multilingual expression, it bridges the gulf between 'tradition' and 'modernity' by something different from a synthetic homogenous fusion: with its 'new and innovative' verbal plays, it produces original creations fit for the specific viewpoint of the actors, beyond the traditional split image of mythic feudality and rational history.

Bibliography

Appadurai, Arjun (1988) 'Putting Hierarchy in its Place,' *Cultural Anthropology*, 3(1) pp.36-49.

Das, Veena (1989) 'Subaltern as Perspective,' *Subaltern Studies* VI, pp.310-24.

Erikson, Eric (1970) Gandhi's Truth: On the Origin of Militant Non-violence, Faber & Faber, London.

Goodwin Raheja, Gloria & Ann Grodzins Gold (1996) *Listening to the Heron's Words. Reimagining Gender and Kinship in North India*, Oxford University Press, Delhi.

---

[18] 'See the *tamasha* that people put up, dear,' 'O *my father*, this woman was caught in a *bad bad* act, dropping her *pallav* in front of the deputy ranger sahib,' etc. (p.106)

[1919] The way the stories of Vac, the vedic Goddess of speech, and Sarasvati, the Goddess of knowledge and music (the musical transmutation of knowledge and speech: story-telling) are intertwinned in the narrative is also significant: Saraswati is also the Goddess who teaches freedom from home-bounds, the power of exile, and creative transmutation of unanswerable questions.

Guha, Ramchandra (1989) 'Dominance without Hegemony,' *Subaltern Studies* VI, pp.210-309.

Guha, Ramchandra (1989) Unquiet Woods: Ecological change and Peasant Resistance in the Himalaya, Oxford University Press, Delhi.

Kabeer, N (1994) Reversed Realities: Gender Hierarchies in Developement Thought, Verso, London/NewYork.

Kakar, Sudhir (1978) The Inner World. A Psychoanalytical Study of Childhood and Society in India, Oxford University Press, New Delhi.

Lannoy Richard (1975) *The Speaking Tree. A Study of Indian Culture and Childhood*, Oxford University Press, New Delhi.

Mawdsley, Emma (2000) 'The Role of Women in the Uttaranchal Regional Movement,' in *Himalaya Past and Present* V, pp.115-26.

Naipaul, V.S (1964) *An Area of Darkness.*

Naipaul, V.S (1977) *A Wounded Civilisation.*

Nandy Ashish (2001) 'L'Histoire de l'identité politique contemporaine,' *La Revue des Deux Mondes*, septembre-octobre, pp.36-42.

Nandy, Ashish (1998) *Exile at home* (1 *At the Edge of Psychology*, 2 *The Intimate Enemy*, 3 *Creating a Nationality*) Oxford University Press, Delhi.

O'Hanlon, Rosalind (1988) 'Recovering the Subject: Subaltern Studies and Histories of Resistance in Colonial South Asia,' *Modern Asian Studies* 22 (1), pp.189-224.

Pandey, M. (1996) *Tales of the Goddess in Our Time*, Penguin, Delhi.

Ramakrishna & al (eds) (1998) *Conserving the Sacred for Biodiversity Management.* Oxford & IBH, Delhi.

Ramanujan, A.K. (1989) 'Where Mirrors are Windows: Towards an Anthology of Reflections,' *History of Religions* 28 (3), pp.188-216.

Shiva, Vandana (1988) *Staying alive: Women, Ecology and Survival in India*, Kali for Women, New Delhi.

Shiva, Vandana (2000) *Stolen Harvest*, Penguin India, Delhi.

Spivak, Gayatri (1985a) 'Can the Subaltern Speak? Speculations on Widow Sacrifice,' *Wedge* 7/8, pp.120-30.

Spivak, Gayatri (1985b) 'Subaltern Studies: Deconstructing Historiography,' in *Subaltern Studies IV*, R. Guha ed. pp.330-63.

Politicised Territory: Nek Chand's Rock Garden in Chandigarh

Iain D. Jackson

Introduction

This paper is commentating on the Indian condition since 1947 and the establishment of a new identity that was to be represented architecturally, through the Modernist agenda of Le Corbusier, and his team of European architects. The politics linked to Chandigarh have always been heated and it continues to test and play with territories and dynamic law, as well as maintaining a strong sense of style and an artistic flank.

Constructed as a series of episodes, the paper commentates on the how the city of Chandigarh was designed and how it has developed in relation to the strict procedure's the architects employed. The aim of the paper is to examine how one man's illegal artistic endeavour undermined, and assaulted, the city's layout and guidelines prepared for its future development, whilst becoming its most important asset in the process.

Nek Chand systematically collected and re-assembled discarded household rubbish to form a series of sculptures. The scale of his production was prolific and covered a considerable area of land adjacent to the Government buildings. The politic of his act was crucial and the polemical decision to allow 'Nek Chand's Rock Garden' to remain upon discovery of it, was indicative of a change in the political and cultural mindset of India.

The post-independence identity of India was never given the opportunity to establish itself, being firmly repressed within the Modernist quest for internationalism and its 'context-free' stance and utopian overtones. India, represented by Nehru, expressed a belief that the Modernist ideals, expressed through the built environment, would signal the freedom of India without resorting to past forms. Despite this, Le Corbusier used the antiquated device of an edict to instil his ideas upon the city. The paper contests the implications of the edict and the indiscriminate use of the 'Modulor Man' to scale and proportion all elements of the new city, whilst examining the contrasting approach of Nek Chands 'hu-man' response, using sculpture and architectural devices to depict folklore.

The notion of 'ruin and transformation' is raised in the penultimate episode. The city is in the process of becoming a ruin, its Modernist origins merely provide a framework for a different city growing within. Chand works with the notion of the ruin transforming 'the ruined' into artefacts.

Chand represents and forms part of a different mindset to Modernity, whilst living and working within it, using it as a raw material to reassess and redefine the new.

The story terminates as it attempts to traverse 'the wall' that now surrounds the Rock Garden. The implications of the wall affect both City and the Rock Garden. The definition of 'self' and the identification of the 'other' are investigated, relating to previous sections and a wider perspective on Indian culture through a spacio-political lens.

Surreptitious Beginnings

This tale begins in 1965, when Nek Chand, a resident of Chandigarh neglected his duties as city road inspector. A small forest in the greenbelt periphery surrounds the Capitol Complex. Without making anybody aware, it was in this forest - almost under the shadow of the best buildings in Chandigarh - Nek Chand began his covert operation of illicit production. He had developed a passion for collecting unusual shaped rocks formed in the Himalayas, as well as, discarded household objects that he salvaged from the city rubbish dumps. As Walter Benjamin so succinctly puts:

> Every passion borders on the chaotic, but the collector's passion borders on the chaos of memories. More than that: the chance, the fate that suffuse the past before my eyes are conspicuously present in the accustomed confusion of [the collection]... Naturally [the collectors] existence is tied to many other things as well: to a mysterious relationship to ownership, to a relationship to objects that does not emphasise their functional, utilitarian value – that is, their usefulness – but studies and loves them as the scene, the stage, of their fate. (Benjamin, 1999, p.65)

His aim was to collect objects that he found interesting in some way, with a view to remoulding the 'raw materials' into a series of sculptures. After several months of reclaiming and rediscovering, he began to labour on the sculptures, working secretly after nightfall by the light of burning tyres. Initially it was just a way of recreation, a therapeutic activity of creating forms out of other peoples discarded refuse. However, Chand had always dreamt about a kingdom that he wanted to recreate. When he saw the patch of land, that is now the Garden, it reminded him of a derelict kingdom and he started to slowly assemble his dream. Without any apparent pragmatic reason behind the production, his creative endeavour continued unabated, making use of broken ceramic tiles, old toilet and basin units, bike saddles, electrical components and dumped hardcore rubble, combining such found material with energy and satiric wit.

As the years passed the statues, which by now had gained some local notoriety, spilt over a greater area and small, concrete podiums were constructed for their display. The critical politic of his creative act, however, must be noted in this occupation of private land and in the illegal development of the greenbelt zone that coupled with the innocent enthusiasm of the pioneer explorer. Despite the land falling within the remit of the city boundaries, it was unused – effectively abandoned scrubland at the periphery of the city. This territorial void, an uncharted wilderness nestling under the shadows of the famous buildings of Sector-1, was both a product of its proximity to the city dumping ground, as well as, of developmental restrictions.[1] Chand used the dumping ground as an open quarry from which his precious base materials could be carefully extracted and refined. From Chand's point of view the space was ideal, he could work undisturbed and with little chance of being caught, his materials were located close by and in regular constant supply. On a local level, his act was exposing the inadequacies of the master plan and its disability to prevent such acts taking place.

However the production of the sculptures was indicative of a fundamental shift in the development of India's political youth and a craving throughout the nation to take the future into their own hands. The adoption of Modernism was essential in creating an immediate physical representation of the Nehruvian concept of independence that expressed an aesthetic that was truly of its time and dreamt of a future free from the shackles of the past.[2] As well as developing the master plan, Le Corbusier ensured that extensive visual controls were in place to nurture a homogenous aesthetic and visual standardisation. This ocular control obsession extended to include materials, textures, boundary gates and even manhole covers. Nehru's enthusiastic participation and active role in the aesthetic decision making process was unusual for a politician but showed how important India viewed the need to establish the correct visual

---

[1] Construction was not permitted north of Sector-I. The space only existed because of Chandigarh's rigid plan that had clearly identifiable limits. The city is very 'clean cut' with the gridiron plan coming to an abrupt end. The Garden nestles at the intersection of the 'fixed' grid (and the sought after plots of the city) and the 'virgin' territory that is uncharted and undesirable because it cannot be officially developed.

[2] Chandigarh, for Nehru, was his new India in microcosm, in both philosophical and practical terms, as he declared: "Let this be a new town symbolic of the freedom of India, unfettered by the traditions of the past... an expression of the nations faith in the future." Nehru, J., *Hindustan Times*, New Delhi, July 8, 1950.

manifestation of the new order, and the capacity image was to play in acting out politician's visions. However, like many other ideological transfers, Modernism proved to be a restrictive and unforgiving importation, working in effect to extend colonial hegemony under the mask of post-independence 'freedom', stifling the development of India's own notion of identity under its vacuous, content-eroded constrictor-like grip. The visual controls that were in place attempted to nurture a homogenous aesthetic and visual standardisation. This ocular control obsession extended to include materials, textures, boundary gates and even manhole covers. Such a notion was given added complexity by the changing attitudes towards development, characterised by the strong presence and continuation of diverse traditions and histories on the one hand and the forces attempting to break away from those precise traditions on the other. It was therefore critical that questions were asked regarding Modernism's true nature, potential, role, contribution and future in post-independence India. It was also imperative that clarifications be sought through a careful understanding of Modernism's close connection with post-independence politics and power.

This is where Nek Chand's work is of fundamental importance. Emerging stealthily out of a context entirely configured and produced by Modernism and Independence, his Rock Garden an ever extending collection of bizarre sculptures, in a very unselfconscious way, began to question and overturn the very conceptual tool employed in the making of Chandigarh - the Modulor - only to re-form the notions of Modernity on the subcontinent, but also tradition, in a 'post-colonial' context. Again, by violating fundamental laws guiding the planning and development of the city, the edict, of which working as a city road inspector he would surely have been aware of, Nek Chand pushed his creation further into this political act of questioning. Without overtly stating a political agenda, Nek Chand's garden, as this paper will argue, can be viewed as a critique of Chandigarh, and by extension, of the Modernist agenda expounded by Le Corbusier. It *is* the 'other' Chandigarh, as we shall see, that emerges, not so much in total 'opposition' to the host through an utter negation of the dominant city themes, but employing, in Saidian parlance, a 'contrapuntal' relationship with the city, that is by establishing precise 'counterpoints'.[3] Nek Chand cleverly constructs these counterpoints by carefully inverting or subverting the rules underlying the various city themes. The Rock Garden acts like litmus paper, responding to its environment and constantly testing the city, using its wreckage as apparatus.

---

[3] This is a view expounded in his influential work, *Culture and Imperialism*, Chatto & Windus, 1993. For a discussion on 'contrapuntal' and 'oppositional' criticism, see, Arac, Jonathan (1998) "Criticism Between Opposition and Counterpoint", *Boundary 2*, Vol. 25/2, pp. 55-69.

Politics of Acceptance

By the time the authorities accidentally discovered the garden in 1972, two thousand sculptures inhabited the under-growth linked via intertwining paths. The 'discovery' could have heralded the bulldozers to return the site back to its status as a conveniently and deliberately maintained wilderness.[4] According to the planning rules development in a 'forbidden area' should be demolished, however news about the garden spread throughout the city and hundreds of visitors came to witness the spectacle. The exodus to the garden had a profound effect on the city bureaucrats and politicians, and probably influenced the views of the planning committee. If they gave the order to demolish the garden they faced widespread public outcry and the serious risk of losing public support. This garden, the authorities realised, had the potential to abruptly end the political careers of many people and had to be handled sensitively. Nek Chand was no longer Nek Chand passing the time forging his sculptures; he was the city's most famous road inspector who defied the Authority without really intending to, whilst still remaining just another resident of the city. Chand's role became one like Dr. Jekyl & Mr. Hyde's: existing within 'the system' during the day, then vividly and actively defying it under the cover of darkness.

His only weapon was recycled rubbish transported to the site on the back of his bicycle. The 'discovery ' was significant as it thrust Chand into the city lime-light and enabled further development on a scale that Chand could not have envisaged nor undertaken by himself. Production was subsequently accelerated and he continued to occupy the site, still working illegally whilst the future of the garden was under debate next door in Sector-1. The pocket of resistance and support developed, as people wanted an association with Chand's success and risk. The home is often viewed as an extension of the self and therefore, the residents of Chandigarh could see themselves present in Chand's production. Pieces of their homes and dispossessed possessions were present and still clearly visible in the Garden, increasing the affinity people felt towards the scheme. It was this attachment through the familiar in which they saw a celebration of their 'mundane' existence in stark contrast to the abstracted and isolated ideas presented in the city and emulated by the authorities with amazing precision in their attitude in dealing with life in the city.

The future of the Garden was debated for a further four years until 1976 when the government officials realised the potency of the situation, its economic possibilities and perhaps the individual merit of the sculptures. The inauguration of the Rock Garden in 1976 was as much an indication of

---

[4] Since any development in these territories would have decidedly lessened the grand architectural impact of the Capitol Complex.

a changing consciousness with regard to Modernist thoughts, as it was the authorities' realisation that the destruction of the Garden was a potential political quick-sand. The 'international art scene' was beginning to take an interest in the 'work', and the garden was to feature in folk art magazines and documentaries. An Indian piece built outside of direct European influence but on the spoils of Modernity. It was almost as if external validation was necessary for the Garden to be taken seriously by the Indian authorities.[5]

The debate would have undoubtedly included the planning issues and the implications of letting such a development remain. The abandonment or flexing of the planning rules to this degree is an oddity for any city to entertain, especially in Chandigarh which had nurtured and insisted on the Modernist principles instilled at its conception – up until this point. Permitting an exception of this scale and setting a precedent for the city in terms of planning could have had serious legal implications for the future of the city; however, the political advantages foreseen in formalising the 'garden' must have far outweighed those. Despite reservations, therefore, the site was officially inaugurated as 'Nek Chand's Rock Garden'.

The high moral planning ground and precise city layout gave way to Nek Chand's unplanned bric-à-brac garden. An official order, presented by Dr. Randhawa, the Chairman of Chandigarh Landscape Advisory Committee, was passed, 'to preserve the garden in its original form, free from the interference of architects and town planners'. This statement almost inverts the agendas of the previous decades after independence, but echoes the same pompous tones. One can detect a shift away from the rigid rules governing the planned city, while a diminishing modernism-instigated faith in the paramount leadership of planners and architects is clear from this statement that was originally made in support of the garden as early as 1973.

Non-Modulor-Modulor

The city of Chandigarh was to be designed according to specific proportions. The chosen system was called The Modulor Man and was devised by Le Corbusier as a, 'harmonious measure of human scale, universally applicable to architecture and mechanics' (Curtis, 1999, p.163). It consists of a six-foot man with his arm out-stretched inscribed into a square. The square is subdivided to coincide with the parts of the body. His feet, his solar plexus, his head and fingertips provide the intervals for the production of the Golden Section. An inter-spiralling 'red and blue series' is

---

[5] This is not unusual in India. The poet Rabindranath Tagore and the filmmaker Satyajit Ray had aroused international acclaim before being taken seriously in India.

formed using the over-all height of the man and again with his arm outstretched. The intention behind the idea was to help architects adapt their designs to human requirements based on dimensions taken directly from an imaginary, but nevertheless, human body.

The Modulor Man was a singular universal entity, to be applied indiscriminately and universally to all forms of design, irrespective of any other peculiarities that may be part of the conditions. The Corbusian Modernist strategy, recognising the potential in the 'anonymity and standardisation based on human dimensions' (Jencks, 1987, p.79), argued for a transformation of the house as a machine to live in. In Chandigarh this was extended into many aspects of the city plan and especially into the buildings of the Capitol complex, but also through more overt representations. It had found its way into the collection of cosmic symbols assembled in the design of the enamelled ceremonial door. The Modulor's central role in making the city was elevated to near mythical status by the celebrated story of how Corbusier lost his hand-made Modulor scroll on one of his many site visits, never to be found again, suggesting that the seed of Modulor was sown into the ground.[6] The Modulor was, and still is, present everywhere.

Working as an administrator but with a difference, Chand became the non-modulor man living in the Modulor Man City. The Rock Garden is clearly not formed or governed by set mathematical formulae such as the Modulor Man or any other proportioning device. The process Chand employs relishes on circumstance and chance, as opposed to proportional precision, resulting in thousands of variations on several themes. The formal and technical details are not his main concern; Chand is more concerned with the 'panorama of visual rhythms created by varying forms, colours and textures.' (Raw Vision Magazine, 1997, p.36)

Curiously, Chand inverts the implied role of the Modulor in mass-producing artefacts [a house is both a machine and an artefact of everyday use, they are "the slaves, the valets and servants"] (Jencks, 1987, p.79) for the use of the liberated man of the industrial age. He takes the debris of mass production – its molecularised fragments - and turns it into the mass; they are almost always presented as a mass - not faceless, standardised and universal, however - but individuals who form a collective through shared anthropological and socio-cultural characteristics, as it were. Their shadows and silhouettes resemble the outline of the Modulor Man; however, no two are the same and each one is in a constant state of flux as it morphs according to the sun path during the course of the day.

---

6 Yosizaka, T., "Chandigarh: A few thoughts on how Corbusier tackled his work", in *GA (Global Architecture): Le Corbusier: Chandigarh, The New capital of Punjab, India, 1951-* , Vol. 30, introductory text with no pagination.

In the fashion of the true cosmic tyrant, trying desperately to hold on to its cosmic and universal claim, the Modulor Man broadcasts a set of instructions for all occasions, resulting in a monologue. The system by its very nature can be extended indefinitely and is a one way process from the Modulor to the built form. Its purity and continual abstraction attempts to preserve and remove the Modulor Man from any contamination through its accidental contact with human activities and rituals, consigning it to a soulless existence. As a result, it managed to produce the Capitol Complex; in spite of the heroic gestures, they are a group of buildings with their life sapped off. The sculptures, on the other hand, are not condemned to a set system, they are not destined to issue a set of instructions to society, but are a product or reflection of and a response to the society from which they originated. They are not overtly cosmic, but very much down to earth, however their constellations transcend their earthy nature. The sculptures provoke interest, inquiry and interpretation; consequently, as we shall see later, they set up dialogues with the viewer in terms of the their origin and the present, to which they are perpetually linked.

The Modulor was also presenting problems for the Design team. Edwin Maxwell Fry refused to blindly accept the Modulor system in some of his designs[7], and for Corbusier, because such a system was in place,[8] he declared that he could design the scheme from his Parisian studio rather than on site with the other three European architects, which they resented. The implications of denying the supremacy of the abstraction of human proportions were severe and the penalties extended into the spatio-political field. Fry and Drew, it was decided, would design the less eminent buildings and the majority of the housing schemes. Le Corbusier, on the other hand, directly correlating prestigious buildings with self-importance, was to take the more prominent buildings and the Capitol complex.

By inverting the claims, intended roles and qualities of the Modulor, Chand manages to slot in his humanistic, but also possibly political, agendas into the uncharted void left on the periphery of Sector-I. For Le Corbusier, the Modulor was an inanimate tool, or more appropriately a mute slave, to build a city he always wanted to build. In the twilight of his career, he was not willing to allow the specificity of humanistic and programmatic

---

[7] When Fry heard that Le Corbusier was to be employed on the project as well as himself he said, 'Honour and glory for him, and an unpredictable portion of misery for me. *ANQ Document, Chandigarh: Forty Years after Le Corbusier*, Architectura & Natura, 1993, p.15.

[8] It was Le Corbusier's intention for manufacturing industries to adopt the Modulor to standardise all production methods. If this idea was accepted, even the discarded products that Chand uses would be Modulor, however the rejection of the idea by most manufacturers should have been a revelation to Le Corbusier.

complexity to upset that smooth passage. As a result, Chandigarh is an abstraction taken to the infinite, Le Corbusier's creation is vacuous and lifeless - a giant *maquette* - notwithstanding the qualities for which it has been held in high regard. In rejecting the Modulor by playing with the Modulor Chand was protesting against the lack of the humanistic spirit and the anthropological content in Corbusier's programme, and by extension, against Le Corbusier. On a wider level the garden seems to be questioning the undue importance often apportioned within certain schools of architectural thought to abstract mathematical logic over a much needed anthropological content. Chand was using the refuse and collected items to provide a commentary on the city, and on the (often denied) past of the city through the debris-lens.

Edict

Chandigarh has a city `Edict' designed and erected to ensure that future planning of the city remains true to the original concepts instilled by Le Corbusier. This, in Corbusier's mind, ensured the city's historic continuity within the Indian tradition. Throughout the long history of India edicts have been established by reigning authorities (e.g. Emperor Asoka), physically manifested through grand stone carvings or through the erection of pillars positioned at the far corners of their kingdoms to demonstrate their power, role and significance. By their very nature edicts were proclamatory and universalising in their content.

The Edict of Chandigarh is on display in the leisure valley on a plaque and its object is:

... to enlighten the present and future citizens of Chandigarh about the *basic* concepts of planning of the city so that they become its guardians and save it from the whims of individuals.[9]

The edict adopts a simplistic approach to a planning guideline, choosing (thankfully) to disregard many rules that burden the construction process today. It only asks for certain areas of the city to be reserved for certain tasks and that materials and scale follow a `truthfulness [and] human scale . . . that puts us in touch with the infinite cosmos.' The extent and limits of this edict were designed to span the globe, universalised in its intention for being applicable to all cities; the proclamation, understandably, did not extend to the appropriateness of building types, densities nor to the demands of future market forces.

---

[9] The Edict was a simplified edition of Le Corbusier's document entitled, 'For the Establishment Statute of the Land' which contained three sections and was presented to the High Level Committee.

One can argue that, overtly consumed with waging arguments and implementing the CIAM manifesto, the views and opinions held by Le Corbusier and others at the time chose, to a great extent, to blindly ignore the realities gripping cities. The dream of the CIAM was to implement the Utopian City and to forge a New Age of Optimism. On the other hand, showing its reluctance, as we have already seen, to address the Indian reality, the authorship of the edict displays an `imaginative poverty', that carelessly side steps the riches this new city could have potentially reaped. The edict is a static relic based on a naïveté that passes rules with very little impact on the real qualities of a city. It is based solely, as would appear, on a `moral discourse of straight lines, right angles a figurative appeal to nature with the worst kind of abstraction.' (Lefebvre, 1997, p.144)

From its proclamation to link with the cosmic, the edict takes an abrupt leap to make an important announcement; stating that the `city is planned to breathe the new sublimated spirit of art', a surprising reminder of the totalising and exclusionary approach to designing human environment often adopted by the early Modernists,[10] the edict bans the erection of statues in the city or parks of Chandigarh. Although the edict refers to the prohibition on erection of monuments of people in the form of statues within the city parks, it also applies to Chand's production that, by the time of its discovery, had already reached monumental status. Sitting on the edge of Sector-I, on a site designated to remain empty - precariously positioned at the intersection of wilderness, parkland and trenching ground - Chand appropriated the site's ambiguity that questioned the applicability of such rules.

The edict and Chand's actions truly reminds us of Loos' attack on the Modernist 'completeness' in his parable 'The Poor Little Rich Man', where the talented architect had 'forgotten nothing, absolutely nothing'. To the suggestion of displaying gifts by the client, the vexed and annoyed architect thundered, 'Did I not consider *everything*? You don't need anything more. You are complete' (Dodds, G. & Tavernor, 2002, p.273). A *self-build* monument that has consistently violated the city plan layout, it is riddled with statues and goes against the nature of the city and such abstract Modernist preferences. In this sense, the slums that emerged from the early days in Chandigarh and the Rock Garden have similar, yet complementary roles to play. While the unplanned housing developments respond to a basic

---

[10] For a lucid discussion of this issue and Adolf Loos' criticism of this attitude see, Leatherbarrow, David (2002) 'Sitting in the City or the Body in the World', in.Dodds, G. & Tavernor (ed.) *Body and Building: Essays on the Changing Relation of Body and Architecture*, Cambridge, Mass. & London: MIT Press, pp.268-89.

need for shelter and somewhere to call, 'home',[11] the Rock Garden in contrast, has no utilitarian purpose, it transcends all necessity, but has developed in response to the forbidding lack of art and spontaneous expression. The city *does* now breathe the sublimated spirit of art *only* as a result of the Rock Garden and the tourists it teases into the city. [12]

'Fettered' by Archaeology'

Chand makes use of discarded objects and, through a change of context and assemblage, brings them back from the brink of their useful existence into his resurrected collection of Rock Garden artefacts, which take on different meanings as a result of this transformation. The sculptures are the product of the ruins and the ruined objects that undergo subtle but profound transformations into artefacts whilst still retaining evidence of their previous incarnation. Twenty-four villages that stood on the site before the city project began were demolished to make way for the city, the residents were offered no financial recompense and the remains of their belongings and homes were discarded in the rubbish dump. It was this rubbish dump that Chand quarried and obtained the initial pieces for his venture,[13] salvaging in the process, many of the ruined objects and structures that occupied the site before Chandigarh. This process has continued, recycling the debris from the contemporary city, with Chand acting as a commentator, narrator and translator of the city and its inhabitants, whilst simultaneously retelling historical folklore into physical daydreams. Nehru wanted Chandigarh to be the new Indian City unfettered by the past - a-historic, to some extent, and definitely un-archaeological. Yet Chand's Chandigarh precisely depends on the past - on the physical debris that resulted from, what can be termed a catastrophic erasure – and alludes to mythological and popular themes re-contextualised in historical debris. The mythological content underpins the resurrection and elevates the otherwise unremarkable fragments.

---

[11] Rather than paying extortionate amounts for a small unhealthy but legal apartment within the city (far removed from their place of work and access to markets, and so on) most labourers have been forced to construct small settlements on vacant land. This enables greater room area, the structure is more suited to the climate and there is no rent to pay. The farming of livestock is also not permitted in rented accommodation, which renders it unsuitable for the lifestyle of many families who rely on the livestock despite living within a city environment.

[12] Tourism is a very significant part of India's GDP (10% according to the Indian Tourist Board 2000), and the Rock Garden is India's second biggest tourist attraction after the Taj Mahal in Agra.

[13] 'Nek Chand Shows the Way', exhibition publication by *Raw Vision Magazine*, 1997.

Chand judges the object on its aesthetic and material properties, generating new readings based on its revised context and form. Chand makes the entire sculpture from one type of object, intensifying its qualities and making direct connections with the occupants of the city through this repetition of the familiar and the mundane, thereby trapping the lifestyles, and by extension, the peoples within the sculptures. Curiously enough, concrete is employed to bind the fragments together, which is also the material preferred by Corbusier in the Capitol complex. However, there is the difference: the concrete used here is the connector (the binder) and not the principal component, relegating it to a secondary status. An important element of Chand's work is that the original function and 'history' of the object is never dismissed or lost; the small inexpensive fashion accessory becomes the portrayal of something much more significant.

A group of the sculptures is clad in thousands of coloured glass and plastic bangles that have been salvaged. The bangles relate to the huge multitude of the girls who once lived, and are possibly still living, in Chandigarh. Broken bangles retained carry misfortune prompting owner discards them forthright. To Chand those are the final and most important materials in completing the sculptures.

The object is stripped of its function and from its conventional reality as a product; its original function as bangle is replaced with something else, as a drape or colourful clothing on an anthropomorphic sculpture. The tragedy attached to most of the discarded materials is in this way reversed as Chand transforms the objects whilst retaining the aesthetic qualities. The bangle that was once worn on a girl's arm is now part of a sculpture of a girl. The bangle as symbolic of puberty and femininity has been writ large: the bangle becomes the girl! Moreover, they confront the audience - an audience, primarily Indian, hailing from the strictures of the male-dominated society. They face the audience in their multitude, as seldom these sculptures are on their own. They ask questions.

The Wall

With the inauguration of the Garden in 1976 came the construction of the perimeter wall, further promoting the 'difference' and acting as a clear sign of established identity, but also as a political device to frame this anomaly. Earlier, the city defined its limits by the extents of its grid, which polarised the city from the greenbelt. The rigidity and finality of the city plan that came to an abrupt end with the grid was now being feathered by the Garden; softened around its edges.

Initially, the Rock Garden occupied an interstitial space. It is these 'in-between' spaces that always, as Bhabha points out:

provide the terrain for elaborating strategies of selfhood... that initiate new signs of identity, and innovative sites of collaboration, and contestation, in the act of defining the idea of society itself. (Bhabha, 1994, pp.1-2)

The development of the Rock Garden gradually enhanced the polarity; however, 'pre-wall', as we have already seen, it was still clearly apart from the city.

The technique of wall building has been used repeatedly throughout history to establish physical and psychological detachment, but also to incorporate; however the city is normally passive in encircling itself rather than proactively ensnaring its attacker.

Of course, the wall must also perform the mundane duties expected of it, such as fortifying the Garden, making it economically viable and raising the expectations of the visitor by hiding premature glimpses. In addition to this it also encloses and forms a barrier between the sculpture's illegitimacy and the pronounced purity of the modernist city. In an attempt to retain the modernist ideology, to preserve the edict and to demonstrate the city's domination and powers to confine, it was absolutely necessary to alienate and dissociate the garden from the city.

The 'other' was instantly distinguished from the city and in a postcursor to the old American freak-shows, voyeurs can pay to see the transformed household objects.

The visitors have their backs fearfully turned on the city when they pass through the threshold of the wall to enter the cage where the misfit and his narrative of the city are impounded.

The wall marks the spot where the city is left behind and the non-Modulor human has inverted and re-presented parts of the discarded Modulor city, reassuring their differences. The wall specifies the volume that contains difference. In order for the city to recognise its own being, to define its 'self', it must differentiate and highlight what it is not; the 'other' must be clearly prescribed in order to confirm, reassure and validate the existence of self. The construction of the wall was also the construction of an identity. The construction of identity establishes 'others' and opposites; this fashioning of identity is under continuous interpretation and then re-interpretation of its differences from 'us'. Edward Said argues that: 'the identity of self or "other" is a... social, intellectual and political process that takes place as a *contest* involving *individuals* and *institutions* in all societies.' (Said, 1995, reprint, p.332, emphasis added)

This was the case in 1947 with the Independence and also with the city of Chandigarh vs. the Rock Garden debate. The contest for identity is essential and leads to recognition as well as exclusion. Said's words puts the idea across succinctly, '...the construction of identity is bound up with the disposition of power and powerlessness in each society.' (Ibid. p.332)

The Garden also needs the duality of the wall to locate its ever-increasing boundaries and to establish an identity that is not Chandigarh, despite existing solely from its excrement. It is pertinent that the Garden only contains the discarded objects from the city; it can only contain what the city throws away and therefore what the city no longer is, or wants to be associated with.

The wall has enabled the Garden to distance itself from the city, of which it is a part, creating a separate faction within a relatively affluent and consumer-dominated city. By setting up this threshold, the city, rather than taking on the Garden, has surrendered this territory to it. Threshold was never a part of the initial garden; it had no frontier that explicitly stated the extents of its boundaries and this made the 'creation' hard to define, impossible to control and therefore volatile. The Garden is now recognisable as being separated from the City but is connected to it as a result of its legitimacy and bona fide operations, as well as the city profiting from its success directly and indirectly, as the city's fame rotates about the garden.

The Knowing and Subverting Amateur

The success of the Garden is dependent on the recognition of its difference from the city, in which it resides, however it is the city that is at most risk of dilution, a city that has struggled to preserve its idiolect in the changing approach to design, planning and discourse. It is through this difference created by the sculptures and their settings, which is also a means of re-appraising Nehru and Corbusier's dream city Chandigarh, that Chand has managed to introduce a popular and critical modernity, independent from revivalist or Modernist doctrines.

The Rock Garden does not dismiss these patterns, to do so would have amounted to a negation of history and its lessons, but also would have been impossible, as these have already impacted, influenced and contributed to the Indian culture. Instead, the Rock Garden has added the syntax into its own rulebook, posing questions by holding up a mirror, as it were, by reflecting, refracting and manipulating through what has been discarded. It has not claimed to be the new 'ism', but through subtle subversions of the Corbusian city-grammar meditates on the city whose boundary it straddles. By doing so, Chand's art does not merely recall the past as social cause or aesthetic precedent; it renews the past, reconfiguring it as a contingent 'in between' space, that innovates and interrupts the performance of the present. (Bhabha, op.cit. 1994, p.7)

However much Corbusier tried to convince the world of architects and city designers, Chandigarh's imposed city grid and architecture was clearly not a translation of the culture. It was a demonstration of Modernism, an exhibition trick-shot in a game that was rapidly approaching its twilight years. Its stubborn pomposity [edict multiplied by the universal Modulor man] was more akin to the Colonial mindset [organisation and efficiency to abet the modes of production] than the liberated and partisan mentality that battled for Independence. The whimsical fantasy that Chand began existed only as a result of Modernity; but as its polar opposite, renewing modernity and disrupting its apparently clean and predetermined course.

The Garden appropriated, developed and defined an 'in-between' territory, its liminal terrain providing the appropriate conditions for unfolding its strategies of selfhood and thereby initiating new signs of identity. The notion of the Indian identity was left undeveloped, possibly untouched by modernity, and was craving attention, to be brought to light by the work of Chand. Chand's work could be described as existing within Modernity but 'otherwise' than modernity (ibid. pp.1-7), reclaiming not only territory but also power, cleverly turning discarded 'modernism' against its source. Chand's polyphony and his 'D-I-Y' approach was amateur in its outlook and more suited to the 'make do and mend' approach of a by-gone era than slick internationalism. Taking Said's notion of amateurism,[14] which involves calling for a rejection of the professional specialisation's contentment in producing their own vocabulary, and speaking only to other specialists. In his essay, 'The Knowing and Subverting Reader', Ben Godber follows in a similar vein to Said substituting the professional :: amateur with the author :: reader. 'The "architect" is established by the representation of his or her works as an author within the institution. All other such works, coming from outside the institution are, by extension, established as being those of a reader (Godber, 1998, p.192).

The creative process can of course be distorted when the 'reader' blindly follows the author at the expense of their own process, however between the two can emerge a 'knowing and subverting reader', being at once within, [road inspector] and without [maverick artist] the institution [the city/architecture & planning]. It is by the virtue of his/her knowledge of the convention, rituals, codes and means of authorship that a number of challenges and provocative interpretations are offered to the viewer. Godber goes as far to suggest that the knowing and subverting reader may suggest more:

---

[14] The literal meaning of the French word amateur is to develop a love of something without being a professional.

1.The top of the Secretariat building.

2. Side elevation of the Assembly building and reflection pool.

3. Front elevation of Secretariat Building.

4. Tribute to the Modulor Man. A sculpture of the Modulor in Sector-10.

5. A manhole cover displaying the city grid layout.

6. Waterfall located within the Rock Garden with sculptures at the bottom

7. A second waterfall with a folly and colonnade construction at the top. The Rock Garden is an artefact itself and extends into the field landscape architecture and minor civil engineering

8. Le Corbusiers enamel door to the Assembly Building. This contains a painting of the Modulor Man alongside other symbols and representations of India.

9. An army of sculptures clad in bangles and displayed on a concrete podium.

10. A simple concrete sculpture and more abstract examples to the rear.

11. Early examples of the sculptures clad in broken crockery

All photographs the authors own except 'manhole cover' used by the kind permission of Dr. Soumyen Bandyopadhyay.

responsive, inclusive, richer, more diverse and potentially more divergent methods of production and representation for both international diplomacy and conventional architecture (Ibid. p.192).

For Ramanujan, it is through the amateur and the 'little traditions' they narrated - through folk-tales and non-literate modes of expression - that helped India define an important part of her identity, putting culture into motion, developing a counter system dependent on other systems to which they responded (Ramanujan, 1999, p.348). The rubbish lies dormant, like words on a page or music on a score. To read those means to read out aloud, to act as an orator. Chand is the orator, transforming space already laden with politics and uncertainty. Chand is 'travelling' in one direction but his field of view is firmly fixed in the opposite direction, he can only see and use what has gone before him.

The Rock Garden has set an encouraging and daring challenge to India to firmly establish an identity in conjunction with, but distinctly separate from modernity and the west whilst repressing any desire to resort to sole-less by-gone façadism. The post-colonial/ post-independence labels must have surely served their purpose and are in danger of stagnation, if not losing their meaning altogether through/ over prolonged use. The term post-colonial can possibly no longer describe the current condition and is used a/pathetically to conveniently cage a contentious issue. The Independence was slow to take effect and of course the implications take time to gradually spread throughout the country; however, to continuously refer back to 1947 rather than building from it, is a tragedy for the future creative development of the nation. The modernist interventions were essential for India to break the mould of imperialism and to commence 'self government' with an architecture that was appropriate. This resulted in a shift, a complete dismissal of the past and perhaps the repression of a more conservative identity, in favour of 'the machine age' and 'utopia'.

A Klee painting named *Angelus Novas* shows an angel looking as though he is about to move away from something he is fixedly contemplating. His eyes are staring, his mouth is open, and his wings are spread. This is how one pictures the angel of history. His face is turned toward the past. Where we perceive a chain of events, he sees one single catastrophe that keeps piling wreckage upon wreckage and hurls it in front of his feet. The angel would like to stay, awaken the dead and make whole what has been smashed. But a storm is blowing from paradise; it has caught in his wings with such violence that the angel can no longer close them. This storm irresistibly propels him into the future towards which his back is turned, while the pile of debris before him grows skyward. This storm is what we call progress (Benjamin, 1999, p.249). Chand continues to demonstrate that the city can prevent itself from becoming a ruin and although the modernist determinism is unacceptable, the framework that it set up with the intention to introduce the spirit of art has, in a curious and circumvented way, been successful. The debate over the city boundaries and the neighbouring states continues, and keeps the city in flux, the Union Territory and neighbouring states have simultaneously built up an arsenal of villages and industrial territories that contribute to its density and maintain Chandigarh as a significant city in northern India. Modernism was the substratum and sustenance for Chand, who has displayed his work all over the world and provides subtle indicators about the changing culture and identity of India.

Acknowledgement

Many thanks and a sincere appreciation of all his help must go to Dr. Soumyen Bandyopadhyay, Department of Architecture, University of Liverpool, who has been relentless in his energy and encouraging in his criticism during the construction of this paper.

Select Bibliography

Anaia Loomba & Suvir Kaul (1994) vol 16, *ON INDIA Writing History Post-Coloniality,* The Oxford Literary Review.
ANQ document (1993) *Chandigarh 40 years after Le Corbusier.*
Benjamin, Walter (1999) *Illuminations,* Pimlico.
Bhabha, Homi (1994) *The location of culture,* Routledge.
Bhabha, Homi (1998) *Anish Kapoor,* Hayward Gallery.
Curtis, William (1999) *Le Corbusier Ideas & Forms,* Phaidon.
Curtis, William (2000) *Modern Architecture since 1900,* Phaidon, third ed.
Desaim, Miki (1997) *Architecture & Independence,* Oxford University Press.
Dharwadker, Winay (1999) *The Collected Essays of Ramanujan,* Oxford University Press.
Foundation Le Corbusier (1981) *The ideas of Le Corbusier,* George Braziller.
Frampton, Kenneth (1992) *Modern Architecture,* Thames & Hudson Ltd.
Heidegger, Martin (1971) *Poetry, Language, Thought,* Harper & Row.
Hill, Jonathan (1998) *Occupying Architecture,* Routledge.
Jencks, Charles (1987) Le Corbusier and the tragic view of architecture, Penguin.
Joshi, Kiran (1999) The Indian Architecture of Chandigarh, Mapin.
Leach, Neil (1997) *Rethinking Architecture,* Routledge.
Narayan, R.K. (1972) *The Ramayana,* Penguin.
Ramanujan, A.K. (1991) *Folktales from India,* Pantheon.
Raw Vision Ltd London. *Raw Vision Magazine #35,* 2001Summer
Raw Vision Magazine, *Nek Chand Shows the Way,* Exhibition booklet
Said, Edward (1998) *Beginnings,* Granta.
Said, Edward (1995) *Orientalism,* Penguin.
Sarin, Madhu (1982) *Urban planning in the third world,* Mansell Publishing.
Spivak, Gayatri (1987) *In Other Worlds,* Methuen.

Steele, James (1998) Rethinking Modernism for the developing world: The complete architecture of Doshi, Thames & Hudson.

Storey, David (2001) *Territory*, Pearson Education.

Tschumi, Bernard (1997) *Architecture & Disjunction,* M.I.T.

Williams, Patrick (2001) *Edward Said versions of Orientalism,* Sage publications.

Part 4: Negotiating Postmodernity: Culture, Hybridity and Critique

Masculinity, Fantasy and *Bhaji on the Beach*

E. Anna Claydon

Bhaji on the Beach (1992) directed by Gurinder Chadha and co-written with Meera Syal (lately of Goodness Gracious Me! fame[1]) is conventionally thought of as a 'woman's film,' a melodrama by, about and for women but as with many contemporary British films, the reality is much more complex than a collection of generic conventions and audience expectations.

The word 'bhaji', to a Western audience is automatically paired with 'onion', but in UK Bangladeshi the term also means, 'anything stir-fried' [2]. This metaphor for the characters within the film is pertinent for the argument I shall set out for *Bhaji on the Beach* as a film, which negates any expectations we might have as an audience about the film. The stir-fried identities of the characters are mixed together as ingredients of a new kind of identity. They do not, however, need to be absorbed into a British variant of the American melting pot but rather retain their cultural specificity and edge, do not become flavours lost or out-done by the stodge of British cafeteria food and culture. Food, nevertheless, does remain central to the narrative of the film as a signifier of identity and so the original meaning of the 'onion bhaji' is not irrelevant as the characters picnic on the beach or in a greasy spoon 'caff' on the promenade.

In his 1994 review of the film, James Berandinelli notes that the Bhaji is it itself a 'snack food whose identity has been 'Westernised' in the British Isles' and that this another reason Chadha chooses bhaji as a metaphor for the lives of the women in the film.[3] Consequently, like the meaning of 'bhaji' which identifies it with a mixing of cultural indices, the westernised snack is also representative of the hybridised influences upon the film.

In this paper, I shall discuss the configuration, or 'stir fry', of the *male* roles in *Bhaji on the Beach* with the narrative and Bollywood style fantasy sequences of the film as representative of the new British cinema: the British cinema which has moved beyond, but not necessarily past, a concept of a homogeneous, British, English culture in which all other cultures are

---

[1] *Goodness Gracious Me!* BBC TV (1998-2000) Meera Syal is also the author of *Anita and Me* (1996) and *Life Isn't All Ha Ha Hee Hee* (1999)

[2] http://www.curryweb.co.uk/glossary.htm Accessed 15.03.2002.

[3] http://www.movie-reviews.colossus.net/movies/b/bhaji.html

Othered[4] by society and, like the characters *Bhaji on the Beach* represents, towards a multiculturalism with which dominant white English culture is not yet at ease.

The day from which this paper is drawn was called 'Picturing South Asian Popular Culture in English' but one of the key activities of most visions of South Asian culture in British films has been the concept of an Anglo-Asian space in which rather than linguistic signifiers being central to identity, the use or non-use of English as a language by South Asian communities, the manifestation of South Asian identities has been an issue of how characters relate to the space, how South Asian culture is pictured in England by both the South Asian and English communities and how the English landscape or cityscape is made into a core of significant meanings for South Asian Britons seeking to understand both their place in Asian cultures and their parallel occupancy in contemporary British culture. In *East is East* (directed by Damien O'Donnell, written by Ayub Khan-Din, 1999)[5] this duality is demonstrated by the oppositional relationships between the Moslem Khan brothers and their secret lives, sneaking out of the house to go to a disco, pretending to be white as they enter the club, or the eldest brother's transformation into one of the 1970s 'beautiful people' after he escapes his arranged marriage; but in Chadha's film, predating *East is East* by nearly ten years yet set at the time it was released, this duality and idea of a culture clash is less evident and is indeed broken down by the film's narrative and its creative use of the Blackpool setting.

Bhaji on the Beach followed Chadha's earlier documentary *I'm British But...*(1989)[6] in focussing on, thematically, the idea that the South Asian communities around Britain feel marginalised from white British culture to a periphery where they take on what we might call English 'mannerisms' and the 'way of life' and appear assimilated into normative British society[7]. In *I'm British But...* Chadha had spoken to many young Asian-Britons, from the son of a farmer in Wales whose farmhouse had been the victim of a racist arson attack, to a young 'westernised' Londoner considering the way in which she considered herself British but not, crucially, English. The argument which emerged from the documentary was that for the young South Asian Briton, the label British was a politico-legal identity but not a social one; a matter of legal rights and privileges sets against the dominant white society's prejudices both *de facto* and *de jure*.

---

[4] Othered: when one culture is identified as different, 'Them' to the dominant culture.

[5] *East is East* (1999) Director: Damien O'Donnell.

6 *I'm British But...* (1989) Director: Gurinder Chadha.

[7] For example the family in *Goodness Gracious Me!* who change their name to Cooper from Kapur and evade all identifications as Asian, even by fellow Asians.

In *Bhaji on the Beach*, Chadha repeats her question to young British-Asians, 'What does it mean to be British and Asian in contemporary British society?' but sets it within a fictional framework in which the generation divide in both the white and Asian communities becomes a metaphor for the changing ways in which the English picture South Asian culture and South Asians picture, equally stereotypically, ideas of Britishness.

A group of South Asian women from Birmingham climb aboard a bus on a day-trip to the 'Kiss me Quick' hat capital of British seaside culture, Blackpool (imbued with all the significance of Donald McGill's cheeky seaside cartoons and images of white children riding donkeys on the beach). Amongst them is a wife who has been beaten by her husband, a student who is pregnant by her black boyfriend, two teenage girls seeking excitement and a middle-aged woman frustrated by her monotonous family life. No sooner have they departed for Lancashire when the husband, his brothers and the student's boyfriend make their way to Blackpool in pursuit and consequently the film's plot is structured as an extended farcical chase sequence with interludes of pathos, drama and comedy set against the clock of the agreed return time to the bus at 8pm.

In Blackpool, unaware of the men chasing them, the women separate: the student seeks information about getting an abortion; the teenage girls transform themselves from demure schoolgirls into highly sexualised Westernised flirts cruising the burger bars for boys; the wife and her small son enjoy a day of freedom from the hostel where she now lives; and the frustrated middle-aged woman wanders reflectively, finding an English 'gentleman actor' on the seafront.

Everything which happens in *Bhaji on the Beach*, despite the female characters being more central to the journeys made within the film towards self-knowledge, that classic narrative structure which inflects many films which question identity, happens because of the men. The events and the actions of the women are influenced by how they relate to the various models of masculinity offered within the film and how these models are interpolated into the way the women view their own identities.

These models are offered by Bulbir, the eldest brother; Ranjit, the husband seeking his wife; Manjit, the youngest brother; the student's boyfriend; the boys at the burger bar; and the 'gentleman actor.' They are frameworks upon which four conceptualisations of contemporary British identity hinge; the Anglo-Asian, the Anglo-Caribbean, the anachronistic Imperialist and the post-modern Anglo-American teenager - each of them in some ways a hybrid of other, equally complex identities and cultures.

It is in this hybridisation of characters and cultures that the definition of new British cinema resides according to the most recent work of Andrew Higson, a man who since the mid-1980s has made the explanation of the

British cinema, and the idea of a British national cinema, his own.[8] In his 2000 essay 'The Instability of the National,'[9] in which Higson articulated the concerns many had already expressed with his concept of a British national cinema, Higson admits that he: 'was perhaps at times rather too ready to find British films presenting an image of a coherent, unified, consensual nation' (Higson, 2000, p.35) and instead now recognises that there has been and 'inevitable' (Ibid. p.38) shift from homogeneity to heterogeneity in British cinema and that this leads to a configuration of a post-national cinema. Surely, he writes:

Some of the identities and positions explored in films like *My Beautiful Laundrette* (Stephen Frears, 1985) and *Bhaji on the Beach* are [...] as much either local or transnational as they are national. Given the transient and fleeting nature of many of the allegiances established in these films it seems problematic to invoke the idea of a singular, indisputable British nation, however complex and devolved - hence my preference for the idea of a post-national cinema. (Higson, 2000, p.40)

Consequently, the hybrid culture which the post-national cinema seeks to represent 'resists the tendency to nationalise questions of community, culture and identity,' (Ibid. p.38) the concept of *différance* is maintained and indeed supported by the reiteration of the local and the transnational.

Différance, of course, is not the same as Otherness. *Différance*, the Derridean term,[10] refers to the way in which we perceive signs, which are otherwise similar, as *not the same*. It is the way in which all things can only be seen as individual by recognising that each object or subject is dissimilar. It is the way in which we construct the world around us based upon comprehending the *différance* of its constituent signs and as such is related to the Lacanian idea of the mirror stage without which humans cannot achieve subjectivity - or perceive themselves as individual, separate, different from the world around them.[11] In recognising *différance* we recognise the equality of signification.

---

[8] Andrew Higson, *Waving the Flag,* (Oxford: Oxford University Press, 1995) *Dissolving Views* (Editor, London: Cassell, 1996) and other collections.

[9] Andrew Higson (2000), 'The Instability of the National', *British Cinema: Past and Present*. Ed. Andrew Higson and Justine Ashby, London: Routledge, 2000.

[10] Derrida, *différance*. See Jacques Derrida (1982) *Margins of Philosophy*, Chicago: University of Chicago Press/Harvester Press, p.14.

[11] Lacan, J. mirror stage. See Jacques Lacan (1949) 'The Mirror Stage as Formative of the Function of the 'I' as Revealed in Psychoanalytic Theory' in *Écrits - A Selection* (1977) London: Tavistock Publications.

Otherness, on the other hand, is inextricably linked to signs of social *difference*, the identification of a 'them' and an 'us'. Some of the key writers on Otherness have focussed on 'Orientalism', issues of imperialism and post-colonial representations; the central figure being Edward Said and his works *Orientalism* (1978)[12] and *Culture and Imperialism* (1994)[13] In identifying a person or culture as Other to the dominant culture (in whatever setting, the act of Othering is not specific to European culture but exists elsewhere), that dominant society identifies the Other as exterior to itself, brushing its boundaries, 'them', alien and a potential enemy. Consequently, when the counterpart is labelled as Other to 'us', it will always, inevitably, become something, which the dominant culture wishes to make abject[14] and in some cases eject it from its borders.

Racism, then, is an ideology bound in the wish to make abject and to eject that which the dominant ideology has identified as Other. What *Bhaji on the Beach* expresses is that difficult configuration between the anachronistic English Othering of South Asian culture as both exotic (which is tied in with the Orientalisation of the East) and abject (such as when the skin-heads abuse the women at the motorway service station on the M6 as they journey northwards) and the contemporary British embracing of *différance*.

In *Bhaji on the Beach* another kind of Othering is, however, also played out in the opposition of the female protagonists and the male antagonists who pursue them. In the remainder of this paper I shall focus on the models of masculinity offered by four of the men in the film, Bulbir, Ranjit, Manjit and the 'gentleman actor', Ambrose. I shall then discuss the way in which fantasy is articulated within the film and how the *mise-en-scène* of fantasy is linked to the masculinism and hybridity of the narrative.

Each of the male characters within *Bhaji on the Beach* manifest a specific commentary upon contemporary hybrid Britishness and function narratively to develop the journey towards autonomy taken by the female characters seeking identities beyond wife, mother, student or lover. This narrative function means that the men are classical antagonists who make things happen to the protagonists. However, the women are not simply victims.

Half way through the film, just after the men have found their way to Blackpool, and triggering the imminent down turn of the narrative after a

---

[12] Edward Said (1978) *Orientalism*, London: Routledge & Kegan Paul.

13 Edward Said (1994) *Culture and Imperialism,* London: Vintage.

[14] abject: disgusting, horrific, that which you wish to get as far away from as you can. See also Julia Kristeva, *Powers of Horror,* Columbia University Press, 1984.

day of escape for the characters, the three brothers stand frustrated at the top of Blackpool tower looking down on the seafront and pier:

> Bulbir: (in tracksuit bottoms, a football shirt, trainers, holding a can of lager) Can't see a bloody thing. (To Manjit, in shirt, jumper, jeans, smart-casual) I said I can't see a bloody thing!

> Ranjit: (in white shirt, black trousers, shoes, business wear) Bulbir... if you could, er, focus. You'd be more bloody helpless.

> Bulbir: I'll tell you what's wrong. Too much brains and not enough balls that's your problem (Leans on Manjit). Look at him.

> Ranjit: fills in the forms and I drive the van; but he ain't nothing special, Manjit man, is he, eh? Look at him. your fancy cigarettes and your degree, they couldn't keep her, eh?

> Manjit: Bulbir, drop it, man.

> Bulbir: Eh?

> Ranjit: Manjit.

> Bulbir: I ain't the stupid one. I know what I am and I know what to do. And I've still got a wife.

> Ranjit looks up and punches Bulbir, a fight ensues. Manjit tries to stop them getting in between.

> Bulbir: Hang on... look they're down there.

The three brothers: Bulbir, the eldest; Ranjit, the middle sibling; and Manjit, the youngest are each representative of what might be labelled three levels of Anglo-Asian hybrid identity - although the hybridity is not instantly recognisable. Bulbir, the chauvinist, who resents Ranjit's education and money, is a conventional representation of the racist white British image of the Asian patriarch. He represents a position nearer to the model of masculinity as the Law of the King (as articulated by Michel Foucault in *Discipline and Punish*[15]) violent, unquestioned punitively requiring the service of his lesser subjects. Bulbir, however, is dressed in the uniform of the football hooligan, with his tracksuit bottoms, trainers and

---

15 Michel Foucault (1977), *Discipline and Punish*, London: Penguin.

perpetual can of lager, and consequently is a hybrid form of masculinity conforming to both the stereotype of the white British 'yob', also a chauvinist, and the Asian patriarch. Ranjit, meanwhile, in his business suit recalls the iconography of the 'yuppie' but also evokes the idea of the Asian businessman. Ranjit, like his elder brother, believes in the right to beat his wife if she does not do as he requires (towards the end of the film he accuses her of making him do it), but instead of Bulbir's acceptance of this behaviour as a marital right, Ranjit's problematic interaction with his wife, oscillating between mannerism of care and hate, shows that, just as the 1980s icon his costume echoes recalls the changes in patriarchal culture in the late 80s with a movement towards political correctness, he acknowledges his problem but does not know how to deal with it. The youngest brother, Manjit, is posited by Chadha and Syal's narrative as the face of the future for Anglo-Asian masculinity. Manjit is the most recently married of the brothers and unlike Bulbir's and Ranjit's confrontational relationships with their wives, Manjit and his wife respond to each other as equals, are more openly affectionate before the men leave for Blackpool. This equality is not recognised by Bulbir, who scoffs at Manjit's promise to call his wife to let her know that he is safely at the seaside town.

Manjit's narrative function, dressed in the garb of a 'college boy' with corduroy trousers and a patterned jumper, is as an intermediary between Ranjit and Bulbir and, further, between them and the women. In the Blackpool Tower scene above, Manjit physically parts his elder brothers, resulting in Bulbir seeing Ginder in the crowds below. Only with his intervention as an arbitrator can progress be made. Later, however, Manjit's interventions fail to prevent Ranjit's attempt to snatch Amrick, his son, and in the final scene of the film, Manjit, punches and kicks both his brothers to the ground.

The relationship between the three brothers, their multiple significations and connotations, shows in *Bhaji on the Beach* that the 'crisis' these men undergo, as figures of frustration, is one of their changing relationship to a less patriarchal society, of their masculinism and not their masculinity.

The English 'gentleman actor' - Ambrose, who befriends Ayesha, the frustrated middle-aged woman, as she stands on the beach, is like Bulbir representative of the anachronism of patriarchy but whereas Bulbir manifests a working-class iconography, Ambrose's demeanour, costume and accent mark him out as upper-class and, with his white jacket, cravat and straw boater, an icon of the colonial era. This is reiterated by the beginning of the scene in which he and Ayesha stroll in the park, bathed I evening sunlight, when she asks if he has seen any Bollywood films. 'Been in them!' he replies. '*Gunga Din!*[16][...] *Bhowani Junction!*'[17] These are, of course, not Bollywood films (and Ayesha lets that slide) but Hollywood visions of Imperial India before 1947 and Ambrose's image of Ayesha is entirely bound up in the colonial and Orientalist discourse of the exotic. As he shows her the theatre, the park, the elderly clapping along to the Wurlitzer organ player in the pier both engage with the performativity of identity as Ambrose and Ayesha imagine each are something they are not.

As a model of masculinity within the film, Ambrose conforms to the E.M. Forster image of the 'good' English in India. He is out of time, out, very literally in this setting, of season, waiting to play Widow Twanky (frequently portrayed as East Asian by British pantomime in her job of washerwoman) in the Christmas panto', wishing he was part of the Empire again. What is interesting, however, is the way in which, in the end, Ambrose is made perfectly harmless. He wants to colonise Ayesha, to keep her with him, but she, having the choice, rejects him and finds her own identity. Therefore, Ambrose (his name alluding to Ambrosia, the utopian English countryside) functions as a metaphor for the British Empire which saw itself as benevolent and patriarchal in a protective manner, whilst Ayesha is India marking out her own identity.

Within *Bhaji on the Beach* fantasy plays a large part in mediating the concepts of English and South Asian identities. In filmic terms fantasy occupies a place both within the narration and the *mise-en-scène* of the plot; these spaces are also a combination of the literal and metaphorical. The literal fantastical space within the film is that shaped by the town of Blackpool itself with the lights, the seaside acts and the sense in which it exists outside reality; a world of Wurlitzer organs and snake charmers. The metaphorical, conversely, is played out in the mind of the middle-aged woman, Ayesha, as the site of imagination, the *super-ego* and romantic interludes, manifested through the language of Bollywood films.

The visualisation of Blackpool as an unreal landscape of the mind is one that has also been used in the Peter Chelsom film *Funny Bones* (1995)[18]. In both films Blackpool provides a surreal backdrop against which characters undergo the entire spectrum of emotions and in which anything is possible. *Funny Bones* is very specifically set within the out-of-season theatrical environment of the 'end of the pier show' and so absorbs the surrealism into the acts or turns which are performed; but in *Bhaji on the Beach* this theatricality is just as present in Ayesha's gentleman friend and his shark-costumed acquaintances in the town centre, or the Wurlitzer player

---

[16] *Gunga Din* (1939) director: George Stevens.
[17] Bhowani Junction (1956) director: George Cukor.
[18] *Funny Bones* (1995) director: Peter Chelsom.

entertaining the pensioners in deck chairs. The surreal, therefore, becomes the discourse through which we identify with and comprehend the phenomenon of the British seaside town.

However, the signs and meanings the English recognise as specifically British (and which are commented upon within the film through the continuing dialogue of the elderly 'Aunties' and the fare offered at seaside eateries) are also interpreted within the film, by the Aunt from Bombay, as signs which also signify South Asian culture. At the beginning of the film, on entering the town centre and seeing the street of Blackpool illuminations, she proclaims, 'Ah! Bombay!' - Blackpool is as much a system of international signs as it is one of nationally specific signification. There are other aspects that emphasise the way in which South Asian cultures (and other cultures) are represented and mediated through English imagery in the seaside town. Images which are shared with all English seaside resorts and tell us a great deal about the relationship of the English to their peripheries, their coasts and ports. Images such as: the tracery in the park's fences which echo Japanese culture; the white man with the snake and the turban on the pier, alluding to the Middle East; the ghosts of Imperialistic imagery in the architecture with elephants and exotic fruits (for example, famously, Brighton Pavilion); the strippers in the American bar at the end of the day. The English seaside resort is a cornucopia of the exotic from around the world and as a contemporary institution of British life, bringing together all the influences from around the world to make it into something which specifically articulates an echo of colonising identities, eventually creates a hybrid which is as much a metaphor for the question Chadha is asking *Bhaji on the Beach* as the characters are themselves.

The fantasy landscape of the English resort, therefore, is a *mise-en-scène* of post-colonial desire in which British white culture represents back to itself what it would wish to be but which the characters of *Bhaji on the Beach* also discover is a landscape which amplifies both their conceptualisation of Britishness and the British conceptualisation of the exotic South Asian. We see this in the burger bar boys interest in the girls and in Ambrose's fascination with Ayesha and their comments about skin tone, culture and clothing (the actor, for example, suggests Ayesha buy some 'moccasins' - a interesting allusion to the early belief that the Native American were 'Indians' of another kind).

Consequently, the journey within the film, from Birmingham to Blackpool is a journey from a realist landscape that restricts the characters to a fantasy landscape in which they are afforded the space to dream. Inevitably, nonetheless, pursued by the men, the fantasy cannot last forever as the space is encroached upon and the fantasy ends in a realisation that the Blackpool illuminations illuminate little more than their already existing problems. Accordingly, in finally accepting that reality is the discourse through which they must live their subjectivities, the fantasy landscape becomes less of an escape and more of an excursion.

In *Making Meaning in Indian Cinema,*[19] Ravi S. Vasudevan comments that:

> The [...] cultural explanation of [Indian cinema] characterises the popular film as a repository of a traditional aesthetic that composed different *rasas* or moods, in line with the ancient canons of Hindu aesthetics. In a folkloristic rendering, the popular film is rooted in the persistent orality of Indian culture, in which music has an expressive equivalence to speech [...] such orality is said to sustain an externalised, declamatory and musical form in the Indian popular cinema.' (p.9)

The 'orality' of popular Indian cinema to Vasudevan refers, combined with the Hindu aesthetics a cultural understanding of popular Bollywood would recognise, plays an important part in the way in which the metaphorical fantasy discourse is articulated in the film.

As I said earlier, these fantasies are seen from the perspective of Ayesha as she interprets and interpolates the implications of the actions in which she is involved. These sequences, used initially for comic effect within the film, function, as Freud argued dreams do,[20] to manifest, condense and replay within the subconscious those aspects which affect Ayesha's life that she perceives as problems to be solved or issues to be addressed. The importance of the fantasy sequences for *Bhaji on the Beach* however, despite their comic value, should not be understated as both a picturing of South Asian culture within an otherwise British social realist narrative style[21] and as a means of emphasising key thematic points within the narration of the film. Indeed, after the title sequences pan across the shop fronts of a street in urban Birmingham, the first narrative scene of the film is Ayesha's first fantasy, lost as a Lilliputian[22] amongst the detritus of the shop with video boxes and torn posters of Bollywood heroes and heroines overwhelming her. The fantasy then takes her into a mythological *mood*

---

[19] Ravi S. Vasudevan (2000) *Making Meaning in Indian Cinema,* New Delhi: Oxford University Press.

[20] See Sigmund Freud (1955) *The Essentials of Psychoanalysis,* London: Hogarth Press.

[21] As associated with the films of Ken Loach (e.g. *Kes,* 1969) or the British New Wave directors: Tony Richardson, Lindsay Anderson and Karel Reisz.

[22] Lilliput - the land in Jonathan Swift's *Gulliver's Travels* (1726) occupied by tiny people.

space with a huge and ominous statue of Vishnu,[23] billowing smoke, with luminous coloured lights and a contrasting set of tableaux comparing how she wished her family were and how they actually are, which propels her back into the reality of the business. The function of Vishnu, the statue of which re-appears a number of times throughout the film as Ayesha's times of need, functions as a Freudian *super-ego* to Ayesha's *id*, that part of her which controls her unconscious and therefore controls her fantasies.[24] Vishnu reprimands her, tells her what to do and, as a representation of Hindu culture, is both Ayesha's spiritual guide and the voice of the dominant ideology, forbidding her to question the performativity of her cultural identity.[25] The questioning of which is instead left to the Aunt from Bombay who presents a modern Indian identity that has little to do with the first generation immigrants from India in Britain: implying that for the generation who immigrated in the 1950s and '60s and their children being Indian or South Asian is as hard to do as becoming British (a subject upon which both Salman Rushdie and Hanif Kureshi have written extensively).[26]

Ayesha's fantasies are mode of interpreting the world, of working through the decisions she considers but they are also a way of re-configuring the Anglo-Asian identity as much through South Asian cultural references as through the relation of the individual subject to Englishness.

One of the key fantasies in Ayesha's metaphorical fantasy landscape is also the last of the film, when unlike the others, where she recourses to another space (to the extent that she is often spatially bewildered on coming back to reality), she appropriates the landscape in which she is already placed. This fantasy, therefore, is a metaphor for what she is considering, albeit romantically, might be possible in the real world.

Ambrose and Ayesha enter a park, the evening light dapples through the trees as they walk alongside the lake and there is a romantic mood established by the lighting and use of sound. Talking of Bollywood films (Ambrose's comments on which I referred to earlier); Ayesha is sent reflectively into her own Bollywood reverie. Imitating of the courtship sequences of many traditionally set Hindi Bollywood films, with a musical

---

[23] Vishnu: the Hindu god considered as a 'supreme god' by those who worship him. See http://www.encyclopedia.com/html/v/vishnu.asp.

[24] super-ego/id - see Sigmund Freud, The Essentials of Psychoanalysis.

25 performativity - with reference to Judith Butler (1989) *Gender Trouble,* London: Routledge. All cultural identities are learnt identities that we perform in order to be integrated into the dominant ideology, in Butler, the 'heterosexual matrix' but equally patriarchy or Imperialism.

[26] See Salman Rushdie, (1991) *Imaginary Homelands,* London: Penguin/Granta, and Hanif Kureshi, (1993) 'The Rainbow Sign' in *My Beautiful Laundrette,* London: Faber and Faber.

song-based soundtrack, Ayesha runs through the trees and sunlight rain in a bejewelled sari and Ambrose, made-up in a wig, traditional trouser suit and with make-up to look South Asian, chases after her. As he finally catches up with her, peeking around a tree, the rain being to wash away the make-up and he is left with streaks of brown pancake streaming down his face, the image of which pulls Ayesha back into the real world of the park and Ambrose's face looking with concern at her own drenched features.

What this fantasy sequence does is to play out both Ayesha's initial perceptions of Ambrose and her realisation that he is little more than a fictional hero and that once the make up, the imitation of identity, is washed away by the rain he cannot be anything other than an Englishman Orientalising and fantasising himself. It is a key scene for Ayesha's own realisation of the failure of the fantasy as a resource escaping reality, finally leading up to her more outspoken actions in the final scenes of the film when she slaps Ranjit in the face for beating his wife; but it also is a scene in which one kind of answer to Chadha's question 'What do it mean to be British and Asian in contemporary British society?' is offered. Cultural identity cannot be acquired, like an Englishman putting on make-up or the teenage girls dressing in mini-skirts and denim. It is learn and it is performed but ethnicity cannot be changed by swapping iconographies.

Is this a hard answer? Yes, but still it recognises *différance* and by manifesting the recognition by characters within the film of the process of Othering by Ambrose and the burger bar boys, looks towards the hybridity contemporary British culture should embrace - not changing cultural signifiers and identities but adding to them and re-shaping them into an iconography of equality.

British culture is no longer homogeneous and British cinema is right to consider the post-national, as a defining factor in the films that are released but neither is British cinema or culture yet heterogeneous. In Higson's paper, he says that contemporary British film is 'as much local or transnational as they are national' (Higson, 2000, op. cit. p.40) and as such, considering the regionality of British British films, I view it as highly unlikely that British films or culture will picture, represent or think about different peoples as heterogeneous and equal for many years to come. Even subtly, the realistic picturing of South Asian culture in English is still perceived by the majority of dominant white society as a novelty, different, not mainstream, on the edge of British culture and consequently, a marginal interest.

Bibliography

Berandinelli, J. (1994) Review of *Bhaji on the Beach*,
http://www.movie-reviews.colossus.net/movies/b/bhaji.html - accessed 15.03.2002

Butler, J. (1989) *Gender Trouble*, Routledge,. London.

Claydon, A. (2001) 'New Perspectives on British Cinema: Going Beyond the Crisis in Masculinity'. Unpublished article originally written for the *Masculinity and Film* conference, University of Newcastle.

Derrida, J. (1982) *Margins of Philosophy*, University of Chicago Press, Chicago.

Foucault, M. (1977) *Discipline and Punish*, Penguin, London.

Freud, S. (1955) *The Essentials of Psychoanalysis*, Hogarth Press, London.

Higson, A. (1995) *Waving the Flag*, Oxford University Press, Oxford.

Higson, A. (1996) ed. *Dissolving Views*, Cassell, London.

Higson, A. (2000) 'The Instability of the National', *British Cinema: Past and Present*,

Higson, A. and Ashby, J. eds. Routledge, London.

http://www.curryweb.co.uk/glossary.htm - accessed 15.03.2002.

http://www.encyclopedia.com/html/v/vishnu.asp - accessed 21.03.2002.

Kureshi, H. (1993) 'The Rainbow Sign', *My Beautiful Laundrette*, Faber and Faber, London.

Lacan, J. (1949) 'The Mirror Stage as Formative of the Function of the 'I' as Revealed in Psychoanalytic Theory'. *Écrits - A Selection* (1977) Tavistock Publications, London.

Rushdie, S. (1991) *Imaginary Homelands,* Penguin/Granta, London.

Vasudevan, R.S. (2000) *Making Meaning in Indian Cinema*, Oxford University Press, New Delhi.

Filmography

Bhaji on the Beach (1992) Director: Gurinder Chadha. Performers: Kim Vithana, Lalita Ahmed.

Bhowani Junction (1956) Director: George Cukor. Performers: Stewart Granger, Ava Gardner, Bill Travers.

East is East (1999) Director: Damien O'Donnell. Performers: Om Puri, Linda Bassett.

Funny Bones (1995) Director: Peter Chelsom. Performers: Lee Evans, Leslie Caron.

Goodness Gracious Me! (1998-2000) BBC TV.

Gunga Din (1939) Director: George Stevens. Performers: Cary Grant, Joan Fontaine.

I'm British But... (1989) Director: Gurinder Chadha. Documentary

Space, Character and Critique: South Asian Identity in *The Simpsons*

Paul Rodaway

South Asian In Springfield

A 'specific Asian cultural space' in English textual and visual representations subsists in myriad forms, produced by both Asians and non-Asians, both in the Indian-subcontinent and internationally. Critically, however, such 'Asian films' and film representations of 'Popular Culture,' do much more than represent or present some 'authentic' Asian culture. In complex ways, these representations both 'create' a specific Asian cultural space, or 'authenticate' particular Asian identities, and, significantly critique both Asian and non-Asian identities. Of particular interest for the present essay, is the function of the 'token' South Asian in Springfield, that is Apu in The Simpsons. This American prime-time TV cartoon is not in the narrow sense an 'Asian cultural space', but nevertheless 'pictures' critical aspects of popular South Asian culture. In particular, it is argued, that the placing of a South Asian character, his values and behaviours within the community of Springfield, opens up a particular cultural space, one which permits a critical discourse on both Asian immigrant identity in North America and a critique of the mainstream American society and values of Homer and his family. A South Asian in Springfield, and the features and events constructed around him, function therefore as a kind of 'space of radical openness.' (hooks 1991)

The Simpsons

The Simpsons has proved to be one of the most popular prime time TV shows in the USA, and increasingly in a number of other countries across the world. The family of cartoon characters first made its television debut on The Tracy Ullman Show on April 19, 1987, and became a TV show in its own right December 17, 1989 (Vogl 2000). To date there have been 12 series, making this one of, if not, the longest running prime time cartoon series on American TV. Even President Bush in 1992 tacitly appreciated the subversive potential of this cartoon when he was recorded as saying, 'we need a nation closer to the Waltons than The Simpsons.' (Sohn 2000) An estimated 14.4 million people watched The Simpsons in the USA during its

1999-2000 season, (Pinsky 2001b) and two episodes aired on 25th and 31st October 1999 reached a combined 28 million viewers in the USA alone. The Simpsons has been described as a satirical sitcom, an adult cartoon and 'one of the most intelligent and literate comedies on television today' (Irwin et al 2001). It is saturated with – perhaps 'articulated by' is a better description – satire, sarcasm, irony and caricature (see Irwin & Lombardo 2001). A key feature of its construction is what Matheson (2001) describes as 'quotationalism' (i.e. 'inter-textuality'), the contemporary habit of multiple cross-referencing cultural (especially popular cultural) representations, nearly always with a strongly ironic (or as Matheson terms it 'hyper-ironic') stance. The Simpsons is widely recognised as critical of mainstream American culture (see for instance, Irwin et al 2001, Vogl 2000, Tingleff 1998) yet it is prime time TV valued for its humour and entertainment, and as such can it genuine offer an effective social critique? (see for instance, interviews with Matt Groening, and other creators: www.snpp.com and www.thesimpsons.com)

Apart from numerous short pieces on the popularity of the series, its creators and its future development, by far the largest body of more detailed commentary has focussed upon religion and moral issues, and these have generated much heated popular and academic debate (Bowler 1996, Durban 2001, Hall 2000, Pinsky 2001a, 2001, Sohn 2000, Vogl 2000). Yet - as reinforced by titles such as 'Saint Flanders' (Pinsky 2001c) - the focus is almost exclusively Christianity (Pinsky 2001a, Hall 2000). Diversity is evident within the community of Springfield, yet critical debates about ethnicity are a largely neglected. Two characters particularly stand out here - Willie, the school groundskeeper from Scotland with his absurd hyper-Scottishness, and Apu, the South Asian owner of the Kwik-E-Mart mini-supermarket in downtown Springfield. Each are ironically constructed as an exotic other but with a critical purchase on mainstream American society and values. Here attention will focus on Apu, the South Asian in Springfield.

Apu And Character

Apu Nahasapeemapetilon has appeared in numerous episodes, but only around 5 episodes centre around Apu himself.[1] It is these we will briefly

---

[1] Of 12 series with around 22 episodes each, Apu only occasionally had his own episode, yet he features quite frequently through the series. There is limited published literature. He is excluded from Vogl's reasonably comprehensive run through the characters, and the extended volume by Irwin et al (2001) only includes passing references (such as Homer and Indian Film, pp.97-98)

focus upon in this paper as illustration of the critical function of the 'cultural space' performed by this character. His fictional biography reads:

> Apu was born in Ramatur, Pakistan, but is no longer an Indian (*sic*) living in America, but an American Indian (not to be confused with a Native American!). In Calcutta he attended CalTech (Calcutta Technical Institute), where he graduated as the top student of his class of 7 million. He was accepted for graduate studies in the USA... (www.scar.utoronto 2002).

Apu is the South Asian immigrant in small town America, not a member of any South Asian community in downtown Springfield, but the lone South Asian shopkeeper and owner of the Kwik-E-Mart, 24 hours a day, 7 days a week mini-supermarket frequented by all the characters of *The Simpsons*. In due course he acquires a South Asian wife, Manjula, and we meet his brother, Sanjay, and his mother, but otherwise Apu's 'cultural space' is largely a personal one, centred around his counter and shelves.

There are numerous 'authenticating' stereotypes to his performativity,[2] notably his dress and appearance (and that of Manjula), his absurd South Asian accent, and the repeated references to his 'exotic' Hindu beliefs, veganism and:

> great disappointment, his attempt to bridge the gap between East and West with tofu dogs, curry crullers, and chutney Squishees (which) met with resounding disinterest from customers. (www.thesimpsons.com/bios)

Yet, Apu is no 'fish out of water' longing to jump back into the Indian ocean. He earnestly seeks out a new life in Springfield as an 'American Indian' (or what is more commonly called 'Asian American'). He is both the exotic outsider and also the accepted token South Asian, and nowhere is there ever any racial animosity shown - perhaps this is the necessary fiction of prime-time TV in a politically correct North American culture?

Tingleff (1998, p,2) makes the important observation that: 'the various characters of *The Simpsons* are less characters of personalities than they are characters of ideas. They are caricatures of the ideologies they represent.' This is an important distinction. And he further adds, 'unlike many sitcoms today, the show is not personality driven; it is about the conflict of ideas.' If

---

[2] 'Performance' might be defined as what individual subjects do, say or 'act out' within particular contexts (see Goffman 1956) 'Performativity' is the broader discursive and reflective, social and spatial practices of subjects within a context, reproducing (and being reproduced), and/or subverting (or being subverted) as identities, or displacements of difference (see Butler 1990)

The Simpsons[3] was played by actors, the family would seem unrealistic and undeveloped. As animated characters they can be merely the ideas they represent. For instance, Tingleff (1998) argues that Lisa Simpson does not have a full personality, she is 'rationality.' A similar interpretation is implied in Bronson's (2001) reading of baby Maggie. In this sense, Apu performs an idea of ethnicity and the South Asian immigrant in contemporary America. Furthermore, this is not merely the representation of South Asian identity, but a strategic deployment of a 'critical other' against both this stereotypical image of South Asian immigrant identity and the taken-for-granted identities and values of mainstream American society represented in Homer's family and Springfield. This construction of characters as a 'conflict of ideas' gives *The Simpsons* its potential social critical power.

Therefore, Apu can be 'read' as the idea of the stereotypical hard working South Asian immigrant shop keeper. He holds to and celebrates his ethnic origins, notably keeping to his Hindu beliefs, his strict veganism, and honouring traditional family values. Yet, he also illustrates a kind of 'hybridity' in his transformation of these cultural values and his non-Asian aspirations (see Bhabha 1994). He seeks to embrace American culture through his friendship with Homer (becoming a member of the bowling team for instance, living for a time at Homer's house etc) and through his efforts to become an American citizen (3F20/0723). Apu is not the subject of overt and aggressive racial harassment, he is not located within any ghetto (the Kwik-E-Mart is downtown and opposite Moe's, Homer's local bar, the Church and Krusty Burger, the burger bar) and he is not presented as part of any South Asian community. Apu's family - especially his wife Manjula - and his links to 'home' (the Indian sub-continent) are reference points that 'authenticate' his ethnicity, but his community and his friends are Springfield. Apu is *almost* the role model of American citizenship, a successful immigrant, but he critically retains his exotic otherness.

In the ironic juxtaposition of Apu, Homer and his neighbours, we are perhaps reminded of Deloria's critical comment about Native Americans and their culture in contemporary America:

the idea of learning from the Native Americans is problematic. Imposed on a variety of Indian peoples are layers of historical oppression, ideological pandering, and symbolic oversimplification... in the twentieth century the imaginary 'Indian'

---

[3] It is interesting to compare the now classic *Flinstones* with this series, and also to contrast it to the more recent *South Park*. In numerous ways these comparisons illustrate how cartoon comedy has developed over the last few decades and the distinctiveness of *The Simpsons* formula.

came to symbolise those mysteries of community, spirituality and harmonious relationships with the environment that the modern world has made increasingly difficult to find. (Deloria in Ballantine & Ballentine (ed) 1993, p.459)

In similar vein, Apu in *The Simpsons* functions ideologically and critically, performing not merely an idea, but critically the conflict of ideas within a simulated cultural space.

Springfield And Space

Cartoon space might, on the face of it, seem somewhat removed from the lived spaces of urban life and social discourse (e.g. Lefebvre 1991). Yet such 'virtual spaces' are far more than mere stylised representations of 'real' or fantasy spaces.[4] Even in the earlier (sub)urban cartoons such as The Flintstones, the landscape representation plays a key role in both establishing a context for the drama and in articulating particular social and cultural values through spatial forms and characteristics of the suburban house, street, and commercial strip. However, in The Simpsons this 'virtual space' is a far more complex (and often ambiguous) component of the performativity of the characters and events of Springfield, and critically its hyper-ironic critique on American society and values.

Springfield is not a representational space, but a hyper-real one in the sense in which Baudrillard (1983) refers to 'simulation' as the dominant order of contemporary culture (see Rodaway 1995). Although 'Springfield' is arguably one of the most prevalent place-names in North America, Springfield does not represent any particular town and its location remains illusive and neatly proximate to geographically disparate 'real' places referenced. In a very direct sense, this is a: 'model of the real without origin or reality: a hyper-real. The territory no longer precedes the map, nor survives it. Henceforth, it is the map that precedes the territory...' Baudrillard, op. cit. p.2)

In exploring the evolution of the image, Baudrillard observes a:

succession of phases of the image: it is the reflection of basic reality, it masks and perverts a basic reality, it mask the absence of a reality, it bears no relation to any reality whatever: it is pure simulacrum. (Ibid p.11)

---

[4] Space does not permit further discussion of the triad of *espace vecu, espace concu* and *espace vecu* (Lefebvre, 1991) but logically this framework could be applied to cartoon spaces.

The 'spaces' which are Springfield, and the performative arena of the characters of *The Simpsons,* might be positioned within this 'phasing' of the image. It is within this 'fluidity' of social and spatial performance that the hyper-ironic critique is articulated.

Furthermore, Apu as the ethnic minority character, the critical other in the Springfield community, might also be seen as performing 'a space of radical openness' (hooks, op. cit.). The black feminist bell hooks identified two types of 'marginality', that which is imposed by oppressive structures and that which one chooses as a site of resistance. This site of resistance she describes as a space of radical openness offering the possibility for segregated cultures to fight back against hegemonic cultures and assert their own identity. The South Asian identity performed through Apu, his Kwik-E-Mart and life in Springfield does not immediately present as a site of resistance yet, as suggested earlier, it does not present as a site of oppression. Apu's performativity is a kind of in-between space, but one with the transformative potential of that marginality to which bell hooks refers, 'a radical openness.' In this case, this 'resistance' is borne from the hyper-irony of character and storylines, at once a critique of mainstream American society and values, and at the same time doubly a critique of South Asian immigrant identity (see for instance Eight Misbehavin' - BABF03/1107). As Soja (1996, p.87) observes:

hegemonic power does not merely manipulate naively given differences between individuals and social groups, it actively produces and reproduces difference as a key strategy to create and maintain modes of social and spatial divisions that are advantageous to its continued empowerment and authority. 'We' and 'they' are dichotomously spatialised and enclosed in an imposed territoriality of apartheids, ghettos, barrios, reservations...

Yet, as hooks and other writers have demonstrated, these marginalities, can in time, through the performativity of segregated cultures transform themselves into sites of resistance, that is spaces of radical openness. Hegemonic power in capitalist societies (and perhaps in general) contains a fundamental contradiction in its articulation. It both differentiates hierarchically (the segregations referred to by Soja) and seeks to normalise these structures, yet to perpetuate itself must repeatedly reconstitute these differentiations. However, within the process of segregation and marginality, there lies the opportunity for the human agency of counter-hegemonic groups to assert alternative kinds of power explicated through their social and spatial practice. (see Gregson & Rose, 2000) With a kind of 'critical othering' between the margin (here the cultural space of a South Asian in Springfield) and the centre (Homer's Springfield), the potential for 'slippage of difference,' displacements of hegemonic power, are created through a hyper-ironic discourse (Matheson 2001) and process of hybridisation (see Bhabha 1994).

Performativity, Space And Critique

If 'cartoon space' is conceptualised as a 'critical cultural space,' it is possible to consider the cartoon characters as articulated in and through that space. In this sense, the character as a 'conflicts of ideas' (Tingleff 1998) 'performs' particular discourses of identity and power. In an earlier and highly influential conceptualisation of the interaction of individuals, society and space, Erving Goffman (1956) took a theatrical analogy, with individuals (or 'subjects') differentially acting out their social roles in varying social and spatial contexts 'as on stage' (e.g. McCannel, 1993) More recently, in the influential Gender Trouble, the feminist Judith Butler (1990) has developed a more politically charged concept of the 'performance' of identities. This is generally referred to as a concept of 'performativity' and is a broader discursive and reflective notion of subjects reproducing (and being reproduced) and/or subverting (or being subverted) as identities, or displacements of difference, within dynamic social (spatial and historical) contexts. 'Performativity' is a more inclusive concept and implies notions of human agency, social practice, and power. Therefore, it is the 'performativity' of the characters, as 'conflicts of ideas,' within the spaces of Springfield, rather than their mere performance as 'representations' of human subjects (or personalities) which gives The Simpsons its potential critical power as a critical cultural space.

Five episodes place Apu more directly in the spot-light and highlight issues of his Asian identity.[5] The idea of South Asian immigrant identity, as presented in the character of Apu, subsists not so much in Apu himself, as in his relationship to the other characters and events of Springfield, and especially Homer, and these are in turn articulated through particular spaces in the map of Springfield - for instance, the Kwik-E-Mart, Homer's home, and the bowling alley. This might be described as 'performativity' not in the restricted sense of drama or behaviour, but rather in the sense of position and articulation between characters, spaces and cultural discourses. It is for this reason that the collage and inter-textuality of representations of places, characters and event in *The Simpsons* is so important since these are the ingredients of irony and hybridity. In this sense, we avoid an essentialist and

---

[5] Episodes are coded alpha-numerically but for the purpose of this article a second four figure signifier is added - series number, episode number - e.g. 0723 represents episode 23 of series 7 which is also coded by Fox as 3F20. The alternative coding provides easier navigation through series.

representational reading of Apu's Asianness, and dig deeper to read the dynamic cultural space of Apu. This is performativity as a critical strategy of displacement of hegemonic discourses.[6] Social identities are constructed in and through social action, and this is articulated in and through particular spaces, and is in turn generative of particular social and spatial forms. Apu's performativity is an articulation of his positioning within (and counter to) Springfield society, a critical positioning which gives his character a critical purchase on hegemonic social values represented by Homer and much of Springfield's community.[7] Apu and his story-lines are therefore performative spaces which through a process of hyper-irony and hybridity operate as sites of resistance or 'spaces of radical openness' which critique both South Asian immigrant and mainstream (white) American values and identities.

At its simplest level, this performativity is dynamically constructed in the repeated interactions between Apu and other characters, most notably Homer. His relationship to Homer (and his family) is kind of 'critical othering.' In a sense, Apu is the critical opposite of Homer. Apu is hard working (behind the counter of his 24 hour, 7 days a week store), whilst Homer is fundamentally lazy and slap-dash (as his reaction to a nuclear melt down at the power plant illustrates, for instance). Apu's home is his counter, Homer's is his couch (with a Duff beer!). However, this is not merely an exotic 'other,' for Apu is not presented as the idea of ethnic oppression. Rather, Apu is the idea of a successful and accepted South Asian in Springfield, the immigrant who has found a position within his adopted society. In an ironic way, it is Homer, the caricature of urban male husbands in contemporary America, which is positioned as 'oppressed' by the very society and values he represents and celebrates. This relationship is further complicated by the degree of mutual adoration between the two, as illustrated in the various episodes where they seek in some way or other to ape each other – where it is Apu seeking American naturalisation, or Homer seeking to be romantic to Marge like Apu is to Manjula. Yet it is this which illustrates the transformative impact of Apu's performativity. In other words, the idea of Apu is not merely an object of subjugation or voyeuristic gaze, but a subject (or agency) of critique and transformative politics.

---

[6] In Butler's case she used this to displace heteronormative alignments of sex and gender, (Butler, 1990)

[7] Other characters also provide a critical displacement, notably Ned Flanders (the born-again Christian), Krusty the Clown (the entertainer) and Willie (the school caretaker).

Apu In Springfield

Homer and Apu (1F18/0513) typifies a key articulation of the character of Apu juxtaposed to Homer, something like his alter-ego. Where Homer is the all American, Duff drinking (beer swilling), couch potato, rather lazy nuclear plant worker, Apu is the immigrant, clean living, hard working, small businessman (Rousseve 2000). Their friendship, which develops throughout the various episodes is typically of a strong degree of mutual respect and a kind of admiration for what the other represents. In Homer and Apu, the Kwik-e-Mart is 'performed' as both a specific space - the place where Apu has sold tainted meat to Homer - and the idea of 'authentic' South Asian immigrant identity. Since Homer has eaten tainted meat from Apu's store, it is closed down. 'As an apology,' Apu moves in with The Simpsons and becomes their personal chef and valet. The 'servant' role is one traditional positioning of the 'exotic other.' Apu is not happy without his store which is the key performative space of his Asian American identity. Apu, with Homer, goes on a trek to the world's first Kwik-E-Mart, high up in the hills of India. This fantasy storyline reinforces the association of the mini-supermarket general store with South Asian immigrants, and seeks to 'authenticate' this South Asian identity. Homer foils Apu's chances of 'Kwik-E-Enlightenment,' and so makes him more depressed than ever. In typical 'happy ever' after style of cartoons, Apu regains his old store after saving the current shop keeper during a failed robbery. The relationship between Apu, the Kwik-E-Mart and the performativity of his Asian American identity is reinforced, but also Homer's American identity is also questioned.

Much Apu About Nothing (3F20/0723) focuses quite explicitly on Apu's attempt to gain a specific 'American' identity. When Proposition 24, an anti-immigrant law, is put into effect, Apu risks being deported as an illegal alien. Apu fails in his attempt to obtain fake papers and Americanize himself (with clothes, behavioural changes etc). Homer comes to the rescue as the 'all American guy' who tutors Apu to pass his naturalisation exam. In typical Simpsons critique of contemporary America, Apu 'proves too smart to be an American' but luckily he passes and is allowed to stay in Springfield. The school groundskeeper, Willie - another exoticised immigrant - is deported back to Scotland. *Much Apu About Nothing* is perhaps rather aptly titled, since Apu is neither rejected as 'authentic' Asian, nor completely 'normalised' as 'an American.' After all, his attempts at performing as an American 'dude' and decorating his store in explicit American symbolism fails. Springfield's residents prefer the Kwik-E-Mart and its owner just as he is, that hybrid blend of exotic other and Americanised South Asian capitalist. In 'proving too smart to be an

American' Apu's performativity reasserts the on-going critique of American mainstream society and values. Is Homer as American as Apu? The question is implicit, but absurd (other episodes articulate a similar theme, such as the Barbershop Quartet - 9F21/0501)

Apu's performativity is not merely a critique of hegemonic society, nor confined to the space of the Kwik-E-Mart. In *The Two Mrs Nahasapeemapetilons* (5F04/0907) we see a critique of a particular interpretation of traditional South Asian/Hindu family values and the arranged marriage, and - as hyper-ironic critique (Matheson op. cit.) - at the same time, a critique of Homer's (and mainstream American society's) values. It is interesting to note here, that this is the only episode where Apu's full name is given such prominence as a re-inforcer of his ethnic origins. Apu's mother visits Springfield to progress his arranged marriage, and Apu enlists Marge Simpson to pretend to be his (American) wife. There are a series of incidents which increases his mother's suspicions and in due course Marge and Apu reveal the truth. Apu's arranged marriage is back on in spite of his reservations. But when he meets his bride to be, Manjula, Apu is smitten with her beauty and 'good taste in movies.' The two are married and live happily ever after. The meeting of two cultures, and the conflicting aspirations of the immigrant are explored, yet at the end of the day, Apu's ethnic identity is presented both generically and specifically in a highly romanticised fashion. Manjula's beauty, taste in movies, and romantic love are what articulate Apu's marriage, rather than the more traditional values of family loyalties, religious belief or tradition.

I'm with Cupid (AABF11/1014) reinforces the romanticised view of Apu's marriage through the increasingly elaborate ways in which he expresses his love for his wife. In a Valentine's Day episode, the message is clearly critically showing up the all-American men of Springfield for their lack of romance. It is also an opportunity to feature the singer Elton John - another unique feature of *The Simpsons*, the 'starring' of famous names from the 'real' world. Throughout this episode, Apu's identity is reinforced as exotic other, but not so much as 'South Asian' other, as an 'American' ideal other, that more wholesome, romantic male juxtaposed to the Duff drinking, couch potato male typified by the men of Moe's bar and Homer Simpson. Again, Apu is not so much represented in his ethnicity, but presented in his critical otherness to both contemporary degenerativeness of American culture, specifically male identities and ironically (re)constructed idea of South Asianness. In these two episodes, the Asian cultural space which Apu, his mother and Manjula perform is a hybrid one, mixing 'Asian' and 'American' values and identities, but critically displacing Asian 'authenticity' and revealing the displacement of contemporary American marriage from its 'authentic' traditions.

This multiple irony (or hyper-irony) is again evident in other episodes where the critique is both of American mainstream culture and of the idea of South Asian culture which Apu represents. In a kind of Baudrillardian melee of inter-textuality, hyperreality and simulation, in *Eight Misbehavin'* (BABF03/1107) Apu and his wife decide to have a baby with the help of fertility drugs. This is the Americanised world of 'more is better' and the 'technological fix' but also the paradoxical construction of immigrant (in)fertility and 'paternalistic' capitalism. Apu and Manjula's attempt to conceive proves very successful and Manjula gives birth to octuplets. The association of large family (or fertility) with South Asian ethnicity is constructed here in a somewhat peculiar way, but Apu's exoticism is reinforced at the same time as opening a space for a critique of mainstream American society and values. The townspeople of Springfield celebrate the arrival of the multiple births, and local companies shower Apu and his wife with free products. But this is the mass media society of 'famous for a day', and when a Shelbyville couple have nine babies at once, all attention switches to them. Apu and Manjula are left to raise their babies, and Apu realises he needs help. He accepts the Springfield Zoo's offer to raise their babies behind the glass of a zoo exhibition. Notions of the exotic other and the freak are reinforced, but also - in typical styles of *The Simpsons* - there is also a critique embedded here of fertility drugs, media hype, and how life is valued as commodity in contemporary American culture.

Cartoon As Critique?

The question is whether humour – satire, parody, irony – can genuinely progress social critique (and ultimately revolutionary change) or does it dilute, defuse and ridicule it – and ultimately disempower, demotivate and neutralise the counter hegemonic. Hyper-irony has a number of 'risks' for any social critique. First it relativises everything, opening up both the hegemonic and counter hegemonic to ridicule. Secondly, - and this is an issue raised by a number of popular authors (see www.snpp.com) the degree and complexity of inter-textuality creates a degree of intellectual elitism[8]which disempowers or excludes a large amount of the audience. For most of the audience, many of the cultural references will be lost and this less informed audience will 'read' The Simpsons at a more superficial and literal level.[9] In other words, - if we can use the term – is 'postmodernism'

---

[8] It is interesting to note how many of the script writers of *The Simpsons* are Harvard graduates!

[9] Pinsky (2001) refers to his 'conversion' to *The Simpsons*, when he moved from this superficial reading to a more inter-textually and intellectually rich reading of the cartoon.

merely an intellectual irrelevance, a kind of grown ups puzzle-play which has little relevance to ordinary people's lives? Is it a strategy to debunk all and everything through irony, which achieves little more than political apathy and disempowerment in the audience/reader? Is Apu (and The Simpsons) therefore merely reinforcing (or reproducing) the very hegemonic values it seeks to question?

This is primetime TV that aims first and foremost to provide popular entertainment. In short, one might ask can multiple layers of irony, satire and inter-textual referencing, in urban soap style cartoon fantasy, effectively do more than make people laugh? This paper has argued that the saturation or articulation of *The Simpsons* by such 'hyper-irony' and hybridity opens up a complex performativity of social and spatial relationships and situations which sustain a social critique of contemporary American mainstream culture and South Asian immigrant identity. It is a 'space of radical openness,' offering the potential for transformative politics, because it escapes the essentialism, dualism and conformity of the merely humorous. Because hyper-irony sets everything against the other and itself simultaneously, dynamically and perpetually, there is no absolute ground or fixed oppositional politic of 'them' and 'us.' Instead, behind the veneer of Springfield's 'sameness' of a small town community and the familiar stereotypes, there is a conflict of ideas, a critical performativity expressed in a continual process of displacement and hybridisation of both the mainstream American society and values, and the exotic other (in this case South Asian immigrant identity). In seeking to identify the effectiveness of this social critique however, we cannot rely on the traditional dualities and hierarchies of social and spatial relationships, and must, in a sense, let ourselves fall into, and participate within, that transformative flow of making and remaking personal and social geographies and histories.[10]

Postscript: Apu And South Asian Culture

Apu describes himself as an 'American Indian' rather than 'Asian American.' (3F20/0723) This typifies the peculiar construction of South Asian culture within The Simpsons. On various occasions the attempt is made to 'authenticate' his South Asian identity, but often in naïve and contradictory ways. As noted earlier, his place of birth is a fictional town in Pakistan, yet he seeks Kwik-e-Enlightenment in the uplands of India. He is

---

[10] In a particularly perceptive reading of Bhabha, Rose (1995, p.365) argues that 'he is performing a subject position symptomatic of the contradictions of post-colonial discourse, contradictions he is also at the same time analysing'. This post Cartesian strategy is also evident in other post-modern writers (e.g. Baudrillard, Butler) and asserts the fundamental (revolutionary?) shift from criticism ultimately within a hegemonic discourse to a genuine counter- or post-hegemonic discourse.

repeatedly referred to as 'Indian,' yet himself asserts his 'American' signifiers at every turn. Even the Kwik-E-Mart is constructed as that all-American convenience store, and his failed attempts to sell tofu, curry and chutney delights are all American hybrid varieties: 'tofu dogs, curry crullers and chutney Squishees' (www.thesimpsons.com/bios). Although Apu is the South Asian immigrant, his South Asian identity is as Americanized as a second or third generation resident.

However, to describe Apu as representative of the South Asian identity of the Diaspora is equally misleading. Apu is the exotic other, yet he is not set apart as part of a wider South Asian immigrant community, nor does he identify with other South Asians in America (or outside the Indian sub-continent). Apu is a resident of Springfield, proud of his heritage, but eager to embrace his homeland - that is Springfield, and the America it represents. As Tingleff (1998) notes, the characters of *The Simpsons* function as 'characters of ideas,' and in particular the conflict of ideas. Apu is not so much the idea of South Asian identity - either diaspora or Indian sub-continent - as the performativity of a critical other. In other words, what is important here, is not that Apu is in any way is 'authentically' South Asian, but that he opens up a critical cultural space in which identities, and in particular American identities, can be questioned and perhaps transformed. Perhaps not surprisingly, Apu is 'about America' and in his own words "I am selling only the concept of karmic enlightenment." (www.scar.utoronto).

Bibiliography

Ballentine, B. & Ballentine, I. (ed) (1993) *The Native Americans: An Illustrated History,* Turner Publishing, Altanta, Georgia – note quote from Philip Deloria, p.459.

Baudrillard, Jean, (1983) *Simulations,* New York: Semiotext(e).

Bhabha, Homi, (1994) *The Location of Culture,* Routledge: London.

Bowler, Garry, (1996) *God and The Simpsons*; *The Religious Life of an Animated Sitcom,* http://www/snpp.com/other/papers/gb.paper.html

Bronson, Eric, (2001) 'Why Maggie matters: Sounds of Silence, East meets West' in Irwin et al (ed) *The Simpsons and Philosophy; The D'oh! of Homer,* Open Court Publishing: London & New York, pp.34-45.

Butler, Judith, (1990) *Gender Trouble,* Routledge: London.

Durban, Gabe, (2001) 'Tones of Morality Through Layers of Sarcasm; *The Simpsons* and its underlying themes,' http://www.snpp.com/other/papers/gd.paper.html

Goffman, Erving, (1956) *The Presentation of Self In Everyday Life,* Doubleday: New York.

Gregson, Nicky & Rose, Gillian, (2000) Taking Butler elsewhere: performativities, spatialities and subjectivities, Environment & Planning D: Society & Space, 18.4, pp.433-452.

Hall, James, (2000) Religious dialogues in prime time http://www.snpp.com/other/papers/jlh.paper.html

hooks, bell, (1991) *Yearning: Race, gender and cultural politics,* Turnaround, London.

Irwin, William; Conrad, Mark; Skoble, Aeon (ed) (2001) *The Simpsons and Philosophy: The D'oh! of Homer,* Open Court Publishing: London & New York (2002 edition)

Irwin, W. & Lombardo J.R. (2001) '*The Simpsons* and Allusion', in Irwin et al. (ed) *The Simpsons and Philosophy; The D'oh! of Homer,* Open Court Publishing, London & New York, pp.81-92.

Knight, D. (2001) 'Popular Parody: *The Simpsons* meets the Crime Film,' in Irwin et al (ed) *The Simpsons and Philosophy; The D'oh! of Homer,* Open Court Publishing, London & New York, pp.93-107.

MacCannel, Dean, (1993) 'Staged Authenticity: Arrangements of Space in Tourist Settings,' American Journal of Sociology 79, pp.589-603.

Matheson, Carl, (2001) '*The Simpsons,* Hyper-Irony and the Meaning of Life, in Irwin et al (ed) *The Simpsons and Philosophy: The D'oh! of Homer,* Open Court Publishing: London & New York, pp.108-125. (also available at snpp.com)

Pinsky, Mark, (2001a) The Gospel According to The Simpsons: The Spiritual Life of the World's Most Animated Family, John Knox Press, Westminster, USA.

Pinsky, Mark, (2001b) 'How big is The Simpsons', Christianity Today, 5th February.

Pinsky, Mark, (2001c) 'Saint Flanders' *Christianity Today* 26th January.

Rodaway, Paul, (1995) 'Exploring the subject in hyper-reality', in Pile S. Thrift N. (ed) *Mapping the Subject,* Routledge, London.

Rose, Gillian, (1995) 'The interstitial perspective: a review essay on Homi Bhabha's *The Location of Culture',* Environment & Planning D: Society & Space 13, pp.365-373.

Rousseve, Dan, (2000) Individualism versus Paternalism: An Analysis of Homer J. Simpson, www/snpp.com/other/papers/dr.paper.html

http://www.scar.utoronto.ca/~95barbar/ (2002) Kwik-e-Mart fan site which includes Biography of Apu, key quotes and other trivia (accessed April 2002)

http://www.snpp.com (2002) *The Simpsons* Archive compiled and maintained by Jouni Paakkinen including interviews, articles, book extracts, academic papers, fanscripts, complete episode listing and synopses. A 'complete' Simpsons Bibliography compiled by Bruce Gomes Sr. (accessed March/April 2002).

Sohn, Jon, (2000) *Simpson Ethics* www/snpp.com/other/papers/js.paper.html

Soja, Edward, (1996) *Thirdspace: Journeys to Los Angeles and other real and imagined places,* Blackwell Publishers: Cambridge, Mass. & Oxford, UK.

Tingleff, Sam, (1998) *The Simpsons as a Critique of Consumer Culture,* http://www.snpp.com/other/papers/st.paper.html

http://www.thesimpsons.com (2002) Fox TV Network's official site including various information such as character profiles, complete list of episodes and synopses. (accessed March/April 2002)

Vogl, Bastian (2000) The Simpsons and their world – a mirror of American Life? http://www.snpp.com/other/papers/bv.paper.html

How the Elephant Forgot its Politics. Cultural Identity and Difference in the Videogame: Taj the Elephant Genie in Rare's *Diddy Kong Racing*

James Newman and Claire Molloy

It has been argued that the power of racialised stereotypes is, in part, located in their ability to traverse historical and discursive contexts (Bhabba, 1997). Through an examination of discourses that constructed notions of 'Indian-ness,' this chapter demonstrates how linkages between nonhuman animals and racialised stereotypes served to emphasise colonial power in the nineteenth century. Concentrating on the cultural significance of the elephant, we argue that the nonhuman animal was discursively positioned in such a way that it has become intrinsically linked to Western European understanding of 'Indian-ness.' Moreover, we examine how this form of racialised stereotyping is reactivated within contemporary cultural contexts. Here we present a reading of the elephant-genie, Taj, that appears in the videogame Diddy Kong Racing and suggest that this character maintains discursive linkages with colonial discourses of the nineteenth century. Accepting that the videogame represents perhaps the current apotheosis of high-level human-computer interaction and that, for many, it is this feature or perhaps function, that marks the uniqueness of the genre, this chapter seeks not to explain gameplay as a complex of practices played out in real-time interaction. While this chapter presents a textual reading of the videogame, it does so neither to merely counterpoint the 'ludological' approaches of, for example, Aarseth (1997, 2001) and Juul (2001) that privilege the experientiality of play nor to simply align (2001) itself with the critical readings of narratologists (see Jenkins, 1993). Rather the approach here is founded on Newman's (2001, 2002a) claims that the simple designation of the videogame as an 'interactive' form masks a multiplicity of uses and experiences, not all of which demand direct engagement, or 'interaction' in its crudest terms, through the interface. Importantly, this approach encourages the consideration of player and non-player perspectives, practices, play and reading.

Introduction

At their 'Spaceworld 2001' trade conference, Japanese videogames developer and publisher Nintendo unveiled footage of their much-anticipated cartoon racing title. Amid the fast-cut footage of the various

Kongs struggling to control their unwieldy rhinoceros and ostrich steeds, a large blue-grey elephant, dressed in ornate faux-Indian garb flashed across the screen. These few seconds of videowall footage at a trade show signalled the return of Taj, the anthropomorphised 'Indian' elephant character that, on its appearance some five years before, had prompted a discussion of racialised stereotyping in videogames.

Generally, the issue of racialised representation depends upon the reduction and normalisation of particular 'fixed' cultural signifiers such that the power of the stereotype is in its becoming a form of knowledge. Thus, the stereotype finds discursive currency in knowledge/power relationships as something that is unchanging and knowable. Homi Bhabha contends that the fixed nature and repeatability of the colonial stereotype has ensured that it transfers easily between different historical and discursive contexts:

> For it is the force of ambivalence that gives the colonial stereotype its currency: ensures its repeatability in changing historical and discursive conjunctures; informs its strategies of individuation and marginalization; produces that effect of probabilistic truth and predictability which, for the stereotype, must always be in excess of what can be empirically proved or logically constructed. (Bhabba, 1997, p.66)

In this sense racial differentiation appears to move effortlessly between discursive moments reasserting the power of the colonial stereotype and the normalisation of 'otherness.'

The reactivation of colonial discourses in videogames is exemplified through the elephant form of the character Taj. Here, the complexity of relationships between Hindu mythology, colonial power and national identity are inscribed upon the videogame character read within a register of racialised stereotyping. As Bhabha has argued, colonial stereotypes have traversed temporal and discursive spheres to emerge within contemporary cultural spaces and practices. In other words, despite an historical separation of more than a hundred years, colonially constructed identities of the nineteenth century, and videogame characters of the twentieth and twenty-first centuries maintain discursive linkages. In *Diddy Kong Racing* the 'Indiness' of Taj references discourses of difference in which the elephant resonates with particular cultural significances. In this way, 'Taj' can be read at the cultural intersection of Western European colonialism, Hindu mythology and Indian national identity.

Context: Nintendo, Rare and *Diddy Kong Racing*[1]

The size, scope and influence of the contemporary videogames industry is considerable, yet in scholarly discourse, it is discussed with a concerning infrequency and often as merely an (immature and inconsequential) adjunct to more 'serious' or 'worthy' mediums such as film or even television. Because it is so poorly understood, it is useful to investigate the contexts in which this important medium presently exists and, more specifically, to interrogate and locate Diddy Kong Racing both as a popular cultural product and as an element of the continuing mythology that forms the Nintendo canon.

Running on the present generation GameCube platform, Spaceworld 2001's *Donkey Kong Racing* is a pseudo-sequel to *Diddy Kong Racing* released in 1996 for the previous generation of Nintendo console hardware, the Nintendo 64 (N64). Based largely around Nintendo's Donkey Kong character originally designed by Shigeru Miyamoto in the early 1980s and now part of the Super Mario mythology, both of the 'Kong Racing' games are developed by Rare (formerly Ultimate Play the Game), a UK subsidiary of Nintendo. Both games ape, to some extent, Nintendo's own seminal *Super Mario Kart* series in gameplay and aesthetic. *Diddy Kong Racing* was a key title in Nintendo's attempts to challenge the dominance that PlayStation has given Sony in the global videogames market. Consequently, the game was aggressively marketed with a US advertising budget of some $10 million. At the time, this was the largest budget for any N64 game. To cope with the anticipated demand arising from the marriage of marketing muscle and a well-designed and balanced game mechanic, in excess of one million cartridges were made available on the day of release in the US.

Nintendo's decision to effectively devolve responsibility for the Donkey Kong franchise to a UK developer is an interesting one as, in much of the videogames industry, character design and, it follows, character-led videogames, are seen as the province of Japanese developers. In short, neither European nor US developers are considered to possess the skills to rival the designs of Japanese developers such as Sega, Squaresoft, and

---

[1] The videogame is an increasingly significant cultural genre. The influence of the form is felt aesthetically and formally on a wide variety of media from film through television and literature. Moreover, in addition to the fact that sales of videogames have outstripped cinema box office takings and video rentals and in the UK since the beginning of this millennium, the sheer amount of time players engage with videogames demands that they be examined in more detail. While there has been some interest from psychologists keen to demonstrate the potentially damaging and harmful effects of videogames and gameplay, it is lamentably the case that there is little scholarly research in the field and that the majority of extant studies are flawed both methodologically and analytically. (see Emes, 1997 for a summary).

above all, Nintendo. However, like its parent, Rare has prided itself, and has received considerable praise throughout the industry and from players, in the strength of its character design. Consequently, while its titles have often featured a Nintendo-designed character in the central role (and we see this trend continuing with the forthcoming *StarFox Adventures*), Rare have lavished considerable effort in providing an original 'supporting cast' of characters. Through the 1990s, Rare developed a Donkey Kong family, for example, members of which would eventually take centre stage in their own titles (see the *Donkey Kong Country* series on SNES and *Donkey Kong 64* on N64, for example[2]). In addition, a number of original characters such as the bear/bird team Banjo and Kazooie (of N64 *Banjo-Kazooie* and *Banjo-Tooie*) cemented the developer's reputation for excellence in, amongst other things, character design.

One notable feature of both Rare and Nintendo's approach to game design is their use of characters 'across' titles. While it is unlikely that we will see Lara Croft outside a Tomb Raider game or engaged in activity other than running, shooting, climbing, and flicking switches, Rare and Nintendo appear keen to place their characters in as broad a variety of contexts as possible (hence Mario go-karting) and, importantly, to mix characters from different games together. In doing so, the boundaries that delimit specific titles are blurred and in place discrete gameworlds and franchises emerges a Nintendo 'universe.' *Super Smash Bros Melée* (GameCube) is a most potent example of this principle, bringing together characters from Nintendo's rich and varied history from manufacturer of portable Game & Watch titles, through the more recent Super Mario series and *Pokémon*. However, while *Melée* brings together and in some cases reunites characters from the videogaming annals, Rare's *Diddy Kong Racing* attempted similar boundary blurring, by mixing together existing characters with those designed specifically for this title along with those intended to presage Rare titles. At least part of the function of the title is to provide coherent context for the burgeoning Rare universe. Both Nintendo and, perhaps partly by

---

[2] The 16-Bit 'SNES' console (Super Nintendo Entertainment System) was released in 1991 in Japan and was the functionally identicial but remodelled and repackaged 'worldwide' version of the Super Famicom ('Family Computer') that had launched in Japan a year earlier. Bypassing the 32-Bit technology so successfully harnessed by Sony in their PlayStation (released 1994/1995), Nintendo's successor to their well-respected and surprisingly long-lived SNES was released in 1996 as the 'N64' (or Nintendo 64). The longevity of both the N64 and, perhaps even more, the SNES was ensured by continued support from Nintendo's own in-house development teams and their 'second party' developers such as Rare. Certainly, with titles like Rare's *Donkey Kong Country* wowing players and other developers, Nintendo were able to take on Sony in the initial stages of PlayStation's life even though their SNES hardware was considerably less sophisticated technically, particularly in its ability to render 3D gameworld environments.

association, Rare take great care to stress the family-friendly and, importantly, inclusive, nature of their products. 'Nintendo is committed to a fun, and safe, experience for kids' ('Information for parents,' Nintendo, no date). When Rare took the bold decision to rework one of their games and present it as the mature-themed, and self-mocking *Conker's Bad Fur Day* (*BFD*) complete with a cursing, swearing lead character, Conker the Squirrel, they went to great lengths to ensure that the game was not confused with the raft of 'family-friendly' titles in the current and back-catalogue, and that the developer's image was not tarnished.

> There were no risks taken with the marketing of Conker'd BFD...it's Mature rating meant that it was only advertised in channels catering to the older market (and not covered in the Nintendo Power website at all), while Nintendo made sure that they weren't selling *Diddy Kong Racing* or Conker's Pocket Tales at the same time as BFD so that there could be no mix-ups. Both Rare and Nintendo still make a wide range of family-friendly games: the occasional foray into older territory doesn't mark us out as adult developers for life (Answers to your Frequently Asked Questions,' Rare, n.d.).

Certainly, a consensus in the industry and among players suggests that Nintendo and Rare specialise in child-oriented, approachable, non-intimidating games. However, *Diddy Kong Racing* was lauded for the sophistication of its graphics, the precision of its vehicle handling routines, and above all, for the way in which it broke new ground by presenting a hybrid of the 'racing' and 'adventure' genres, praise was not unanimous.

In a letter to respected UK videogames journal Edge, Girish Mekwan highlighted concerns over some of Rare's characterisations.

> In light of the last two games from Rare, *Diddy Kong Racing* and *Banjo-Kazooie*, I'd like to point out that the largest games company in Europe is promoting stereotypical racism. The characters - Taj in *Diddy Kong* and the snake charmer...in *Banjo-Kazooie* - both speak with clichéd Indian (Asian) accents (even though the snake charmer is supposed to be Egyptian), which I find hard to stomach in this day and age...to see this type of content in games is frankly just bad taste and offensive. (Mekwan, 1998, p.153)

Girish Mekwan's comments echo the criticism of videogame commentators like Eugene Provenzo, who for over a decade have claimed that racism is rife within a videogames industry that is essentially purveying what are at best antisocial, or at best asocial, products. Citing research originally presented in Provenzo, he states that:

During the past decade, the video game industry has developed games whose social content has been overwhelmingly violent, sexist, and racist...Of the 47 most popular games...40 had violence as their main theme...13 included scenarios in which women were kidnapped and had to be rescued i.e. the idea of women as victims. (Provenzo, 1994, p.15)

The character of Taj in *Diddy Kong Racing* can be read as an example of racial stereotyping, reactivating colonial expressions of difference and 'otherness,' exoticism and mythology and reducing the historical and cultural complexity of 'Indian-ness' to a collection of essential characteristics. The 'Indian-ness' of 'Taj' is implied through recourse to a set of apparently fixed signifiers, the political currency and historical legacy of which have tended to be overlooked. Within colonial discourses the elephant functioned to emphasise the naturalised mastery of humans over nature; the submission of so large a beast to the will of 'man' could be offered as proof of the power of the human over nonhuman animals. However, the elephant also embodied a national identity and, as such, the relationship between the elephant and 'Indian-ness' discursively located it at a juncture between exoticism, docility, mythology and 'otherness.' Reading nonhuman animals within human social structures, the exhibition of Indian elephants in European zoos served to amplify the dominance of colonial power and constructed discourses within which nonhuman animals played a significant role in the politics of colonialism.

Colonial discourses

The elephant has been a main attraction in European zoos since the nineteenth century and contemporary zoos such as the San Diego Wildlife Park still offer the audience the opportunity to view 'African and Indian animals in realistic landscapes from the vantage of a slow moving monorail' (Franklin, 1999, p.63). Earlier zoos of the nineteenth century offered exotic nonhuman animals in barred cages for public display. The exhibition of nonhuman animals allowed Western European publics to view 'exotics' and configured the zoological gaze as an educational and scientific experience. As the opening statement of the Zoological Society of London proclaimed:

Should the Society flourish and succeed, it will only be useful in common life, but likewise promote the best and most extensive objects of the Scientific Nature, and offer a collection of living animals such as never existed in ancient or modern time...animals to be brought from every part of the globe to be applied to some useful purpose, or as objects of scientific research, not of vulgar admiration. (Mullan and Marvin, 1987, p.109)

As sociologist Adrian Franklin points out, nonhuman animals in zoos of the nineteenth and early twentieth century were read socially and:

> it was quite useful for non-Europeans to be represented as infantile and worse, animal-like. Because zoos contained exotic, non-European animals, this form of colonial condescension was clearly extended to them. (Franklin, 1999, p.69)

Nonhuman animals were often thought of in human terms and their behaviour read as humanlike. The authorial style of natural history writers offered readings of nonhuman animal action as suffused with human intention and agency (Crist, 1999, Molloy, forthcoming). In this way, nonhuman animals were considered to have emotional life-worlds similar to those of humans. The success of Charles Darwin's (1985, 1998, originally 1859, 1872) scientific writings at the end of the nineteenth century aimed to consolidate a scientific view of the shared emotional history of human and nonhuman animals with claims for evolutionary and emotional continuity between humans and the natural world. As the distinction between human and nonhuman animal was blurred at the level of agency, intention and emotion, so too was the distinction between non-Europeans and nonhuman animals. Discursively positioned as 'other', non-European peoples were summarily aligned with notions of animality, 'wildness' and 'exoticism.' Thus, the relationship between the humanness of nonhuman animals and the 'animality' of non-Europeans was blurred within colonial discourses. In this sense, the collection and exhibition of nonhuman animals from 'exotic' continents could be viewed as practices that served to emphasise Imperialist power (Ham, 1997).

Hunting and capturing elephants was a colonial leisure pursuit dating from the eighteenth century. With the influx of British women into India, leisure practices became clearly gendered by 1780. Tales of 'The Great White Hunter' were sent back to England to confirm a British masculinised dominance of wild exotic lands and their inhabitants. By the nineteenth century, these stories were accompanied by photographic evidence of successful hunts typically showing the hunter standing proudly beside the lifeless body of a 'foreign animal'. The elephant was not only hunted and captured but also used as a preferred mode of transport by colonial hunters intent on killing tigers. Elephants it was claimed, unlike horses, were not afraid of tigers (Ritvo, 1987, p.24). Colonial hunting expeditions intertwined with the leisure practices of India's aristocracy and it was common for Indian princes to arrange hunting parties for European guests. Mughal imperial entertainment had long included the hunting and capture of elephants. As the British elite became the 'Nabobs' of the late eighteenth century, aristocratic Mughal leisure pursuits were subsumed into colonial practices. Thus, the 'Indianisation' of colonial leisure added an exotic aspect to the tales of the White Hunter. Moreover, the elephant was clearly linked to the mysterious glamour of non-European aristocracy as evinced by the prose of a nineteenth century English naturalist writing for a young audience,

'The elephant is tame and wise, / And grows to a majestic size, / He carries Princes, in the east, / And is esteem'd a noble beast.' (cited in ibid. p.25)

Western Europeans could share a part of the exotic experience by visiting zoos where elephants were used to give rides to children and adults alike.

Despite claims for the nobility of the elephant, colonial hierarchies reinforced readings of the pachyderms as beasts that could be controlled and trained into socially acceptable roles, unquestioningly biddable to the demands of the European publics. Within the European zoo, the elephant was one of a range of specimens that reminded visitors of the continuing dominance of Imperialist power. With the correct training and control, the elephant could be trusted to come into contact with European bodies. Peculiar in that it was one of a small range of 'exotics' that interacted with humans in close physical proximity, the elephant was not just an object of the zoological gaze but a beast of burden, an entertaining form of transportation and a link to the mysterious 'east'.

The elephant was imbued with considerable symbolic significance. In Hindu mythology, characteristics such as patience, devotion and truth were inexorably imprinted upon it. According to Hindu myth, the elephant was the mount of the eight guardian deities, Indra, Agni, Yama, Surya, Varuna, Vayu, Kubera and Soma. Of these deities Indra, the god of the firmament, was the most important and his mount Airavata was the king-god of elephants. Also called Ardh-Matanga (elephant of the clouds), Arkasodara (brother of the sun) and Naga-Malla (the fighting elephant), Airavata was said to be completely white and have four tusks. Legend claimed that eight elephants had come from an egg held by Brahma, one of which was Airavata who then later emerged from the ocean when the gods churned up the waters. Ganesha, the elephant-headed son of Shiva and Parvati, was very popular with Indian nationalists during colonial occupation. Revered as a remover of obstacles, Ganesha was invoked prior to the commencement of any undertaking or significant event. According to the Shiva Purana, Ganesha was beheaded whilst standing guard at his mother's door. To console Parvati, Shiva ordered that the head of the first living thing that could be found was to be brought to him. The head of an elephant calf was delivered and Shiva used it to restore Ganesha's life. The mythological significance of the elephant was not lost on a European zoo-going audience but reconfigured as another aspect of Indian exoticism. Zoos housed elephants in inappropriate accommodation that included stylised Indian temples. References to the mystery of 'eastern mythology' were reinforced through the temple-like accommodation and thus constructed a colonially bound intersection between exoticism, animality and Indian-ness.

A colonial penchant for reading nonhuman animals in social terms meant that the elephant assumed a national identity and was discursively linked to forms of racialised stereotyping and moral judgement. Distinctions between Indian and African elephants exceeded those of the place of origin or externally perceived physical differences by also focussing on idiosyncratic humanlike attributes. As Harriet Ritvo explains,

> ...the only wild animals to receive the unqualified praise of natural history writers were those that could be persuaded at least partly to abandon their unregenerate state. Elephants were the major recipients of such appreciation. They could not be considered domestic animals because only the Indian elephant was routinely tamed. (Ibid. p.24)

The temperament of the Indian elephant was considered 'docile', 'mild' and 'magnanimous' ensuring that its larger African relatives did not have the same relationship with colonial hunters and European zoo-goers. The Indian elephant was routinely pictured carrying English ladies, gentlemen and children on its back and tales of the submissive nature of such a large beast served to amplify colonial power and human mastery (Ibid.).

The imposition of human structures on the natural world extended to the organisation of space within zoological gardens. Routes through zoos were described in guidebooks and would often suggest a single course through the exhibits based upon taxonomic classificatory systems. However, British sensitivity to the national identity of 'exotic animals' combined with the recognition of class distinctions was evident in the arrangement of exhibition spaces within the British Zoological Gardens at the turn of the century. Animal collections could be allocated space within zoos based upon criteria other than scientific classification as evinced by an article written for the Strand Magazine in 1906. Aimed at the educated middle-classes of the early twentieth century, the Strand article took its reader on a 'rapid tour' of the Zoological Gardens illustrated with one hundred photographs of the exhibits mentioned. Heading the article, a plan of the Zoological Gardens clearly showed a section of the zoo entitled 'The Prince of Wales' Indian Collection' where the reader was invited to:

'view the magnificent collection of Indian animals presented to the Zoological Society by H.R.H. The Prince of Wales on his return from his recent tour in India.' (Strand, 1906, p.534)

The maintenance of the relationship between national identity and social hierarchies meant that 'Indian animals' collected by a member of the British Royal family could be classed as a distinct grouping and allocated with their own space within the zoo. Consequently, a young Indian elephant was exhibited in the Zoological Gardens with the Indian antelope, Indian wild dogs and the Calcutta monkey but kept apart from the elephant house where all the other Indian elephants were located. Similarly the accompanying hundred illustrations in the Strand Magazine made a clear distinction between the two types of Indian elephant. The 'Young Elephant' included in the Princes' Indian collection was photographic illustration number 79, and the 'Indian Elephant' number 97 (1906, pp.532-533). Thus, colonial social hierarchies eclipsed scientific taxonomies, effectively subverting classificatory systems and reordering spatial arrangements, within the Zoological Gardens.

Taj the elephant genie, a case study

This ancient Genie, traditional guardian of Timber's island, isn't exactly pleased at being evicted from his mountain home. With Wizpig's magic keeping him cut off from his lamp and trapped in the outside world, Taj goes in search of a champion racer to challenge the uninvited guest and teach him a lesson in manners! ('The Cast List: *Diddy Kong Racing*: Taj', Rare, n.d.)

Upon starting a new Diddy Kong Racing session, the player is treated to a series of establishing shots panning across and swooping around the initially available spaces of the gameworld, outlining their interconnectedness and imbuing the gameworld with a spatial coherence. Importantly, the player is then located within the gameworld as the virtual camera comes to a halt placing the player's character centre-screen. Following some initial exploration, a further movie sequence introduces Taj. The elephant, standing upright on hind legs, bedecked in jewelled headdress and elaborately decorated waistcoat that Spaceworld 2001 attendees glimpsed in the Donkey Kong Racing teaser trailers traces his roots to this point. Here, however, he takes no part in the racing and is a supporting character. His first appearance is nothing if not grand, emerging from one of the many tunnels that lead from the central hub to the main play areas of Diddy Kong Racing's gameworld, riding a magic carpet, leaving a trail of magical stars in his wake. This strikingly exotic entrance, like every encounter with Taj in the game, is accompanied by the swirling drone of the tamboura and the musical shorthand of the flattened second, dominant seventh and sitar sample. Before long, the clichéd Indian accent that so enraged Girish Mekwan is heard as Taj announces himself to the player, offering his services. Taj's principal functional role in the game is to enable the player to select a series of options, for example changing their current vehicle from a selection of kart, plane or hovercraft. It is important to note that Taj is a non-playable character (NPC). That is, unlike Diddy Kong, Banjo et al that the player can select and race around Diddy Kong Racing's many tracks and locations, the player can not exert direct control over Taj per se. However, Taj is under the control, or perhaps, command of the player. That the character cannot be controlled directly by the player should not encourage us to consider him as independent or autonomous. Taj's role in the game is wholly subservient, literally doing the bidding of the player, powerless to resist. The player's wish is his command. Taj's few moments of freedom from the player are found in his pacing the grounds of the central hub space of the gameworld. However, even this minimal liberty can be halted at any moment by the player who, with a single blast of their vehicle's horn can summon Taj to them. Immediately appearing before the player as though by magic, Taj obeys each request for a change of vehicle with the same unquestioning obedience. No sooner has the player demanded a plane to replace their kart than, in a cloud of smoke, the plane appears.

Although not a directly selectable or playable character within *Diddy Kong Racing*, it is interesting to note that Taj quickly became something of an emblem for the game. Rare's dedicated *Diddy Kong Racing* webpages, for example, show Taj's beaming visage rather than that of the eponymous Kong. Taj's literal and functional centrality (literal in that he inhabits the hub of *Diddy Kong Racing*'s gameworld from which the various themed racing levels are accessed and functional in that it is Taj's mystical powers that allow the player to change vehicle) has ensured that the character is inexorably linked with the game despite the lack of playable control. The character's reappearance in the yet-to-be-released sequel (perhaps in playable form, though this has not been confirmed) is illustrative.

The discourse of difference – character selections

The player's first encounter with Taj takes place some way into the game. The elements and sequences that precede and frame the encounter(s) play an instrumental role in priming the player, and can be seen to encourage a particular type of engagement with Taj. The character selection screen is useful in exemplifying the ways in which the player is gently yet forcibly located within the gameworld's discourse of difference. Diddy Kong

Racing, like many games, and almost all racing games[3], presents the player with a choice of characters to choose from. Often the choice is offered at the beginning of each new level (as in Super Mario Bros. 2), or even at the end of a predefined series of tries or 'lives' (as in the Street Fighter II series). In Diddy Kong Racing, the choice is made at the commencement of a new game, essentially the beginning of a new adventure through Diddy Kong Racing's gamespace. Each of the characters available for selection is assigned a set of cultural characteristics that can be read in the register of racialised representation. As a consequence, cultural difference is foregrounded as a means of character differentiation and selection.

Diddy Kong Racing's character selection screen is not functionally dissimilar to that presented in *Super Mario Kart*, for example. The player is required to select their choice from the roster of possible characters available in the game (because the revelation of new characters occupies a central position as a staple of the contemporary videogame reward system, it is not uncommon to find that the roster of characters increases through time and with subsequent, and more successful, play). While it is possible to identify changes in the motivation for character selection through time, commensurate with experience and knowledge of the game and the matching of character capabilities and capacities to the demands of particular elements of the simulation such as specific tracks, objectives (imposed by the game or perhaps by the player) or even individual playing style and preference (see Newman, 2001, 2002a, 2002b) the character selection screen does not immediate enable decisions to be made on such bases. Gameplay-affecting functional differences of characters are not presented to the player, there are no statistical comparisons of acceleration, top-speed and cornering ability, for example as found in some games (eg *Ridge Racer Revolution*). In *Diddy Kong Racing*, these characteristics must be revealed through repeated play and experimentation. For many commentators, this tactile, exploratory deduction of the rules of the game, or perhaps, the parameters of the simulation, is one of the defining qualities of the videogame. (see Friedman, 1995, 2002). However, irrespective of whether it can be considered to represent a defining quality of videogaming and a mechanism through which pleasure is derived from gameplay, *Diddy Kong Racing*'s character selection screen presents the choice of character not in terms of the values of a system of objects within a simulation but rather in terms of aesthetics. Characters are designated and differentiated audio-visually. Each character has its own unique appearance, its own theme tune that is dynamically introduced as the player's cursor moves

---

[3] There are a few exceptions to this truism. Most notable is Sega's single-car *F355 Ferrari Challenge* (Dreamcast and coin-op).

across the lineup, and can be prompted to utter a few words of sampled speech introducing themselves.[4] In fact, the characters also have their own dance routine to complement the theme tune and vocalisation, their gait and co-ordination further embellishing their characterisation and potentially giving the more astute player clues as to the relative strengths and weaknesses of the character as an object within the simulation. Even a cursory examination of the available characters reveals that Taj is by no means *Diddy Kong Racing's* only stereotype. 'Banjo', the brown bear appears as an ungainly, somewhat oafish 'Hillbilly', accompanied by bluegrass, fingerpicking banjo; Diddy Kong, the cheeky monkey's are accompanied by congas and bongos. While it is clear that longer-term character selections shift away from simple selections of appealing or cute characters as the player better understands the simulation and the role each character allows them to play within it, the presentation of character selection in terms of aesthetics initially encourages the player with no knowledge of the simulation to discern and discriminate on the grounds of audio-visual appearance.

For many players and even developers, the character selection process is often bracketed with sequences such as pre-rendered movie cut-scenes, high score tables or even (on-screen) instructions and tutorials. Because there is typically limited or perhaps even no direct input from the player, these sequences are often seen as existing 'outside' the game, or more accurately, outside 'play'. Regardless of the appropriateness of such binary distinctions (see Newman, 2002b for example) the impact of the choices made here, and more importantly, the very fact that choices are made at all, impacts significantly on the player and the manner and mode of their subsequent engagement[5].

Representing Indian-ness and Indianicity

Exposing the discursive connections between colonial notions of Indian-ness and videogame characterisations, Taj exemplifies the ability of racialised forms of representation to maintain linkages between seemingly disparate historical contexts. As a consequence, it can be argued that Taj is revealed as a stereotype that references colonial discourses of the nineteenth

---

[4] The themed music is not limited to this selection screen as upon selection, the 'appropriate' style continues to accompany the remainder of the gameplay.

[5] Moreover, differentiation is not confined to the initial character selection screen and continues through the game. In fact, Taj is rendered instrumental in perpetuating the consideration of difference. While the initial character selection cannot be reversed within a session of play, further options are available to the player. As we have seen, one of Taj's roles within the game is to do the bidding of the player, magically transforming their mode of transport, from kart to plane to hovercraft.

century. The power of the stereotype is located in its fixed nature whereby cultural complexity can be reduced to a set of essential characteristics and naturalised as 'truthful' within power/knowledge relationships. In this way, the cultural complexity of Indian-ness is reconfigured within discourses at the juncture between colonialism and the politics of cultural identity. This discursive framework makes reference to historically specific moments in the construction of Indian-ness, reactivating colonially determined notions of otherness and relocating them within a contemporary cultural context. The naturalisation of racialised stereotypes tends to disguise the historical contexts within which they are constructed ensuring that the politics of such representations are not immediately apparent. However, a close reading of the character Taj reveals that representations of 'Indianicity' within the videogame Diddy Kong Racing rely upon the reactivation of colonial discourses wherein Hindu mythology, exoticism and national identity were intrinsically linked with 'animality' and anthropomorphised nonhuman animals. Thus, the body of the elephant becomes a site upon which 'Indianicity' can be inscribed through reference to particular cultural signifiers and discourses. Moreover, the anthropomorphisation of the nonhuman animal (in this case the elephant) enables the ascription of racialised characteristics, which are then configured as 'Indian-ness'. This would tend to imply that relationships between cultural identity and nonhuman animals, or between Indian-ness and the elephant, rely on more complex interconnections than simply referencing the place of origin of an indigenous species. In other words, the Indian-ness of Taj does not rely upon any sort of accurate representation of an Indian elephant (as opposed to an African elephant for example). Taj is a stylised depiction of an elephant that is attributed and ascribed with signifiers of Indian-ness. What is constituted as Indian, in the case of Taj, must then necessarily reference discourses that construct Indian-ness and appropriate the 'relevant' cultural signifiers to establish the cultural identity of the videogame character. Depoliticising the racialised framework within which the characters are constructed, cultural identity becomes a functional element in the videogame whereby character selection is facilitated. However, the example of Taj reveals that notions of Indian-ness and Indianicity maintain connections with the colonial reconfigurations of Hindu mythology and Mughal leisure practices which centralise the elephant as something distinctly 'Indian' through its exoticism, mythological symbolism and via its significance in aristocratic hunting practices. Signifiers of each of these aspects of 'Indian-ness' are apparent in the representation of Taj, and as such, their referencing of colonial constructions of Indianicity means that Taj is burdened with the politics of racialised representation.

Postscript

Since their arrival in the console videogames marketplace, Microsoft has been keen to establish an in-house development programme so as to alleviate its reliance on third-party studios. Consequently, wishing to benefit from franchises such as Perfect Dark, during summer 2002 it purchased Rareware from Nintendo. However, while details of the buyout remain cloaked in commercial secrecy, it is understood that the rights to the franchises and characters with the Nintendo canon will remain with the Japanese corporation.

Bibliography

Aarseth, E. (1997) *Cybertext. perspectives on ergodic literature,* Johns Hopkins University Press, Baltimore, Md. London.

Aarseth, E. (2001) 'What kind of text is a game?' paper presented at International GameCultures Conference, Bristol, 29 June-1 July.

'Answers to your frequently asked questions' (n.d.) Rare corporate website, http://www.rareware.com/ accessed July 2002

Bhabba, H. (1997) *The location of culture* London: Routledge.

Crist, E. (1999) *Images of animals: anthropomorphism and animal mind* Philadelphia: Temple University Press.

Darwin, C. (1985) [1859] *Origin of species,* Penguin, London.

Darwin, C. (1998) [1872] The expression of the emotions in man and animals, Harper-Collins, London.

Emes, CE. (1997) 'Is Mr Pac Man Eating Our Children? A Review Of The Effect Of Video Games On Children' *Canadian Journal Of Psychiatry,* 42, (4) pp.409-414

Franklin, A. (1999) Animals and modern cultures: a sociology of human-animal relations in modernity, Sage, London.

Friedman, T. (1995) 'Making sense of software: computer games and interactive textuality' *in:* Jones, SG. (ed) *Cybersociety: computer-mediated communication and community,* pp. 73-89)

Thousand Oaks, CA: Sage Publications (also available online at http://www.game-research.com/art_making_sense_of_software.asp)

Friedman, T. (2002) 'Civilization and its discontents: simulation, subjectivity, and space,' *in:* Greg Smith (editor). *Discovering discs: transforming space and place on CD-ROM.* New York University Press, New York (also available online at http://www.game-research.com/art_civilization.asp)

Ham, J. (1997) 'Taming the beast: animality in Wedekind in Neitzsche' *in:* Ham, J. & Senior, M. (1997) *Animal acts,* Routledge, London, pp. 145-164

'Information for parents' (n.d.) Nintendo (of America) corporate website, http://www.nintendo.com/parents.jsp/ accessed July 2002

Juul, J. (1998) 'A Clash between Game and Narrative', paper presented at the Digital Arts and Culture conference, Bergen, 26-28 November.

Juul, J. (2001) 'Games Telling Stories - a brief note on games and narratives', *GameStudies: the international journal of computer game research* 1(1), http://www.gamestudies.org/ accessed Sept 2001

Jenkins, H. (1993) ' "x Logic": Repositioning Nintendo In Children's Lives' *Quarterly Review Of Film And Video*, 14 (4) 1993, pp.55-70

Masson, J. & McCarthy, S. (1996) When elephants weep: the emotional lives of animals, Vintage, London.

Molloy, C. (forthcoming) Anthropomorphism and the popularisation of science.

Mullan, B. & Marvin, G. (1987) *Zoo culture*, Weidenfeld & Nicholson, London.

Mekwan, G. (1998) 'Letter to the editor' *Edge* (63) October, Future Publishing.

Newman, J. (2001) *Reconfiguring the videogame player* Paper presented at 'GameCultures international computer and videogame conference', University of the West of England, Bristol, 29 June-1 July.

Newman, J. (2002a) 'The myth of the ergodic videogame' *Game Studies* Vol 2 (1) [online] available at http://wwwgamestudies.org/0102/newman

Newman, J. (2002b) 'In search of the videogame player: the lives of Mario' *New Media & Society* Vol 4 (3) pp.407-425

Provenzo, E (1991) *Video kids: making sense of Nintendo,* Harvard University Press, London.

Provenzo, E. (1994) 1993 Joint Hearing Before the Subcommittee on Juvenile Justice, 103 Congress, serial no J-103-37, Dec 9, 1993, Mar 4 & July 29, 1994, p15

Ritvo, H. (1987) The animal estate: the English and other creatures in the Victorian age, Harvard University Press, Massachusetts.

The cast list: *Diddy Kong Racing*: Taj', (n.d.) Rare corporate website, http://www.rareware.com/ accessed July 2002

'Our '100 picture' gallery: no II – round the zoo' in *Strand Magazine*, Vol xxxii, November 1906, no 191, pp. 530-535

Notes on Contributors

Dr Anna Claydon is Lecturer in Film Studies at Edge Hill College of Higher Education. Her Ph.D. upon masculinity and sixties British cinema, was gained at the University of Kent at Canterbury, where the ideas for her chapter began to take shape. She is currently continuing work upon British cinema, teaching, and is academic co-ordinator of the Christopher Roby Archive of Film Text (CRAFT) at Edge Hill.
e-mail: claydona@edgehill.ac.uk

Karen D'Souza   An Associate of the   International Centre for Development and Environmental Studies (ICDES),   teaches English Literature at Edge Hill and jointly runs a module on the Popular Culture of South Asia in Human Geography. She writes creatively and is currently editing a forthcoming volume of poetry. Her prominent current research includes South Asian women's writing in the postcolonial period and has a long association with India where she has travelled extensively.
e-mail: karen@dsouza121.freeserve.co.uk

Dr Stephen Gregg is a lecturer in English Literature at Edge Hill. Publications include various articles on masculinity in Defoe and early eighteenth century sermons. He is currently researching male-male friendship in the eighteenth century and the literature of Eighteenth-century Empire.
e-mail: greggs@edgehill.ac.uk

Dr Clive Grey studied linguistics at Bangor and Cambridge. After teaching English as a foreign language in the south of England he worked in various Swiss universities, then came to Edge Hill to teach sociolinguistics and phonetics. He researches extensively into issues of language, identity and expressions of cultural difference and conflict and he advises Taylor and Francis (Routledge) on the suitability of new texts on sociolinguistics for various audiences.
e-mail: greyc@edgehill.ac.uk

Iain Jackson studied architecture at the Liverpool School of Architecture. He is currently in private practice in Manchester. His interests revolve around urbanity, the representations of space and the effects of colonialism on UK and Indian cities. His architectural strategies and designs are currently under publication along side other schemes by the University of Westminster. e-mail: lowlife90@hotmail.com

Claire Molloy is a lecturer in Media and Communication at Edge Hill. Her main research interests are cultural histories of nonhuman animals; anthropomorphism as cultural practice and relationships between institutional discourses and moral philosophy. Recently has completed joint research on 'cultural hybridity' of Indian Cinema in the 1950s. e-mail: molloyc@edgehill.ac.uk

Annie Montaut, former fellow of Ecole Normale Supérieure, presently professor of Hindi and Indian linguistics in Inalco, Paris, and translator (Hindi contemporary literature: KB Vaid, N. Verma, A. Saraogi, J. Kumar, A. Mishra). Director of a research unit on south Asia literary and aesthetic creation in the Centre d'Etudes sur l'Inde et l'Asie du Sud in CNRS/EHESS, Author and editor of a dozen books (including Voix, Aspects et diatheses en Hindi, Peeters, Les langues d'Asie du Sud, Ophrys, Le Rajasthan, ses dieux, ses cultes, son peuple, Presses de l'Inalco, Le Datif (Cahiers de Linguistique de l'Inalco). e-mail: Annie.Montaut@ehess.fr

Dr James Newman is Senior Lecturer in Media and Communication and Programme Leader for BA (Hons) New Media at Edge Hill. His main research interests are in computer and videogames; interface design, usability and accessibility, and audience ethnographies. Recent publications include 'In search of the videogame player' New Media and Society, 'The myth of the ergodic videogame' Game Studies. Current projects include a volume on videogames for Routledge (2003). He is the Managing Editor of the e-journal GBER (Global Built-Environment Review). e-mail: newmanja@edgehill.ac.uk

Dr Paul Rodaway is Head of School of Sciences & Sport at Edge Hill. His research interests include individual and sensuous geographies, socio-spatial experience within electronic media, and postmodernism. Recent publications include the book Sensuous Geographies: Body, Sense & Place (Routledge) and contributions to a number of collections, including Mapping the Subject (Routledge). e-mail: rodawayp@edgehill.ac.uk

Dr Tasleem Shakur was elected as a Fellow of the Royal Society of Arts (FRSA) in 1996. Having taught at Oxford Brookes, University of Sheffield and SOAS (University of London) is currently the Co-ordinator/Senior Lecturer in Human Geography and Director of ICDES (International Centre for Development & Environmental Studies) at Edge Hill. He has published extensively on Development, Environment and South Asian Cultural Studies. He edits the e-journal on Architecture, Planning, Development and Environment (GBER: www.edgehill.ac.uk/gber). Recent major publications include *Unsustainable Environment and the Cities of the Developing World* co-authored with N. Dasgupta and D. Treloar, published simultaneously by Hegemon, City Press and Vrije Universiteit (Amsterdam).
e-mail: shakurt@edgehill.ac.uk

Professor John Simons is Head of the School of Humanities and Arts at Edge Hill. His main interests are in English popular culture of the early modern period and literature and the environment. Recent major publications include his monograph 'Animal Rights and the Politics of literary Representation' (Palgrave) and an edition of Robery Parry's romance 'Moderatus' (Ashgate).
e-mail: simj@edgehill.ac.uk

Claire Spencer-Jones is a lecturer working at Edge Hill. She is working on her PhD thesis on James Joyce's Ulysses at Manchester University. Her publications include 'Kristeva and the Magpie' in Manuscript and 'Mosquitoes and Magnolias' in The James Joyce Quarterly.
e-mail: claire@spence-n.demon.co.uk

Sylvia Woodhead, currently Senior Lecturer in Human Geography at Edge Hill, has a long background in geographical education. Her research interests include investigations into how people perceive places, both local and distant.
e-mail:woodhs@edgehill.ac.uk

Index

Open House Press

Open House Press is a new publishing venture that has as its primary remit the sharing of information on global issues by writers around the world.

Open House Press welcomes manuscripts from authors wishing to write on issues to promote and share knowledge and information about multicultural, social and political development in the non-western world.

Writers on post-colonial development or environment affairs are strongly encouraged to submit manuscripts for possible publication.

Open House Press is not a political publisher as such: it offers authors the opportunity to write from any contemporary or historical political perspective, as long as the views expressed do not cause offence to potential readers.

Open House Press publishes manuscripts written from a strongly academic perspective by experts in their field, by people working in the third world, not necessarily first language speakers of English.

If you have a title that you would like us to consider for possible publication please contact: mail@openhousepress.co.uk

Forthcoming from Open House Press:
Architecture and Planning around the World:
Emerging Trends in Built Environment Practice

Editor: Tasleem Shakur

This volume represents a synthesis of recent articles that appeared in the electronic journal: Global Built Environmental Review, a journal devoted to architecture, planning, development and the environment.

MY BACK HURTS!

A GUIDE TO UNDERSTANDING WHAT'S WRONG AND CHOOSING THE BEST TREATMENT

RICHARD M. WESTMARK, MD, FAANS

Paperback ISBN: 978-1-970079-92-0
eBook ISBN: 978-1-970079-93-7

Published by Opportune Independent Publishing Co.

For permission requests, write to the publisher, addressed "Attention: Permissions Coordinator" to the address below.

Email: Info@opportunepublishing.com

Address: 113 N. Live Oak Street
Houston, TX 77003

TABLE OF CONTENTS

INTRODUCTION

Has your back pain prevented you from sleeping or sitting properly? Or, have you been unable to do daily activities with ease because of pain and discomfort? Every day there are millions of people living with back pain and suffering in silence. Thanks to **My Back Hurts!**: *A Guide to Understanding What's Wrong and Choosing the Best Treatment*, you no longer have to be a part of that group. This handbook has been designed to be the No.1 resource for those suffering from back pain.

As a noble Harvard-trained neurosurgeon, with fellowship training in spine surgery, Dr. Richard Westmark has thoughtfully created this guide to help the non-medical person get closer to understanding their back problem and choosing the proper treatment. While reading, you will begin to understand the specific terms and concepts that will assist in making decisions about diagnosis and treatment options. Oftentimes, reading medical-related books can be very confusing and the information can easily go over your head. This guide is very unique because a medical background is not required in order to understand what is wrong with your back and what to do about it.

Dr. Westmark has "de-coded" the complicated terms and acronyms commonly used by doctors and has written this handbook in everyday plain English so that you can clearly understand your problem and possible treatment options. It is designed to avoid having to Google every other word or giving up because you can't understand the terms being used.

This book is an organized solution for people with many types of back pain. Ranging from those with a new onset of pain who are concerned that it could be something more serious, to the person with months to years of back pain who can't stand in the grocery store checkout line. This jewel will make the possibility of living pain-free part of your future!!

To keep it simple and straightforward, this book has been organized so that you can get through the fluff and find your path quite quickly. Each section is arranged for you to go into as much depth as you'd like, or to get right to it.

THE SIX SECTIONS INCLUDE:

1. Frequently Used Medical Terms

This section will help you better understand all of the odd words and acronyms you've heard doctors say. You can use it as a very basic *back pain dictionary.* You can also use these terms as a way to describe what's going on and/or to communicate better when consulting with your doctor. These are not necessary to know to get to the solution and treatment of your back pain, but it is always good to know as much information as possible for you to communicate your experience.

2. Introduction to Back Pain and Understanding the Types of Back Pain

It's easier to solve problems when you know all of the possible answers! Back pain sounds very general, but many dynamics are in play all at once. Knowing the specific type of back pain you are having can save you a lot of time looking in the wrong places.

3. Diagnostic Testing and the Spine Doctor's Office Visit

It is important to know and understand the tests that may be ordered by your doctor to help to identify the source of your pain and suffering. When you are going to see the doctor, it's valuable to understand the tests you may have to undergo and why they are important. This information potentially could help you save money and decline specific tests as well.

4. Treatment options
Once the cause of your back pain has been identified, you typically have multiple options for treatment. This section will describe what each treatment will entail, how and why it's done, and advice for helping you decide which to choose. This is a very critical part of the book because it holds the key to put you on a path towards the solution of your suffering.

5. Being proactive
The old adage, "An ounce of prevention is worth a pound of cure," definitely applies here! This section will offer steps you can take to have a strong back and keep it well. Getting rid of back pain is one thing, but keeping it from ever getting started, or worse yet, returning is even more important!

6. Frequently Asked Questions
Dr. Westmark has constructed a list of questions he most commonly is asked over the last 30 years of treating patients for back pain.

SECTION 1
Frequently Used Medical Terms

Unless you have been to medical school, you probably wouldn't know all of the medical terms that doctors regularly use to describe your condition. Most people have been in a situation where they are clueless about what the doctor is talking about because he/she is throwing out terms and acronyms that you've never heard before. This is always an uncomfortable situation because obviously, you want to know exactly what is wrong, but asking "What does that mean?" after every other word is even more prickly.

This section is here to assist you in uncovering some of those mysterious terms and acronyms. You can use this as a reference during your doctor's visits, and can keep this pocket-sized book at your fingertips anytime you hear something new about your back.

COMMONLY USED MEDICAL TERMS:

Anterior: Toward the front of the body.

Posterior: Toward the back of the body.

Superior or cranial: Towards the top of the head, upwards.

Inferior or caudal: Literally towards the tail, downwards towards the feet.

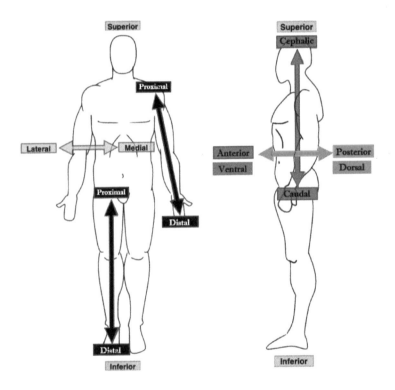

Vertebrae: The individual bones that make up the spine. This is the plural form, meaning more than one. When talking about just one bone, doctors use the singular form, vertebra. In the majority of people, there are 7 cervical vertebrae (bones in your neck); 12 thoracic vertebrae (bones of your spine that have ribs and are in your mid to upper back), and 5 lumbar vertebrae (bones of your spine in your lower back).

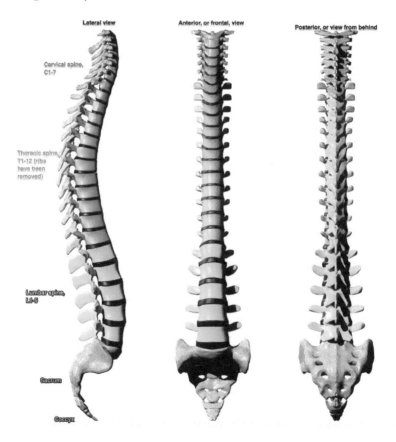

Lateral view   Anterior, or frontal, view   Posterior, or view from behind

Cervical spine, C1-7

Thoracic spine, T1-12 (ribs have been removed)

Lumbar spine, L1-5

Sacrum

Coccyx

Thecal sac: A sack filled with spinal fluid inside your spine that surrounds the spinal cord and nerves.

Intervertebral disc: The structure between the vertebrae that absorbs impact and, along with the facet joints, allows the spine to bend. Often described as similar to a jelly-filled donut, the inner (jelly) portion is actually the consistency of boiled shrimp meat. The disc has a tough outer band which is like a belt and is called the annulus. This is the structure that may be torn, thus allowing the inner jelly portion to herniate or "slip out".

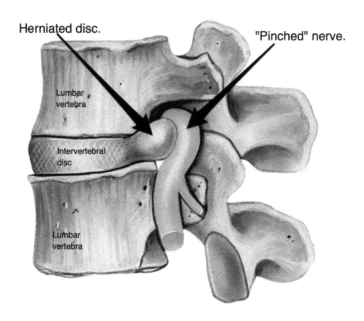

Herniated disc.

"Pinched" nerve.

Lumbar vertebra

Intervertebral disc

Lumbar vertebra

Herniated intervertebral disc ("Herniated disc" or "slipped disc"): The "pillow-like" cushion between the vertebrae has a tear in the outside lining that allows the inside of the disc to come out into the back of the spine where it may pinch a nerve root or narrow the spinal canal. Most herniated discs don't cause symptoms so just being diagnosed with one only matters if it is thought to be the source of your pain.

Spondylo*sis*: This is a very non-specific term used to describe any non-traumatic degeneration of the spine. It effectively is the same as "arthritis" of the spine.

Spondylo*lysis*: A broken bone that is present in the posterior part of the vertebra, almost always involving the lowest lumbar vertebrae. In the majority of cases, this is something that occurred very early in life rather than something that you develop as an adult secondary to trauma.

Spondylo*listhesis*: (aka "slipped vertebra) The vertebra has slipped abnormally forward or backward relative to the next vertebra below it. In young people, this is usually at L5/S1 and related to spondylolysis. In older people, this is more likely at L4/L5 and is due to degeneration. This is graded 1 through 5 based on the percentage of slips. Grade 1 is up to 25% and grade 4 is up to 100%. In grade 5, the entire vertebral body has slipped in front of the one below it.

Degenerative changes: Like spondylosis above, these changes can be thought of as "arthritis" of the spine. As we age, the tissues supporting and cushioning the spine also age and begin to wear out. This may result in the bony part of the spine becoming larger (called **bony hypertrophy**) and pressing in on the spinal canal (**spinal stenosis**) and nerve roots. Degeneration of the discs and facet joints may be painful but are also very common with age and don't necessarily lead to pain.

Osteophyte (aka "bone spur"): an abnormal growth of bone in response to degenerative change. It can protrude and possibly result in symptoms if it contacts a nerve root or severely narrows the spinal canal.

Facet joint disease: (aka **facet** syndrome, spinal osteoarthritis, **facet** hypertrophy, or **facet** arthritis), is a spinal condition when the joint on the back of the vertebra that connects one vertebra to another may become enlarged due to degenerative change. This is a common cause of back pain.

Spinal stenosis: A "stenosis" simply means narrowing regardless of the cause. Stenosis doesn't always cause symptoms. If it does, it can cause symptoms from compressing individual nerves (sciatica) or the entire sac of nerves causing claudication.

Claudication: This is the onset, or worsening, of back and leg complaints that gets progressively worse with walking. If claudication is from spinal stenosis (known as neurogenic claudication), it is typically relieved by bending forward. For example, a person with neurogenic claudication will walk further and with less pain when leaning forward on a grocery cart. The other type of claudication is "vascular claudication" from poor blood flow to the legs. This is typically not relieved by bending forward. Because the problem is blockage of blood flow to the legs, the pulse (sensation of the heartbeat sending blood to your legs that the doctor feels on top of your foot and behind the inside of your ankle) may be reduced and discoloration of the feet and lower part of the legs may be seen.

SECTION 2
Introduction to Back Pain and Understanding the Types of Back Pain.

For all people suffering from back pain, the description of the pain varies widely and the potential causes are incredibly diverse. The back is composed of many elements and is a pretty complex area of the body to diagnose. When you say, "My back hurts," that can mean one of many things. For example:

- You are having muscle spasms
- You pulled a muscle
- You have a kidney issue
- You have a herniated disk
- You have arthritis, or
- Something else

These examples represent vastly different conditions in terms of consequences and treatment options. But all of these can be translated into "My back hurts." That's why it's great to have a guide like this one so that you can better explain and understand the difference in pain and be able to effectively communicate it.

MIMICKERS OF BACK PAIN

There are some important mimickers of back pain where pain "radiates" to the back and is incorrectly attributed to it.

Key Mimickers of Back Problems

- Abdominal Aortic Aneurysm (AAA)—pain seems to bore through to the back, older adult patients are more commonly affected, pulses in the feet may be reduced.
- Kidney stones—Typically severe pain that radiates around into the flank rather than down your back, posterior thigh and into the leg. Blood in the urine is an important clue that this may be the cause of your back pain.
- Kidney infection (aka pyelonephritis)—As above for kidney stones except also burning with urination and fever.
- Other intraabdominal problems including: pancreatic cancer or pancreatitis (inflammation of the pancreas); diverticulitis; appendicitis; and gallbladder disease.
- Pelvic abnormalities in females such as endometriosis and ovary related abnormalities.

The most important and difficult task for your doctor when evaluating your back pain is identifying the source, or cause, of your pain…the so-called "pain generator." No single test or part of your story alone will be able to uncover the source of your pain. The history, or story, you tell your doctor is just the starting point in defining the pain generator.

Oftentimes, the pain in your back can come from a wide variety of things. So paying attention to your back and what's going on is very important when having to describe what's wrong with it. Unfortunately, it's not like other parts of your body where you say one thing that's happened and your doctor can immediately know the solution. For example, if you take an antibiotic and break out in a rash, then your doctor knows that you are allergic to it. The back is much more complex than that.

Luckily, MOST back pain is not life-threatening, is not caused by cancer, and does not require urgent evaluation. There are, however, certain DANGER SIGNS that suggest that more immediate attention is warranted.

- *Severe, persistent pain (especially if it continues to worsen)*
- *A history of cancer and new-onset back pain*
- *Pain that is worse at night and awakens you*
- *The presence of fever and/or chills*
- *Severe abdominal pain*
- *Loss of bowel and/or bladder control*
- *Numbness or tingling in both legs (as opposed to just one)*
- *Numbness or tingling across the chest, abdomen or groin*
- *Weakness in both legs*
- *Trouble walking due to weakness (not pain)*
- *Ankylosing spondylitis (arthritis in the spine) with a history of any trauma or change in posture or new pain, weakness, numbness, and tingling in your body*

If you are experiencing these symptoms, then you may have a more serious condition than you realize and you should see a doctor immediately. ***This book should not be used as a substitute for medical attention***. Fortunately, the vast majority of those suffering from back pain will not have these serious conditions.

Typically, when we think of back pain, it's associated with an event that caused it to hurt. Maybe you lifted something that was too heavy or slept the wrong way. But this isn't always the case. Sometimes back pain is caused by more serious conditions.

Cancer patients often experience back pain as well. Here are some clues that your back pain may be caused by cancer and needs immediate evaluation:

- Pain is relentless and progressively worse
- Pain awakens you at night
- A prior history of cancer
- Age less than 20 or older than 65

Although a serious concern, the vast majority of back pain is not caused by cancer. But even if you haven't been diagnosed with cancer and you can relate to any of the situations above, then you should get checked for cancer to be on the safe and proactive side of things. Some people have discovered something was wrong because their back pain was the indicator and after further testing, they got to the root of the real problem. Pain is simply your body's way of telling you something is wrong. So, when you feel pain, especially relentless and progressively worsening pain or pain that wakes you from your sleep, pay attention, and get it checked out. Also, ignoring the pain could possibly make matters worse and you could end up with a more complicated and expensive problem to deal with later.

Back pain can sound and seem very simple and specific, but it's not at all. In fact, there are many types of back pain conditions to consider:

- Herniated disc(s)
- Muscle strains (from overuse or poor posture)
- Muscle injury
- Pinched/compressed nerves
- Narrowing of the spinal canal (spinal stenosis)
- Vertebral fracture(s)
- Osteoporosis
- The natural processes of aging
- Spondylitis (a spinal infection that creates inflammation)
- Scoliosis
- Tumors
- Degenerative disc disease
- Sacroiliac joint dysfunction and degeneration
- … and more

TYPES OF BACK PAIN

Understanding the time course of your back pain helps the doctor to figure out the diagnosis and therefore treatment. Pain can be either relatively new (acute) or present for a long time (chronic). It can be sporadic (occurring randomly) or constant. Its onset can be sudden or come on more gradually, and worsen in severity. It's very important to understand this and be able to articulate these features of your back pain in order to help your doctor establish your diagnosis.

New onset (acute)

- Often sudden onset—in some cases, there is a clear-cut link to an activity such as heavy lifting. More often than not, it occurs without a known trigger.
- The back pain may be accompanied by leg pain that typically radiates from the lower back down to the buttock, and into the back of the thigh and leg, often, going into the foot, this is commonly termed **"sciatica."**
- This type of pain is usually due to a herniated disc but can be from a bone spur.
- Leg pain is greater than or equal to the degree of back pain.

Long-standing (chronic)

- Most often without associated leg pain.
- Back pain is greater than leg pain.
- May occur in some people with spinal stenosis, or diffuse narrowing of the spinal canal.

When a patients experience long-standing back pain, slowly worsening bilateral leg weakness, and pain which is especially made worse by walking but is improved by leaning forward (i.e. walking further when using a grocery store cart), the diagnosis of neurogenic claudication may be suggested. These symptoms can mimic vascular claudication, as similar complaints will exist but the cause be secondary to a blockage of blood flow to the legs. Diagnostic imaging and the physical examination can almost always sort out which one is responsible for your symptoms.

Expert spine doctors will classify your chronic back pain into three types:

1. Mechanical

- Characterized by pain that is minor in the morning and becomes progressively worse by the evening.
  - — This is the result of mechanical factors such as bones rubbing together; the more they rub the more they hurt. Therefore, evening pain is worse!
- This type of pain is more likely to have a defined pain generator and therefore more likely to have a surgical treatment option
- Often (but not always) associated with a history of *sudden onset*.

2. Inflammatory

- Characterized by pain that is worse in the morning with stiffness but improves throughout the day with activity.
- This type of pain is typical of arthritis or hereditary spine disorders and should prompt blood work to try and identify a cause.

3. Medication-related (This is rare!)

- Statin drugs prescribed for high cholesterol:
  — Can cause leg complaints that mimic sciatica
- Drugs for erectile dysfunction (ED):
  — Common prescription medications for ED can cause severe lower back and leg pain.

ALWAYS INFORM YOUR DOCTOR ABOUT ALL OF THE MEDICATIONS YOU ARE TAKING!

There are some key clues based on your pain and other symptoms that strongly suggest your back pain is due to an inflammatory condition. If you answer yes to most of the following questions listed below, your back pain is likely inflammatory and not mechanical.

Clues that you are suffering from inflammatory back pain

- Did your back pain start before you were 40 years old?
- Does your back pain wake you up from sleeping and prevent you from falling back asleep?
- Do you have less back pain if you exercise or move around?
- When you rest or sit for long periods does your back pain feel worse?
- When you wake up, does your back feel stiff for at least 30 minutes?
- Does your back pain feel better when you take NSAID drugs, such as ibuprofen?
- Has your back pain been, on and off, for more than three months?
- Do you have any other symptoms that may seem unrelated, including eye inflammation, inflammatory bowel disease, psoriasis, or pain in your peripheral joints, such as your ankles or knees?

Many structures in your back can cause pain

Your back is subjected to various strong forces throughout the day, such as from twisting, sudden jolts, or poor posture when sitting hunched over. Any of your spine's many interconnected and overlapping structures are capable of becoming injured and producing back pain. Common anatomical causes of back pain include:

- Large muscles that support the spine
- Spinal nerves that exit the spinal canal and may go to the legs or elsewhere
- Facet joints that connect the vertebrae along the back of the spine
- Intervertebral discs that provide shock-absorption for the bones
- The sacroiliac joints-large joints that connect the spine to the pelvis

SACROILIAC JOINT PAIN

Yet another cause of lower back pain, especially pain in the buttock and upper thighs that does not extend below the knee, is sacroiliac joint or SI joint dysfunction. The sacroiliac (SI) joints are paired joints in the pelvis that connect the lowest part of your spine, the sacrum, to the iliac bones, which are the fixed part of your hips (the large flat bones on both sides of your pelvis).

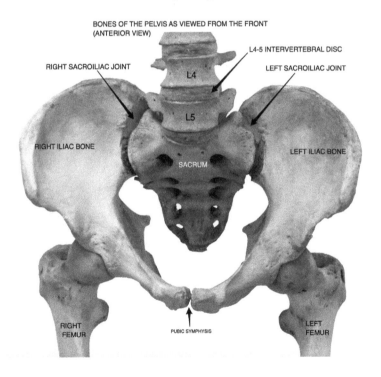

BONES OF THE PELVIS AS VIEWED FROM THE FRONT
(ANTERIOR VIEW)

L4-5 INTERVERTEBRAL DISC

RIGHT SACROILIAC JOINT

LEFT SACROILIAC JOINT

L4

RIGHT ILIAC BONE

L5

LEFT ILIAC BONE

SACRUM

RIGHT
FEMUR

PUBIC SYMPHYSIS

LEFT
FEMUR

This type of pain is usually, but not always, on one side only and may be "sciatica-like" in that it radiates from the back down the back of the thigh, but again, it rarely will go below the knee. The pain typically gets worse when climbing stairs, or jogging, or lying on one side-turning from one side to the other. What that means is that the pain is made worse by anything that asymmetrically puts more load on one half of your pelvis than the other.

Although it may occur with no known cause, it is associated with leg length discrepancy and also pregnancy or recent childbirth. There are certain tests the doctor will do as part of the physical examination if they believe that your pain may be coming from the SI joints.

Surprisingly, many doctors do not realize that a routine MRI ordered for lower back pain (i.e. Lumbosacral MRI) only visualizes a small portion of the SI joints and frequently will not include images the radiologist needs to specifically evaluate these joints. So, if the routine lumbosacral MRI does not reveal the source of your back pain and the doctor feels that, due to the history and physical exam findings, it is a real possibility that your pain is coming from the SI joint(s), a targeted MRI examination of the SI joints may be indicated. Even if this exam is unrevealing, if your exam and history support SI joint dysfunction strongly enough, some doctors will refer you to pain management doctors who can directly inject the joint with numbing medicine and steroids as an outpatient. Relief of pain is a strong indication that the source of your problem has been correctly identified.

SECTION 3
Diagnostic Testing and the Spine Doctor's Office Visit

After many long days and nights, the only thing you are searching for is relief from your agonizing back pain–chronic or new-onset. When you are dealing with daily discomfort, sharp pain, and/ or sleepless nights, your best chance at achieving relief from back pain starts with figuring out the right diagnosis.

Diagnostic testing is one of the most important pieces of the puzzle to understanding the source of your pain. As many different conditions may cause back pain, your doctor will take a thorough medical history as part of the examination. Some of the questions may not seem relevant to you, but the questions are important to your doctor determining the source of your pain.

Your first appointment will include a physical exam, but one of the most important clues needed to determine the source of your back pain comes from sharing a thorough history of your symptoms with your doctor.

He or she will ask questions about the onset of the pain, luckily for you, you already know how to answer these because you learned it in the last section on page 22. They may also ask questions to try to relate it to something you did or experienced recently (or in the past). For example, "Were you lifting a heavy object and felt an immediate pain?" "Did the pain come on gradually?"

The doctor usually wants to understand the full story. He or she will want to know what makes the pain better/worse (i.e., sitting, standing, or walking) and whether the pain occurs at different times.

The doctor also will ask about recent illnesses and their symptoms such as coughs, fever, urinary difficulties, or stomach illnesses. If you are a woman, they will want to know about any vaginal bleeding, cramping, or discharge.

When is further testing most probably going to be ordered?

- Complaints for less than 8 weeks without "DANGER SIGNS" (outline on page X) do not routinely require further testing.

- Plain X-rays of the spine are sometimes appropriate to exclude severe bony problems like tumors or infection but are very insensitive which means that the problem must be very severe in order for the problem to be visible with this test. The upside is that it's a fast, easy test that does not need advanced equipment nor do you have to worry about being claustrophobic or unable to lie still for prolonged periods.

- If you have any of the "DANGER SIGNS", complaints lasting longer than 8 weeks, or weakness, further tests will be required.

THE PURPOSE OF DIAGNOSTIC TESTING

In a nutshell, the purpose of testing is to try and figure out where your pain is coming from, and if you are suffering from a condition, pinpointing it. This is often far harder than you would imagine. The doctor has to gather a lot of information including your medical history, recent experiences, and test results (sometimes multiple), and then compare them to all of the possible conditions you may have. This is like identifying the "suspects" and the "crime" is your pain.

In the case of leg pain or sciatica, your doctor is trying to find the cause and location of a pinched nerve from a bony spur or herniated disc. The doctor starts with the history and physical exam, as there are frequently very characteristic areas of numbness or weakness that relate to each nerve.

The nature of your pain, whether it came on gradually or suddenly with an event, like moving furniture or weight lifting, also provide important clues. Once your doctor has a theory as to the cause of your pain, they will order appropriate diagnostic testing, or review any imaging studies you have already had, to look and see if there is an abnormality on the testing that fits with your complaints and examination abnormalities.

THE BEST FIRST TEST—MRI

Magnetic Resonance Imaging (MRI) is the most useful test and most likely to be ordered first. It is a non-invasive diagnostic tool that uses energy similar to radiowaves and a very strong magnetic field to produce detailed images of the inside of a body. Doctors can use them to examine not only the spine but also the surrounding soft tissues and the nerves in and exiting from the spine.

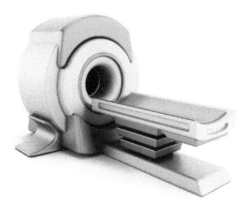

MRI is usually the first test ordered for patients with back pain and leg pain or numbness and tingling.

Pros:

- No radiation!
- Excellent for diagnosing a herniated disc and excluding tumors.
- Considered the best screening test for all conditions of the spine.
- Non-invasive. Unless you have had prior surgery, you have cancer in your spine or your history suggests infection, no contrast (sometimes called "dye") injection is required.

Cons:

- Difficult to get "good pictures" if you can't lie still due to pain or claustrophobia
- Weight and body size limits
- High field magnets ("closed in" magnets) create by far the best images (sometimes

called "pictures") but can create feelings of claustrophobia in sensitive patients as the hole you must enter is smaller than low field ("open") magnets.

- Some metal implants may keep you from being able to get an MRI.

Because you will be in a powerful magnet, you MUST inform the staff of any metal in your body (medical implants or bullets/shrapnel) including prior exposure to ironworks that could have resulted in a metal fragment in your eye. If you have a medical implant, like a stent in your heart or a pacemaker, it's very important to have a note or card from your doctor detailing the type of implant.

The MRI center will have you fill out an extensive screening form and will request more detailed information should you have a medical implant.

TYPES OF MRI

An "open" MRI is of lower field strength and has reduced quality of imaging in comparison to a closed MRI. That said, a new open MRI may be superior to a very old closed MR machine with outdated software.

Open vs. Closed MRI
- Some patients with severe claustrophobia request open MRI's.
- It is important to recognize that open MRI image quality is inferior and may miss problems and take longer. So, if you can tolerate it and fit inside, a closed, high-field MRI is always **in your best interest**.
- Closed MRI machines deliver better pictures within a shorter amount of time in the machine.
- New closed MRI machines are **overall the best** and now have significantly larger openings to allow for heavier patients to be imaged and lessen the sense of claustrophobia.

Many people fear the tunnel and will readily jump at the chance to get in an open magnet, which provides **much lower quality**. It's highly recommended that, when possible, you choose the high field (1.5 tesla) option. Otherwise, you could end up with money wasted, your problem missed or so poorly defined that the doctor ends up ordering a CT myelogram (which includes radiation and a needle inserted into your back through which contrast is injected).

COSTS ASSOCIATED WITH MRIS

- MRIs in a hospital-affiliated center, even if free-standing, are routinely MUCH more expensive than in a free-standing, outpatient MRI center not associated with a hospital.
- Often a free-standing MRI center can offer a cash price that may be lower than your insurance deductible! The downside is that the cash payment will not go towards meeting your deductible…but the savings can be dramatic and make it worthwhile.
- Low field MRI may give poor quality images that, in some cases, are insufficient and will create the need for further, more expensive, and perhaps, more invasive testing.

PLAIN X-RAYS (or plain radiographs)

This is the simplest imaging test. A radiology technician will position you with a "radiographic plate" behind you and use an X-ray tube to take "pictures" of your spine.

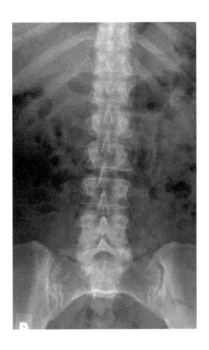

Pros:

- Fast
- Images can be performed with you in various positions, like bending forward and backward, to look for abnormal movement (slippage) of one bone on the other which is called instability.
- Full-length images of the spine are sometimes taken while you're standing to look for the abnormal position of one bone on the other as well as to assess the curvature of your entire spine.
- Lateral bending films may be taken when your doctor is evaluating you for scoliosis, or abnormal curvature of your spine.

Cons:

- X-rays involve radiation exposure so it's best to limit this. Although a lead shield can be used, it is still best to avoid radiation exposure especially in pregnancy and young patients.

Although they should ask, be sure and tell the doctor and radiology technologist if you think you might be pregnant!

Typically, 5 views are taken:

- **AP** (front)- the X-ray beam travels from the anterior (front) of your body to the posterior (back) of your body. When looking at the AP film, the left side of your body appears on the right side of the film, so that it is viewed as you would be looking at the person standing in front of you.
- **Lateral** (side)- the X-ray beam travels from one side of your body to the other.
- **Two oblique (angled) views from either side**- you are turned slightly to one side and then the other, for two pictures.
- **Coned-down lateral view of the sacrum**- This is a small image that is taken just of the lowest portion of your lumbar spine where it connects with the sacrum, which is the center portion of your pelvis.

CT SCAN

A computerized tomography (CT) scan combines a series of X-ray images taken from different angles around your body and uses computer processing to create cross-sectional images (slices) of the bones, blood vessels, and soft tissues inside your body. CT scan images provide much more detailed information than plain X-rays.

A CT scan has many uses and is particularly well-suited to quickly examine people who may have internal injuries from car accidents or other types of trauma. It may also be used to give a spine surgeon additional information specifically about the bony anatomy of your spine if the MRI suggests this is necessary or you can't get an MRI.

- Involves ionizing radiation exposure, unlike MRI. As the radiation dose is greater than plain X-rays, this should be avoided especially if you are pregnant!
- In the emergency room setting, with NO trauma, and simply back pain, the CT scan is NOT a good test.

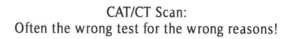

CAT/CT Scan:
Often the wrong test for the wrong reasons!

Most emergency rooms can perform a CT scan but not an MRI, so they may be biased to want to perform this test. This does not mean that you should have a CT scan, only to be told that an MRI is by far the better test with no radiation. So, if you are going to end up getting an MRI anyway, you would rather just pay for the MRI and not the CT scan.

Only in the setting of acute trauma presenting in to the Emergency room is a CT of the spine superior to MRI.

Also, for patients that cannot get an MRI due to metal implants, a CT may be the only choice.

Pros:

- Shows the bony structures like osteophytes and fractures more clearly than MRI
- Fewer restrictions than MRI. You can have a CT even if you have metal in your body.

Cons:

- All CT scans involve radiation.
- CT scans are not suggested for women that are pregnant, even if shielded unless it is a medical emergency.
- A plain CT scan is inferior to MRI for showing the nerves of the spine so that a myelogram is often needed (see below).

CT Scan Versus MRI

CT and MRI of the lumbar spine are examining the same area of your body but are totally different tests. While the MRI can see certain elements of the bone, it is best for evaluating the spinal cord, nerves and discs. The CT Scan is best for imaging the bones of the spine and is the best test if there has been serious trauma and there is concern for a fracture.

CT MYELOGRAM

A CT myelogram is an invasive test requiring iodine-based dye to be injected by spinal tap into the fluid inside your spinal canal followed by a CT scan. It's a two-part procedure performed to detect abnormalities including:

- Tumors
- Herniated discs
- Arthritis
- Spinal narrowing and/or nerve impingement of the spinal canal.

The CT myelogram should only ordered by a spine specialist and is usually reserved for people who cannot get an MRI (typically due to metal fragments in the eye, pacemakers that are not MRI compatible, etc). Sometimes it's ordered for patients with prior surgery, especially if they have metal screws or plates in the spine which limit MRI scans.

It's an outpatient procedure and can be done in a hospital or outpatient facility—as with MRI, the same price differences apply. The hospital-affiliated settings, even if free-standing, will be more expensive.

Pros:
- Far better exam than just a plain CT scan for looking at nerves.
- An excellent test for those who have had prior surgery with lots of metal rods in their back. The metal can severely limit the ability of the MRI to detect abnormalities.
- The CT scanner is more open than an MRI scanner and the scan time is much faster making it better tolerated for people with claustrophobia than MRI.

Cons:
- This is an invasive test! A needle is placed into the sac containing your nerves and spinal cord.
- There is a risk of infection and bleeding that does not exist with other tests. Although the risk is low....it's not zero!

Certain medications related to diabetes and all blood thinners need to be stopped before this test.

Be sure and tell the doctor (typically a radiologist) about all medications you are taking before having this test.

BONE SCAN

A bone scan is a nuclear imaging test that helps diagnose several types of bone disease. Your doctor may order a bone scan if you have unexplained skeletal pain, bone infection, or bone injury that can't be seen on a standard X-ray. This is NOT the same as a bone density scan.

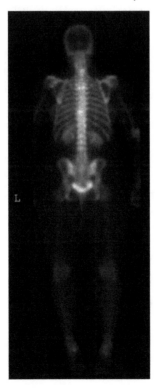

This is a nuclear medicine test performed primarily to evaluate long-standing back pain. A nuclear medicine tracer or dye is injected into a vein and you lie under an imaging camera. The material injected is completely different than the contrast injected for MRI, i.e. gadolinium, or the contrast that is injected for CT scans that contains iodine. "Hot-spots" of uptake of the dye are potential areas of inflammation that could be the cause of your pain. Performing this test ordered with "SPECT" increases the accuracy.

If this test comes back as "negative" this does not mean you have no pain generator, but rather that the test was not able to find it. Conversely, many degenerative discs and facet joints may appear "hot" on bone scan. It is up to your doctor to correlate the nature of your pain and MRI results to decide if the bone scan "hot-spot" is meaningful.

Pros:
- Involves the injection of radioactive material into your bloodstream but does not involve injection directly into your spine like a CT myelogram.
- Patients with metal in their body or for other reasons can't get an MRI, can still get a bone scan.
- You do have to lie still under the camera for the bone scan but the area is much more

open and less likely to cause the feeling of claustrophobia than an MRI.

Cons:
- This does not take the place of plain films, CT scan, CT myelogram nor MRI but rather it is in addition to other tests to add information about which degenerated area of your spine is more likely to be the source of your problem when it isn't apparent on the CT, CT myelogram or MRI alone.
- Involves a low dose of radiation exposure.

EMG AND NCV

Electromyography (EMG) and nerve conduction velocity (NCV) are electrodiagnostic tests that measure the electrical activity of muscles and nerves. These tests may be an important part of a spine patient's work-up by their doctor. EMG and NCV join forces to help get to the bottom of why symptoms are occurring.

This test can help pinpoint which specific nerves are being affected and can also help tell if other problems are present such as neuropathy or "pinched" or injured nerves in the legs themselves rather than in the back. The EMG helps the doctor "rule-out" other causes of your complaints and thus helps to avoid wrong diagnoses and treatments.

If you have pain, numbness, tingling, or weakness in your legs, an EMG may be ordered. Needles are inserted in the legs to evaluate the electrical activity of the nerves and muscles. This test sounds scarier than it is and is not an IMAGING test. The amount of pain associated is usually mild and no sedation or recovery is required.

Pros:
- Unlike an imaging test, this exam is trying to determine if a particular nerve is really being affected in a way that could result in your pain.
- Can diagnose non-spine causes of your complaints.

Cons:
- Sometimes the test gives meaningless information that does not fit with your symptoms.
- Invasive and uncomfortable test where needles are inserted into your muscles for the recordings of the nerve and muscle activity.

All of These Diagnostic Tests MAY NOT GIVE THE ANSWER!

Dr. Westmark has been treating back pain for more than 30 years. In his experience, most patients often want to know with all the improvements in medical technology, ***Why does the treatment of back pain often fail?***

An analogy that Dr. Westmark gives is that a doctor treating back pain is like a detective solving a case.

Sometimes there is a "body" (the pain) and no "clues" (a meaningfully positive diagnostic test result). In back pain scenarios, this is the patient who has back pain but essentially negative diagnostic tests. This is often surprising to the patient as their back pain is very real to them. Similar to the crime with no suspects and no one to convict, without identification of a specific cause ("suspect"), there is no surgical solution. When the patient's pain is not explained by diagnostic testing and no surgical solutions are offered, they may become frustrated, thinking it is being implied that their pain is not real. To the patient, this is irritating and illogical just as the absence of suspects certainly does not mean a crime did not occur!

The ideal scenario is to find the dead body, a gun with fingerprints, video of the crime, and 10 witnesses. Then, we would all agree, it is most probable that the case will be solved. This is similar to a patient with back pain who has a single, very focal abnormal area on diagnostic testing that clearly relates to their back and/or leg pain. This leads to a confident consideration for surgery given that the pain generator is well defined. There are no other suspects!

The third, perhaps most common scenario is that there are too many suspects and not enough evidence to confidently identify the perpetrator. This corresponds to diffuse, multilevel abnormalities on imaging studies. While some abnormalities appear more significant than others, any of the areas of degeneration or disc herniations could potentially be the cause of pain. If surgery is contemplated for this scenario, the options are: pick the most guilty-looking and hope you got the right one or convict them all. The advantage of picking one is that this would lead to a much smaller surgery but lower the probability of succeeding, as the odds of having identified the pain generator are reduced. The other option is to treat multiple levels. Now, the odds are higher of having addressed the pain generator but treatment is a much larger surgery with a greater risk of blood loss, infection, and further complications.

Again, using the analogy of detective work, just because someone looks guilty doesn't mean they are. As shocking as it sounds to many people, just because your MRI has one or more abnormality, there is no guarantee that ANY of these abnormalities are causing your pain!

Key Points to Remember When Seeking Help for Back Pain

- The history and physical exam are not nearly as helpful in making the diagnosis as to the cause of pure, mechanical back pain as they are in people with sciatica or "nerve pain."

- The specific location and characteristics of your back pain are seldom helpful beyond deciding if it is mechanical or inflammatory

- Abnormal findings on your MRI and/or CT scan do NOT NECESSARILY MEAN we have found the cause of your back pain as these abnormalities could simply be the result of aging.

- Bone spurs, herniated discs, and degenerative discs are present in many patients and are the consequence of normal aging. Further, asymptomatic small tears and degenerative change in the lumbar vertebral discs are seen on MRI in up to 30% of normal patients with no back pain! Therefore, it's impossible to say if they are definitely the cause of your back pain.

SECTION 4
Treatment Options

Most back pain goes away on its own, usually within eight weeks. This is known as "the natural history of the disease." Unfortunately, this means that you can hurt for a while before you have relief, or it simply goes away. But, if your pain is severe enough you will probably seek some sort of treatment.

The treatment options and their goals vary based on how long your pain has been present—**i.e. is it short-lived or chronic.**

SHORT-LIVED COMPLAINTS
(pain has been present for less than 8 weeks)

The good news is short-lived complaints, no matter how severe, will likely resolve on their own. For example, when you have a sprained ankle the pain can get worse before it gets better, and it usually peaks 10-14 days after the pain begins.

There is no one path to recovery, as some people get better quickly and others improve more gradually. However, unlike a mild sprained ankle, back problems don't <u>always</u> resolve by themselves. When the complaints are <u>mild-to-moderate</u> in severity, you have the following options:

MILD TO MODERATE PAIN TREATMENT OPTIONS:

Do nothing:
- Since all treatment options carry risk, this is the preferred treatment for those with tolerable complaints.
- Realize that the time course for improvement is variable.

Anti-inflammatory medicines:
- Commonly called NSAIDs (non-steroidal anti-inflammatory drugs) such as ibuprofen (Motrin) and Naproxen (Aleve).
- Very effective at fighting inflammation, and therefore pain, as inflammation is what causes the pain.
- These drugs are generally safe at the recommended dosage but do have definite side effects including the risk of kidney damage and bleeding in the stomach. Kidney damage usually results from taking high doses of these medications for a prolonged

period of time. If you have kidney problems or diabetes you are more at risk and should check with your doctor. Bleeding risk is increased if you have a history of ulcers or are taking blood thinners. <u>You should not take NSAIDS if you are on blood thinners without checking with your doctor first.</u>

Physical therapy:
- Proven to be useful not only in treating an episode of back pain, but also in preventing future back pain as well.
- Short term - may be effective for symptomatic relief.
- Long term - may prevent future episodes by strengthening core muscles.

Chiropractic therapy:
- Shown to be a useful treatment for back pain with or without sciatica.
- Treatment consists of manipulation of the spine and/or multimodality therapy, which may consist of heat, ultrasound, electrical stimulation, and a device known as an activator that is a form of muscle release.

Massage therapy:
- Works to relax muscle spasms associated with back pain.

Acupuncture:
- Little understood modality.

- Currently, the National Institute of Health (NIH) has studies looking at the utility of this therapy in the treatment of pain.

If your pain is <u>moderate-to-severe</u>, other options may be considered:

MODERATE TO SEVERE PAIN TREATMENT OPTIONS:

Steroids:
- The common treatment for people with back or leg complaints that are incapacitating to them.
- Side effects may be very significant but are very uncommon. The most severe side effect is known as avascular necrosis (AVN). This can result in very serious problems with your hips. AVN can occur with steroids taken by shot or by pill.
- Can make you feel better but there is no evidence that it will affect your overall outcome. You will either get better or you won't.
- Can be given by mouth, IV, or by shot. The most convenient is a Medrol Dosepak which is a pre-packaged set of pills that deliver a dose that tapers off with time.
- Trigger point injection is a shot that can be given in the doctor's office.

- Involves local injection of a long-acting anesthetic agent and steroid at the site of your maximal pain. The injection is superficial, which means into the muscles and soft tissues OUTSIDE of the spine. No "downtime" or recovery period and you can drive home that day as no general anesthesia or sedation is used.
- The most invasive shots are called "epidural steroid injections" (ESI's). Epidural steroid injections involve the placement of a needle into the epidural space in your back which is inside the spine but outside the sac that contains your nerves.
  - Typically administered by a specialist in an ambulatory surgery center.
  - Uses X-ray guidance to ensure the drug is being put into the proper place.
  - Typically, you are sedated so there is little or no discomfort.
  - If sedation is given, you are unable to drive the day of the procedure. No other restrictions or recovery is typically needed.
  - Epidural shots are typically given in a series of 3, separated by 10-14 days.
  - Epidural steroids should not be repeated on an ongoing basis and would typically not be repeated for one year
  - They carry a small risk of infection,

bleeding, spinal fluid leakage, and damage to the nerves.

- <u>These injections cannot be performed while you are on blood thinners</u>

Surgery:

- A last-resort treatment for people with short-lived complaints.
- Not recommended for the first 8 weeks of pain, unless experiencing the Danger Signs listed on page 22.
- Typically reserved for people with severe pain down the leg that are unable to tolerate the pain long enough to know if it will get better on its own.
- If pain persists longer than 8 weeks.

Even with more than 8 weeks of complaints, patients can continue to pursue all aforementioned options. However, surgical options are now more appropriate as the chance of getting better naturally has diminished.

If surgery is contemplated, then you will likely get bending X-rays (flexion/extension views). It is unlikely you will have abnormal motion of your spine but if you do, the only surgical option would entail fusion (explained on page 63).

The surgical option for incapacitating sciatica or sciatica for more than 8 weeks **WITH** imaging that documents a pinched nerve on the MRI or CAT scan myelogram but **WITHOUT** instability (abnormal motion shown on flexion-extension X-rays of your back).

- Outpatient surgery to relieve pressure on the nerve root(s).
- For patients suffering from sciatica, the typical surgical option is that of decompression. In order to assure that this is an appropriate treatment, you likely would undergo X-rays of your spine bending forward and backward to assure that there is no instability of your spine. Should there be instability, this would require fusion surgery.
- Often performed in an ambulatory surgery center.
- Generally involves a relatively small incision on the back. This is often done with a microscope and can be done with a tube.
- During the surgery, portions of bone and ligament are removed. Beyond this, sometimes the disk material itself is removed or bony spurs if they are encountered. Regardless of what is actually done during the surgery, your recovery and the overall experience should be the same.
- If you are in good health, a typical regimen would be that there would be no driving allowed for 3-5 days. No showering allowed for 1-3 days and no lifting or twisting for

8 weeks. From a practical standpoint, this means no more lifting than 10-15 pounds. A brace is sometimes prescribed by surgeons post-operatively.

Even if pain persists past 8 weeks, it does not always mean there is a medically serious underlying cause or one that can be easily identified and treated. In some cases, treatment successfully relieves chronic back pain, but in other cases, pain continues despite medical and surgical treatment.

Chronic complaints - Pain has been present for more than 8 weeks and usually for many months to years.

Living with one's complaints is probably the best advice that could be given to a patient given the fact that there are currently no risk-free, guaranteed outcome options for people with chronic back pain. The primary question: *Is this acceptable to you?*

Chronic back pain typically is past the point of healing on its own, so using an alternative method for treatment is the only resort for a path to a possible pain-free future. The same treatment methods as short-lived complaints can still help at this point, but there is a more serious option available in some cases—fusion surgery.

The only surgical treatment option for chronic back pain, without sciatica or an imaging study documenting a pinched nerve, is a spinal fusion. However, this should be the last resort, as fusion surgery is a considerably tricky surgery with very definite risks and no guarantee of relief of your complaints. Further, fusion surgery carries the risk of developing new or worse complaints.

Chronic pain can be treated with all of the same options listed previously for short-lived complaints:

Nonsteroidal anti-inflammatories
- There are risks associated with prolonged use. However, most of these risks can be reduced by regular follow-up with one's primary care physician and appropriate laboratory testing.

Physical therapy
- Particularly useful for people with chronic back pain in terms of core strengthening. There is very good literature to support the proposition that weight loss and core strengthening can significantly decrease back pain.

Massage, chiropractic, and acupuncture therapy

- Useful in terms of relieving the ongoing perception of pain. That said, there is very little suggestion that this would improve the long-term outcome of back pain.

Pain management

- This could consist of medical therapy meaning the prescription of medications that result in the management of one's pain. This can be a complicated process balancing the side effects and risks of the medication versus the medication success in relieving symptoms. With that said, if a medical regimen can relieve a patient of enough pain that they become functional and with a reasonable quality of life, this certainly remains a viable option despite the risks and side effects associated with this.
- There are long-term strategies for pain management that involve injection therapy. The longer-term options remain the possibility of receiving epidural steroid injections no more than once a year. Some patients note that they gain enough benefit from this that they can go a year or two without receiving further injections.
- Another way of receiving pain management injections is for it to be delivered into the joints of the spine. The injections can be

administered in the form of steroids. If this is proven to be beneficial to you, the nerves to the joints can be burned by a process called radiofrequency ablation which can offer longer-term relief.

Steroids taken by mouth are not a viable option for people with chronic back pain.

FUSION SURGERY

The last option for long-standing back pain.

- Demonstration of abnormal motion (slippage of one vertebral body on another which gets worse with flexion and/or extension of your spine), means your spine is unstable and will require fusion if surgery is contemplated.
- Doctors may suggest spinal fusion if you have had several decompressions for a herniated disc but continue to re-herniate. Rather than simply go in yet again and remove the disc, the surgeon will very possibly suggest spinal fusion because it is felt that the reason the disc continues to herniate is because there is abnormal motion between the vertebral bodies, and abnormal motion is best treated with spinal fusion.

For all other conditions, that may or may not

be causing your back pain, the results are, in general, worse and definitely not guaranteed. As noted in the diagnostic section, the hardest challenge of contemplating surgery for back pain is identifying the source of the pain. This is the most important step in terms of trying to achieve the highest probability of a favorable outcome. It is this part of spine surgery that tends to be the least certain. The outcomes of surgery for back pain are highly dependent on multiple variables, but most importantly depend on the accuracy of determining the source of the pain.

What is specifically done during Fusion Surgery?

First, if needed, decompression surgery is performed to get pressure off of the nerves. This would be followed by a stabilization procedure or fusion. This stabilization procedure fundamentally involves attempting to get one bone to grow to another bone. This involves bone graft. This bone graft can come from you, at either the site of the surgery or from one of your pelvic bones. There has been a tendency to move away from taking the bone from your pelvis as this can often lead to severe pain and slow recovery. Other substances can be used to try and achieve fusion by getting bones to grow one to the other. This could involve cadaver bone, something called demineralized bone matrix, and something called bone morphogenetic protein (BMP). The decision as to which of these are used would be between you and your surgeon as each has relative risks and benefits.

Beyond placing the bone graft, fusion surgery typically involves stabilization with hardware. This typically consists of screws and rods being placed in the spine. These are typically made of titanium so that patients can still undergo MRIs following the placement. Today, these screws could potentially take different trajectories throughout the spine. However, they share all common traits. They are associated with misplacement of the screws, which is the consequence of the fact that one cannot see where these screws are going. I liken this to placing a screw into a wall to hang a bookshelf. You can know your starting point, but you cannot know where the screw ends up. This could potentially be life-threatening including involving arteries or veins. The greatest statistical risk of hardware is the risk of infection. This risk goes up both in terms of how often it occurs and how severe it is if it does occur. Antibiotics are given to reduce the probability of this. That said, the overall benefits of hardware today are found to be greater than any potential risks associated with them. Certainly, the hardware allows for earlier mobilization and has been shown to lead to higher fusion rates.

Fusion surgery can be done from the front of the

spine (throughout the abdomen), the side of the spine (lateral approach), the back of the spine, or in some combination thereof. Each approach has a specific risk/benefit profile. The literature does not favor any particular approach and therefore this is typically a matter of surgeon/patient preference.

What is minimally invasive surgery for spinal fusion?

There is a discussion in spine surgery regarding the designation of "minimally invasive surgery." This certainly remains a viable option and can be discussed with your surgeon. That said, today there is no consensus opinion that the type of surgery performed whether it be from the front of the spine, the back of the spine, the side of the spine, combined, or "minimally invasive" has any long-term bearing on the outcome. Each technique has its advantages and disadvantages.

Unfortunately for the patient, fusion surgery remains significant surgery regardless of the approach utilized for it.

The name "minimally invasive surgery" might suggest this surgery is less serious than other approaches to fusion surgery. The process of attempting to obtain a fusion involves scraping of bones and placing screws. Regardless of any technique used, this remains a painful and traumatic event with very definite risks.

The only non-fusion option currently available in the literature beyond decompression alone is that of a device that is used between the so-called spinous process. This is being compared favorably in research studies to fusion surgery. This device has been used in a limited number of people who are considered to be candidates for it. This option should be discussed with your surgeon should you be interested.

If your doctor recommends that you have spine surgery

It's important to ask the doctor the following questions:

1. Is surgery **recommended** or is it a treatment **option**?
2. What are the dangers if I don't have surgery?

Remember: A second opinion is your Right! Never be afraid to ask for one.

Surgery has been "RECOMMENDED" or "SUGGESTED AS AN OPTION." These statements are not the same! While it may seem that these two statements are implying the same thing, technically, they are completely different.

If surgery is "suggested as an option" or that you "should possibly consider having surgery," this means the decision is yours and, if you don't choose surgery, you are not creating a more dangerous situation. Another term commonly used for this is "elective." In cases like this, if you went to 5 different spine surgeons, you might end up with 5 different opinions! In this situation, there is no consensus on what is best…but also no guarantee that having surgery is going to help.

On the other hand, if your doctor says, "Surgery is recommended," this implies that the vast majority of spine surgeons would operate to treat your condition. Another legal term extensively used is "Standard of care." This legally means, what would the vast majority of well-trained doctors do under the same circumstances.

For example, if your spinal canal is severely narrowed to the point that you are not only having difficulty walking but also cannot control your bowel or bladder and the diagnostic imaging testing clearly shows a severe narrowing, surgeons would reasonably recommend surgery. It would not be offered to you as "an option" but rather it would be strongly recommended! Plainly stated, there is no other, non-surgical treatment, to correct this problem and not fixing it may lead to permanent loss of function and bladder and bowel control!

For back pain alone, without any evidence of

compression of nerves or the spinal cord, surgery should never be "recommended". It is always an option…it is always elective. Whether the surgery is LIKELY or UNLIKELY to help you depends largely on whether the pain generator has been wisely defined.

If your doctor says he or she knows where your back pain is coming from, ask them the following questions:

- How certain are you and on what are you basing that opinion? This is an extremely important question because your treatment success will be based largely upon whether the pain generator has been ACCURATELY defined. Failure to accurately define the pain generator is a major cause of failed back surgery.
- Who would you recommend for a second opinion given that fusion surgery is a big deal? Don't be embarrassed to get a second opinion. The magnitude of this surgery is great enough that this is a prudent step.

Risks of surgery

General anesthesia has become a very safe and routine procedure in the vast majority of cases. There are important risks with general anesthesia of which you should be aware that include heart attack, stroke, coma, and even death. These risks generally increase with age and poor overall health; however, even young, healthy people die from general anesthesia. During and after surgery, there is the risk of blood clots forming in the legs and traveling to the lungs which is a serious problem that could result in death. Care is taken to reduce this risk by placing special compression stockings during surgery. However, the risks are not completely eliminated. Staying well hydrated after surgery also decreases this risk.

The risks of surgery to your spine include infection, which is minimized by sterile conditions of the operating room. Infection, although rare, is most often superficial and may be treated as an outpatient with antibiotics, debridement, and dressing changes. Deep infections are much less common but can be life-threatening. Returning to the operating room to wash out the infection may be necessary. There is the risk of bleeding which, in worst cases may require a transfusion. This is very uncommon, however. There is the risk of blood clots forming under the skin and putting pressure on nerves that could require additional surgery.

In order to remove the pressure off of your nerves, the nerves must be manipulated. Because of this, there is the risk of new pain, numbness, tingling weakness, or loss of bladder/bowel/sexual function which may be either temporary or permanent. There is also the possibility of scarring around the nerves. A spinal fluid leak is a potentially serious problem that can result in meningitis and may require a return to the operating room. This is very uncommon.

Some surgeries weaken the spine. A surgery to simply remove a herniated disc is unlikely to result in spinal instability, however, it is possible that a future spinal fusion may be required.

Finally, there is no guarantee you will get better. The nerves themselves cannot be directly operated on to make them better. Therefore, as only pressure can be taken off the nerves, there is a change that they will not recover. Your symptoms may not improve and could even be worse.

For surgery on the front or side of the spine, there is the risk of injury to the organs of the abdomen as well as to the large blood vessels to the legs. These complications can be life-threatening and should be discussed with your surgeon.

Males undergoing surgery on the front of the spine are at risk of getting retrograde ejaculation. This risk should be discussed with your surgeon.

Surgery on the side of the spine (lateral) has an increased risk of damaging a nerve that could make it where you cannot walk for a period of time and potentially permanently. This risk varies based on the level of the spine being fused but should definitely be discussed with your surgeon.

SECTION 5
Back Pain Prevention

Once you've achieved relief from your back pain, it is important that you keep it gone by taking some preventable measures. The most important thing you can do to take care of your spine is to keep your body weight within a normal Body Mass Index (BMI) range where 25.0 or more is considered overweight. There are many online calculators you can use to identify where you are on the chart. Although it can be somewhat misleading in that a very muscular person can have a high BMI but not be overweight, this is certainly superior to a simple weight range for your age as it attempts to take into account differences in size among individuals.

Equally important in proactively protecting your back is the incorporation of frequent core-strengthening exercises. Core muscles are defined as those that support the trunk and stabilize the back. These muscles act to take the burden off of the bony structures of the spine as well as the discs. Exercises that emphasize this include walking and targeted exercises to strengthen your core. (discussed later in the chapter).

Don't smoke! Smoking interferes with blood flow to your body's tissues and actually leads to disc degeneration!

High-stress levels will weaken your coping mechanisms for your back pain. Although stress cannot be totally eliminated, finding a routine that decreases stress is important. Walking, doing yoga, and meditation are all great options. You need to seek a positive outlet for stress that works for you which will help decrease your back pain.

Exercise and Diet

There is no easy way to keep your body weight at its ideal level. Just like your car will suffer if you never changed the oil or replaced the tires, your body needs maintenance.

For the mature adult, it is not possible to maintain body weight with diet alone and it is not possible to exercise enough to eat anything you want!

There are not enough hours in the day to exercise yourself out of a bad diet! Diet is responsible for 90% of your body weight and appearance. Exercise determines how toned your muscles are and the ability of your body to be able to respond to challenges of everyday living which involve stress, movement, and weight loads.

Exercise

Exercising regularly (at least 4 out of 7 days) and maintaining a strong core doesn't guarantee you won't hurt your back but the odds of this happening go down tremendously. So, think of daily exercise as buying a very inexpensive but worthwhile insurance policy!

Pick an activity that you will **actually do** and **start slowly**. Walking is probably the best starting point if you haven't exercised in a while (remember to be sure your heart is healthy enough for exercise). Swimming and biking are excellent exercises that do not put much strain on your lower back. Walking up an incline on a treadmill is a good alternative.

Interval training

High-intensity effort x 1 min alternating with recovery is one of the best ways to jump-start weight loss with exercise.

For example:

- Track or treadmill - run the long stretch and walk the turn.
- Stair climber - vary the speed for 1 min intervals (low, medium, high, and repeat).
- Swim - speed burst x 20 strokes and slower pace to recover.

Most importantly, mix it up! Don't do the same exercise for the same amount of time every day. Not only does this increase the chance of repetitive stress-type injury but it also decreases effectiveness and continued weight loss from activity and increases the chance you will stop exercising altogether because of boredom. Join an exercise class that is mindful of warming up and stretching at the end of the class and have a friend who counts on you to join them at the park, jogging track or gym.

Core strengthening exercises

I highly recommended putting these exercises into your routine as they can protect your back! It shouldn't take more than 10 minutes a day and doesn't require a gym or other equipment.

Gradually increase the amount of time of a static hold for the following exercises. Try to build up to working your core muscles 4-5 times per week.

Begin at 30 sec and increase to 1-minute hold for each of the following:

Plank:

Side plank:

Leg lift - Lie on back with hands under your lower back and lift legs off the ground 6-8 inches. Closer to the ground makes this exercise more difficult.

Weight Lifting

The mature spine becomes more brittle and less flexible no matter how fit you are. Any exercise that puts an undue amount of stress on your lower back becomes increasingly more dangerous as you get older.

Lighter weights at higher repetition are the answer.

Dead-lifting is a well-recognized cause of lower back pain. Unfortunately, many people coming to my office for new-onset back pain after lifting can tell me that they had a trainer and their form was perfect. True, being mindful of proper form and good posture are always important. However, if the amount of weight you are lifting exceeds what your back is capable of lifting, an injury will be the result regardless of form!

Overall rules in the gym:
- No weights that push your shoulders toward your pelvis (military press, deadlifts, etc
- No exercise where you are concerned about keeping your spine straight (sit-ups, etc)

Diet

To be clear, weight loss is hard, especially if you already have back pain!

Goals to completely change your diet are likely to fail but incremental changes can be quite successful. Here are some small changes you can make:

- Don't buy things that you know you shouldn't eat. No one can ignore the chips calling them from the pantry.
- Eliminate ALL fried foods.
- Eliminate ALL sodas including diet sodas-drink only water or tea
- No cheese or special sauces on the burger—only ketchup and mustard
- No creamy salad dressings-use plain vinegar instead
- Limit chips—try carrot and celery slices
- When eating out:
  - Say no to the bread
  - Ask to substitute a vegetable for the potato or rice
  - No gravy or sauces
  - Say no to the french fries
  - Don't supersize
  - If available, pay attention to the calorie guide on the menu
  - Say no to dessert
  - Limit alcohol to the weekends and special occasions

These are relatively easy and painless changes that can reduce your calories by well over 1,000 calories per day!

SECTION 6
Frequently Asked Questions
Questions about diagnosis, testing, and
treatment options

How often is it that back pain indicates that I have cancer?
Cancer is a very rare cause of back pain. If you have a history of cancer, especially breast cancer or prostate cancer, then of course the odds go up tremendously.

What are symptoms that indicate I should seek attention immediately?
Please see Section 1, Red Flags on page 22.

What is the best way to find a spine surgeon and/ or get a second opinion if I am concerned about the doctor's recommendation?
The American Association of Neurological Surgeons and the North American Spine Society publish lists of board-certified surgeons in your area. I would look for a spine fellowship-trained neurosurgeon or orthopedic surgeon if possible.

I'm severely claustrophobic. What do I lose if I insist on having an open MRI?

A brand new open MRI may actually be better than a very old, out-dated closed MRI. However, as a general rule, the image quality is much worse on an open MRI. Worst-case scenario, if the open MRI is of very poor quality, the surgeon may actually need another test. Sadly, the insurance company may then refuse to pay and the surgeon is forced to order a more invasive test that has associated risk of infection and radiation relative to MRI, namely the CT myelogram.

Is there any difference between one imaging center and another in terms of quality?

Almost always there are differences. Although when talking about brain MRI, a 3 Tesla magnet is better than a 1.5 Tesla magnet, this is not true for spine imaging. A new, updated 1.5 Tesla magnet often does a better job when imaging the spine especially if you have had prior surgery.

I have metal in my body (specific examples are numerous...i.e. joint replacement, piece of metal in my eye, aneurysm clip in my brain, a pacemaker, etc, etc)....how do I find out if this is a problem for MRI?

It is critical to tell the physician about any metal in your body or prior surgery. They should know this before scheduling the MRI because if you have a metal implant, the imaging center will request documentation as to the exact type. It is ultimately up to the head MRI technologist and radiologist to make the decision as to what is safe and what is not for MRI.

Should I take aspirin, Motrin, or Tylenol for my back pain?

Motrin is typically more effective but has an increased risk of causing kidney injury and affecting blood clotting and causing stomach upset including bleeding.

Tylenol at higher than recommended doses may damage your liver and result in death.

If my work involves carrying heavy objects, did this cause my back pain?

Most people who have low back pain cannot identify a specific cause, so it's hard to say whether any isolated event is responsible. That said, certainly repetitive lifting puts you at greater risk.

Should I see a chiropractor to "Crack my back?"

Chiropractors are often very helpful and LOWER spine manipulation may be very effective. Whereas manipulation of the neck carries some risk of damage to blood vessels and the spinal cord, this type of injury is not a major concern when the therapy is directed to the lower back.

Should I get a new bed/mattress?

If your bed is too soft and doesn't support your

spine, it is very possible that getting a new, firmer bed will be helpful. The firmer, the better.

What are the best pillows to use?
Regardless of the pillow type, the goal is for the pillow to support your spine in a neutral position.

Is practicing yoga going to help me?
Yoga may increase flexibility, improve your core muscle strength, and decrease stress. For all of these reasons, yes, yoga may be helpful.

QUESTIONS ABOUT SURGERY

Will I have to wear a brace?
A brace is commonly worn if a person has had fusion surgery where metal implants have been put into the spine. For routine surgery for a herniated disc or stenosis, a brace may or may not be prescribed.

Should I have surgery in a hospital or outpatient surgery facility? When is one type of center better than the other?
This decision is ultimately up to you and your surgeon and where you are most likely to get the best care and be safe. That said, for a routine laminectomy and discectomy, outpatient surgery centers are less expensive and less likely to be associated with infection and other complications.

If the surgery is more complex, like a spinal fusion, it will almost always be performed in a hospital with an overnight stay.

How long is a person typically out of work after surgery for a herniated disc?

The restrictions are mostly related to lifting and twisting so return to work is highly dependent on the type of work. For desk type work, seven to ten days is reasonable.

How long is a person typically off work after fusion surgery?

The same comment applies to fusion surgery and to disc surgery, as noted above. However, fusion surgery is typically more painful with a longer anticipated recovery. For desk type work, four to six weeks is reasonable.

What type of work or exercise can I do and how soon?

Walking can and should begin immediately. Vigorous exercise and all weight lifting should be avoided for 6 weeks in order to give the tissues a chance to heal and decrease the chance of re-herniating more disc material.

What are the chances that I would lose a lot of blood and need a transfusion?

This would be rare in all circumstances but the risk is higher in fusion surgery and increases the longer the surgery takes. Your blood is drawn and the coagulation profile is measured before surgery to assess you for unusual increased risk.

What precautions are taken to prevent infection during surgery and what is done about it should it happen?

All surgery is performed under sterile conditions and a dose of antibiotics typically is given right before the surgery is performed. After surgery, you will be told to not immerse the incision in a hot tub, pool, tub bath, etc and to keep the incision clean and dry.

I've heard that running an elevated temperature (low-grade fever) after surgery does not always mean there is an infection. How does the doctor figure this out and how do I know if I have to go to the emergency room after surgery?

The most common reason for a low-grade fever in the first few days after surgery is actually NOT an infection of your surgical site but rather due to a small part of your lungs not getting adequate air and closing down during and immediately after the surgery (called atelectasis). You could also have a urinary tract infection. Your doctor may tell you to go to the emergency room where, in addition to blood work to look for signs of infection, a chest x-ray and urinalysis will likely be done. If the low-grade fever is due to atelectasis, deep breathing helps. In fact, practicing deep breathing and walking after surgery may prevent this complication from happening in the first place. Importantly, your doctor cannot diagnose you over the phone and you cannot diagnose yourself. If you think you have a problem after surgery and are running an elevated temperature, you must contact your surgeon and you very well may be told to go to the emergency room for further evaluation.

Will fusion surgery decrease my range of motion?
Fusion surgery is always done on ABnormal discs and typically on people with preexisting, severe limitation of range of motion due to pain. Successful surgery therefore typically increases the effective range of motion of the spine if it eliminates the pain generator.

Will fusion surgery cause my discs above or below to wear out?
So, it is well known that after fusion surgery, the disc above or below the fusion may become degenerated and future surgery possibly required. Surgeons call this adjacent segment disease. What is not known is whether the newly affected disc would have degenerated without the adjacent fusion surgery.

Fusion surgery is done (in the vast majority of cases) on ABnormal disc levels. This is an important distinction. The fusion of normal discs would always lead to extra stresses above and below. However, abnormal discs can themselves cause stresses above and below so the net effect of fusion may be the same as the stress that preexisted the fusion and occurred simply from the degenerative disc alone. Yes, It is possible that the surgical technique could add to the occurrence of adjacent segment disease.

ABOUT THE AUTHOR

Dr. Richard M. Westmark, MD, FAANS

After completing his neurosurgery training at the Harvard teaching hospital, Massachusetts General Hospital, Dr. Westmark trained in advanced spine surgery techniques at the world-famous Barrow Neurologic Institute in Phoenix, Arizona. He has also worked with pioneers in spinal cord injury and regeneration research at the University of California San Francisco and the University of Florida.

Dr. Westmark is board certified, a Fellow of the American Association of Neurological Surgeons (AANS) and a member of the AANS/CNS

(Congress of Neurosurgeons) Joint Section of Disorders of the Spine and Peripheral Nerves.

Dr. Westmark has been treating patients with back pain for over 35 years and has performed over 5,000 spinal surgeries. He has written numerous publications including several chapters in key medical textbooks on the diagnosis and treatment of spinal disorders.

Having such vast practical experience has prompted him to help those suffering by writing My Back Hurts: A Guide to Understanding What's Wrong and Choosing the Best Treatment. This fact-filled guide has been written specifically for the person suffering from back pain with no prior medical training!